N G BERRIDGE and
J PATTISON

Geology of the country around Grimsby and Patrington

Memoir for 1:50 000 geological sheets 90 and 91 and 81 and 82 (England and Wales)

CONTRIBUTORS

Stratigraphy and structure
M A W Abbott
J D Cornwell
D W Holliday
I E Penn

Engineering geology
A Forster

Hydrogeology
M F Davenport

Marine geology
P S Balson

LONDON: HMSO   1994

First published 1994

ISBN 0 11 884496 2

Bibliographical reference

BERRIDGE, NG and PATTISON, J. 1994.   Geology of the country around Grimsby and Patrington.   *Memoir of the British Geological Survey*, Sheets 90, 91, 81 and 82 (England and Wales).

Authors

N G Berridge, BSc, PhD
J Pattison, MSc
formerly *British Geological Survey, Keyworth*

Contributors

P S Balson, BSc, PhD,
J D Cornwell, MSc, PhD
A Forster, BSc
D W Holliday, BSc, PhD
I E Penn, BSc, PhD
British Geological Survey, Keyworth

M A W Abbott, BSc
M F Davenport, BA, MSc
formerly *British Geological Survey*

Other publications of the Survey dealing with this and adjoining districts

BOOKS

British Regional Geology
Eastern England from the Tees to the Wash (2nd edition, 1980)

Memoir
Kingston upon Hull and Brigg (80 and 89), 1991

MAPS

1:625 000
Solid geology (south sheet)
Quaternary geology (south sheet)
Aeromagnetic anomaly (south sheet)
Bouguer gravity anomaly (south sheet)

1:250 000
53N 02W Humber–Trent
   (Solid geology), 1983
   (Aeromagnetic anomaly), 1977
   (Bouguer gravity anomaly), 1977
53N 00 Spurn
   (Solid geology), 1985
   (Quaternary geology), 1991
   (Sea-bed sediments), 1990
   (Aeromagnetic anomaly), 1983
   (Bouguer gravity anomaly), 1982

1:126 720
Hydrogeology, north and east Lincolnshire, 1967

1:125 000
Hydrogeology, east Yorkshire, 1980

1:50 000
Sheet 80   (Kingston upon Hull), 1983
Sheet 81   (Patrington), 1991
Sheet 89   (Brigg), 1982
Sheet 90   (Grimsby), 1990
Sheet 103 (Louth), 1980

Printed in the UK for HMSO
Dd 292039   C8   3/94

CONTENTS

One Introduction 1
Outline of geological history 1
History of research 2

Two Structure 5

Three Concealed strata 10
Carboniferous 10
  Namurian 10
  Westphalian 10
Permian and Triassic 11
  Basal Permian Sands 13
  Don Group 13
  Aislaby Group 15
  Teesside Group 16
  Staintondale and Eskdale groups 16
  Sherwood Sandstone Group 16
  Mercia Mudstone Group 16
  Penarth Group 17
Jurassic 17
  Lower Jurassic 17
    Lias Group 17
  Middle Jurassic (excluding Callovian) 22
    Inferior Oolite Group 22
    Great Oolite Group 23
  Upper Jurassic (including Callovian) 24
    'Ancholme Clay Group' 24

Four Cretaceous 26
Lower Cretaceous 26
  Claxby Ironstone 26
  Tealby Formation 26
  Roach Formation 28
  Carstone 28
Upper Cretaceous: The Chalk Group 29
  Ferriby Chalk 30
  Welton Chalk 30
  Burnham Chalk 32
  Flamborough Chalk 37

Five Quaternary 38
Anglian 38
Hoxnian 40
'Wolstonian' the Basement Till of Holderness 40
Ipswichian 43
Devensian 43
  Dimlington Silts 44
  Skipsea Till 45
  Withernsea Till 48
  Glacial Sand and Gravel 50
  Glacial Silt and Clay 53
  Proglacial deposits 54
    Fluvioglacial Sand and Gravel 54
    Glaciolacustrine Silt and Clay 56
  Kelsey Hill Beds 56

Devensian to Flandrian 58
  Older Blown Sand 58
  Head 59
  Dry Valley Deposits 59
  Lacustrine Alluvium 59
  Peat and Submerged Forest 61
  Landslip 62
Flandrian 62
  Alluvium 63
    Marine and Estuarine Alluvium 65
  Storm Beach Deposits 66
  Coastal Blown Sand 70
  Present-day estuarine and marine sedimentation 70
  Made Ground 71

Six Coastal changes 73
Geotechnical properties of Holderness tills 74

Seven Economic geology 75
Brick Clay 75
Chalk 75
Coal 75
Evaporites 75
Geothermal energy 75
Hydrocarbons 76
Hydrogeology and water supply 76
Ironstone 79
Phosphates 79
Sand and gravel 79
Tidal power 80
Underground storage 80

Appendices
Boreholes 81
BGS photographs 82

References 83

Fossil index 89

General index 90

FIGURES

1 Topography of the district xii
2 Simplified geological map 2
3 Cleethorpes seismic profile 4
4 Deep boreholes and seismic profile location map 5
5 Post-Lower Palaeozoic structure map 7
6 Cleethorpes seismic profile, upper part: geological interpretation 7
7 Structure contour maps showing the structural evolution of the district 8
8 Bouguer gravity anomaly map 9
9 Aeromagnetic anomaly map 9

vi

10 Namurian strata: Tetney Lock borehole 11
11 Westphalian strata: Tetney Lock borehole 12
12 Permo-Triassic strata: borehole correlation 14
13 Relationship between late-Permian formations of the district 15
14 Relationship of the Lias of the district to that of adjacent regions 18
15 Geophysical log correlation of Jurassic and Cretaceous strata 20
16 Lower Cretaceous stratigraphy 27
17 Cenomanian stratigraphy 31
18 Welton and Burnham Chalk stratigraphy 33
19 Evidence for the Burnham Chalk–Flamborough Chalk boundary 36
20 Quaternary stratigraphy 39
21 Rockhead contour map 41
22 The limits of the Dimlingtonian ice sheet 44
23 Cliff sections from Easington to Tunstall 47
24 Distribution of sand and gravel at the base of the Devensian in Lincolnshire Marsh 51
25 Distribution of Dimlingtonian sand and gravel deposits 52
26 Flandrian and Devensian stratigraphy: Roos Bog 60
27 Contours on the concealed surface of Pleistocene deposits: Humber estuary 63
28 Flandrian evolution of the Humber estuary 64
29 Diagrammatic section through the Flandrian deposits of Lincolnshire Outmarsh 65
30 Flandrian sediments: comparative borehole sections 67
31 History of reclamation A. Sunk Island B. Lincolnshire Outmarsh 69

PLATES

1 Ludborough Quarry, North Ormsby: Welton–Burnham Chalk boundary, general view 34
2 Ludborough Quarry, North Ormsby: Welton–Burnham Chalk boundary, close-up 34
3 Ludborough Quarry, North Ormsby: North Ormsby Marl and contiguous strata 35
4 Sea cliff, Dimlington High Land: Basement, Skipsea and Withernsea tills 42
5 Foreshore, north of Easington: Dimlington Silts on Basement Till 45
6 Sea cliff, Dimlington High Land: faulted Skipsea Till 46
7 Foreshore, north-west of Holmpton: general view of deformed Chalk in Skipsea Till 49
8 Foreshore, north-west of Holmpton: deformed Chalk in Skipsea Till 49
9 Old Hive, Out Newton: Glacial Sand and Gravel 53
10 Irby Dales: subglacial channel 54
11 Keyingham Gravel Pit: general view 55
12 Keyingham Gravel Pit: flat-lying gravel facies 57
13 Keyingham Gravel Pit: folded silt, sand and gravel 58
14 The Runnell, Holmpton: postglacial mere section 61
15 Humber shore, Sunk Island: eroded Estuarine Alluvium and tidal flats 68

TABLE

1 Representative chemical analyses of ground-water 78

PREFACE

This memoir describes the geology of the area about the mouth of the Humber estuary. It is a district of contrasts in scenery and land use, with a considerable geological influence on both, and it includes the port of Grimsby and its hinterland together with the eastern outskirts of Hull on the other side of the estuary.

The district includes green-field flat-land development potential with a modernised road network adjacent to a traditional main seaway facing mainland Europe and the North Sea oil and gas fields. These factors have fostered industrial development, particularly around Salt End and Killingholme on opposite banks of the Humber. In contrast, agricultural and conservation interests are important in a region of highly productive arable land and extensive wetland natural environment.

The district contains some of Britain's best-developed and best-exposed deposits of the most recent (Devensian) glaciation: indeed, the Dimlington Stadial takes its name from a site described herein. Study of these rocks is of course critical to the analysis of the history and predictability of climatic change. The sites of best exposure, the Holderness sea cliffs, are subject to an even more immediate environmental problem in that they are being eroded at an average rate of 2 to 3 m per year although there is net land accretion occurring a few miles to the south across the mouth of the Humber.

Diverse mineral resources are present but many are not economically viable in the context of current technology and commodity prices. A notable exception is water supply, particularly in South Humberside where the main aquifer, the Chalk, crops out as the Wolds and dips north-eastwards under a thick Quaternary cover to provide artesian supplies in the Grimsby area.

This account, describing the results of a survey which took place between 1971 and 1987, is the first systematic study of the district since the primary one-inch survey of 1878 to 1883. It includes not only the evidence available at the surface but also deductions from subsurface and remotely sensed data such as borehole records and gravity, geomagnetic and seismic measurements, permitting the interpretation of concealed strata and the structure of the crust at depth.

Peter J Cook, DSc
Director

British Geological Survey
Kingsley Dunham Centre
Keyworth
Nottingham NG12 5GG

September 1993

HISTORY OF SURVEY OF THE GRIMSBY AND PATRINGTON SHEETS

The district covered by this memoir comprises the area of 1:50 000 geological sheets 81 (Patrington) and 90 (Grimsby), with adjacent land areas of sheets 82 (including Kilnsea Warren) and 91 (Saltfleet).

The original survey was carried out between 1878 and 1883 by A C G Cameron, J R Dakyns, A J Jukes-Browne, W H Penning, C Reid (the major contributor) and A Strahan for the Old Series sheets 83 to 86 inclusive: mapping was at the scale of 1 inch and 6 inches to the mile, south and north of the Humber respectively.

The resurvey at 1:10 000 scale (or 1:10 560 where 1:10 000 base maps were not available) was done between 1971 and 1987 by Dr N G Berridge, Dr T P Fletcher, Dr G D Gaunt, Mr H Johnson, Dr P W Jones, Mr M C McKeown, Mr J Pattison, Mr E G Smith and Dr I T Williamson.

The following is a list of 1:10 000 geological maps included in the district, with the initials of the surveyors and the dates of survey of each map.

TA 10 NW	Great Limber	HJ	1981–82
TA 10 NE	Riby	ITW, NGB	1982, 1985
TA 10 SW	Cabourne	NGB	1983
TA 10 SE	Swallow	NGB	1983–84
TA 11 NW	North Killingholme	EGS	1968, 1977–80
TA 11 NE	Killingholme Refinery	EGS	1980–81
TA 11 SW	Brocklesby	ITW	1981
TA 11 SE	Immingham	ITW	1981–82
TA 12 NW	Marfleet	GDG	1971, 1977
TA 12 NE	Hedon	MCMcK	1985–1986
TA 12 SW	East Halton Skitter	EGS	1980
TA 12 SE	Paull Holme	EGS	1980–81
TA 13 SW	Summergangs	GDG, MCMcK	1971, 1986
TA 13 SE	Preston	MCMcK	1985–86
TA 20 NW	Laceby	ITW	1980–81
TA 20 NE	Grimsby	ITW	1980
TA 20 SW	Barnoldby le Beck	NGB, JP	1984
TA 20 SE	Waltham	ITW	1980
TA 21 NW	Stone Creek	EGS, ITW	1980, 1982
TA 21 NE	Sunk Island	JP	1985
TA 21 SW	Healing	ITW	1981
TA 21 SE	Grimsby Docks	ITW	1980
TA 22 NW	Burstwick	MCMcK	1985–86
TA 22 NE	Halsham	JP	1985–86
TA 22 SW	Cherry Cobb Sands	MCMcK	1985–86
TA 22 SE	Ottringham	JP	1985
TA 23 SW	Elstronwick	MCMcK	1985–86
TA 23 SE	Roos	JP	1986
TA 30 NW	Cleethorpes	ITW	1980
TA 30 SW	Tetney	ITW	1980
TA 30 SE with part of 30 NE	Northcoates Point	PWJ	1980
TA 31 NW	Outstray Farm	JP	1985
TA 31 NE	Skeffling	ITW, NGB, JP	1982, 1985–86
TA 31 SE	Spurn Head	ITW, JP	1982, 1986
TA 32 NW	Withernsea	NGB	1985
TA 32 SW	Patrington	NGB	1985–86
TA 32 SE with part of 31 NE	Holmpton	NGB	1985–86
TA 33 SW	Tunstall	NGB	1985
TA 40 SW	Pye's Hall	PWJ	1980
TA 41 NW with part of 42 SW	Kilnsea	ITW	1982
TA 41 SW	Old Den	ITW, JP	1982, 1985
TF 19 NW	Nettleton Bottom	TPF, NGB	1983, 1985
TF 19 NE	Thoresway	HJ, NGB	1981, 1985
TF 19 SW	Walesby	HJ, NGB	1981, 1983
TF 19 SE	Stainton le Vale	TPF	1983
TF 29 NW	Wold Newton	NGB	1983–84
TF 29 NE	North Thoresby	NGB, JP	1984
TF 29 SW	Binbrook	TPF	1983
TF 29 SE	North Ormsby	NGB	1984
TF 39 NW	Fulstow	EGS	1981
TF 39 NE	Grainthorpe	PWJ, EGS, JP	1980, 1981 1983
TF 39 SW	Utterby	EGS, JP	1981, 1984
TF 39 SE	Alvingham	EGS, JP	1981, 1983
TF 49 NW	North Somercotes	JP	1983
TF 49 NE	Sand Haile Flats	JP	1984
TF 49 SW	South Somercotes	JP	1983–84
TF 49 SE	Saltfleet	JP	1984

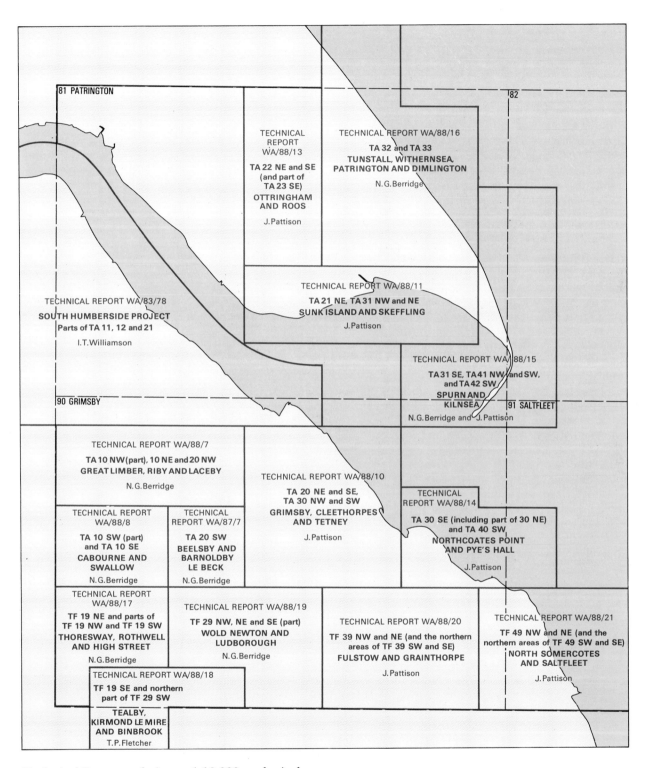

Technical Reports relating to 1:10 000 geological maps.

ACKNOWLEDGEMENTS

NOTES

The main authors of the memoir were N G Berridge, who was also the compiler, and J Pattison. There are major contributions from Dr D W Holliday (first part of Concealed Strata and parts of Economic Geology), Dr I E Penn (second part of Concealed Strata) and Mr M A W Abbott (Structure). Contributors also included Dr P S Balson (Present day estuarine and marine sedimentation), Dr J D Cornwell (Structure), Mr M Davenport (Hydrogeology) and Mr A Forster (Coastal Changes). Specialist geophysics and engineering geology contributions are incorporated within Structure and Coastal Changes respectively. The photographs in the text were taken by Mr T P Cullen and Mr M C McKeown; the complete collection of BGS photographs is listed in Appendix 2. The memoir was edited by Dr R G Thurrell and Dr R W Gallois.

Grateful acknowlegement is given to all landowners and tenants for their cooperation and assistance. We would also like to thank the following organisations for the use of their data and the help of their management and staff: Air Products Ltd., B P Chemicals Ltd., B P Petroleum Development Ltd, British Gas, British Steel Corporation, Geostore Ltd, Holderness Aggregates Ltd, Holderness Borough Council, Howard Humphreys and Partners, Humberside County Council, Lincolnshire County Council, Ove Arup and Partners, Scops Services, Trafalgar House Oil and Gas Ltd, University of Hull and Wimpey Laboratories Ltd. Particular mention is due to Mr T S Whittaker for his keen assistance with the Kelsey Hill Beds at his Keyingham gravel pits, and to Mr C J Wood for his active participation in and editing of Chalk studies. Dr J R Flenley kindly checked and sanctioned the publication of Figure 25.

Throughout the memoir the word 'district' refers to the land area covered by the 1:50 000 geological sheets 81, 82, 90 and 91.

National Grid references are given in square brackets: those beginning the second set of figures (northings) with 9 lie in the 100 km square TF; northings beginning with 0, 1, 2 or 3 lie in the 100 km square TA.

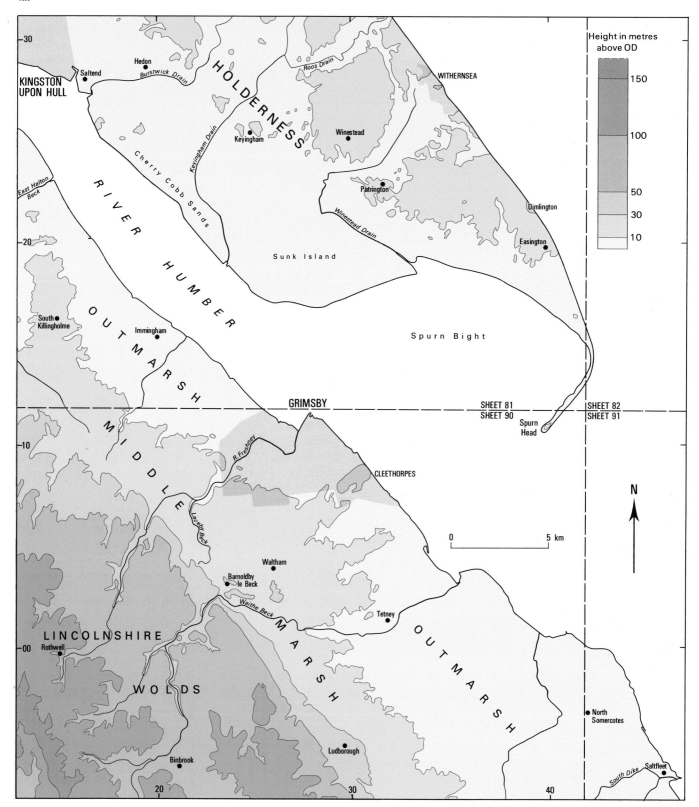

Figure 1   Topography of the district.

ONE

Introduction

The district lies astride the Humber estuary and mostly falls within the county of Humberside, although it also extends into Lincolnshire. The main topographical features are shown on Figure 1 and an outline map of the geology in Figure 2. A generalised geological sequence is given on the inside of the front cover.

The greater part of the district is a low-lying coastal plain drained towards the Humber Estuary and the Lincolnshire North Sea coast by small rivers and artificial waterways. The only significant hills are the Lincolnshire Wolds, which are typical chalk downlands. They consist of a plateau which is thinly draped in the east by glacial till and dissected by a dendritic system of narrow, steep-sided valleys floored by fluvioglacial and postglacial deposits; the main valley is that of Waithe Beck. In the south, the plateau rises to about 165 m above OD, but farther north, inland from Grimsby, it barely reaches 100 m. The indented Wolds scarp, which terminates the plateau on its south-west side, is capped by the Chalk, and the lower slopes are stepped by successive outcrops of interbedded sandstones, mudstones and limestones of Jurassic and early Cretaceous age. The scarp face is subject to widespread landslipping. Lower Cretaceous strata also crop out in the deeper Wolds valleys to the east of Thoresway and Stainton-le-Vale. On their seaward side, the Wolds end in an east-facing slope which is thought to be a degraded and partly buried interglacial sea cliff. In the southernmost part of the district, this slope forms a steep and remarkably straight edge to the Wolds, but it is less distinct north of Barnoldby le Beck.

The Chalk also underlies the coastal plain, which is everywhere covered by thick drift deposits. They mostly consist of till clays and associated glacial sand and gravel, partly overlain by postglacial marine and estuarine sediments. Where thick glacial deposits are at surface, the landscape is commonly gently undulating. It rises to more than 30 m above OD only adjacent to the Wolds and around Waltham south of the Humber, and near Dimlington on the north side. The highest cliffs along the rapidly eroding Holderness coast are at Dimlington. They provide some of the finest exposures of late Pleistocene glacial deposits in England. The surface of the till outcrop south of the Humber generally slopes gently towards the coast. At Cleethorpes, the till forms the only sea cliffs between the Humber and the Wash, but they are now obscured by sea defences.

The coastal plain south of the Humber, known as the Lincolnshire Marsh, is divided into the 'Middle Marsh' on the till and the 'Outmarsh' on the marine alluvium. The Outmarsh and the comparable alluvial plain on the north side of the Humber are underlain by up to 20 m of marine and estuarine clays, silts and sands. These plains are remarkably level at about 2 to 3 m above OD and are thus below the level of high spring tides. They are protected by sand dunes or man-made sea walls, and are drained via sluices. Much of the Outmarsh south of Cleethorpes, and Sunk Island with Cherry Cobb Sands north of the Humber, have been reclaimed from the sea in the last 400 years.

The youngest geological deposits in the district are the beach sand, shingle and, in places, dune sand which partly overlie and fringe the marine alluvium. Inland beach deposits mark the position of old coastlines on both sides of the Humber, and the Spurn peninsula is the most recent of a succession of shingle spits to have projected across the estuary from the north. The flatness of the Lincolnshire 'Outmarsh' is also broken by the extensive waste tips of the medieval salt industry.

Most of the population of the district is concentrated in the Grimsby/Cleethorpes conurbation and in the eastern suburbs of Hull. Commuter settlements extend eastwards from Hull and southwards from Cleethorpes. The greater part of the district is given over to arable farming, much of it in very large units, especially on the grade one soils of the reclaimed areas. The main crops are sugar beet (south of the Humber), wheat, barley and oilseed rape. Pig farming is common in Holderness and market gardening is locally important, notably on the sandy soils of the old beach at North Somercotes and under glass around Keyingham. Produce from the former area partly goes to the food-freezing industry of Grimsby/Cleethorpes, which is still a major employer despite the drastic decline of the Grimsby fishing fleet. Grimsby remains an active port, although not as busy as Immingham and Hull which offer roll-on, roll-off facilities. Hydrocarbons are the bases of the largest new industries: the refinery at Killingholme, petrochemicals at Salt End and the pipeline terminal (from offshore production) at Easington. The coast attracts many tourists, mostly to the resorts of Cleethorpes and Withernsea. However, much of the shoreline, where flanked by wide mud flats and salt marsh, is undeveloped and long stretches of it are reserved for Ministry of Defence use and/or environment conservation.

OUTLINE OF GEOLOGICAL HISTORY

Pre-Upper Palaeozoic metamorphic rocks probably comprise a crystalline basement throughout the district. Major sedimentary sequences displaying tectonic and erosional breaks characterise the overlying Carboniferous. From the Permian onwards there was fluctuation between sedimentation, uplift, tilting and faulting, but comparatively little folding.

Throughout the Permian and Triassic, the district lay at the western margins of an epicontinental basin in an arid climatic environment. Thereafter, variations between

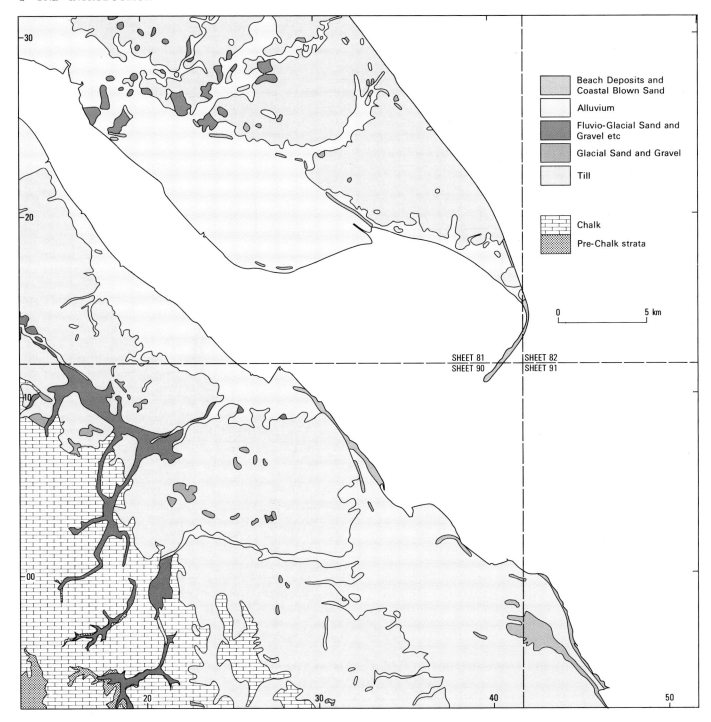

Figure 2 Simplified geological map of the district.

subaerial, estuarine and marine conditions prevailed in a more humid climate throughout the Jurassic and Cretaceous. During much of this period of plate migration, a persistent tectonic 'high', the Market Weighton Block or Structure, reduced sediment thickness from south to north across the district. No trace of topmost Cretaceous or of any Tertiary sedimentary rock is preserved in the district. Younger deposits relate to ice ages and interglacials from the Anglian Stage of the Pleistocene to the present; deposits of the last 15 000 years are particularly widespread

HISTORY OF RESEARCH

Given the extensive cover of drift deposits across the district, it is not surprising that much of the past geological interest has been centred on the Quaternary, and espe-

2

cially on the late Pleistocene glacial history. However, the solid geology of the Lincolnshire Wolds has attracted study since the middle of the nineteenth century and boreholes and modern geophysical methods have provided much information on the concealed rocks of the coastal plain since the Second World War.

Study of the sub-Chalk succession in east Lincolnshire has been primarily aimed at an understanding of the widespread facies variations and depositional breaks represented within it. Judd (1867) established some of the currently accepted divisions and related them to wider Upper Jurassic and Lower Cretaceous classifications. The primary Survey work produced minor amendments (Strahan, 1886; Lamplugh, 1896). Notable twentieth century contributions have been made by Swinnerton (1935, 1941) and Casey (1973).

The Chalk of the northern province (Lincolnshire and Yorkshire) has been a subject of special interest, its nomenclature having often been inadvisably related to that of south-east England. Early classifications of the Chalk of the region were a mixture of the litho- and biostratigraphical (Hill, 1888; Burnett, 1904). They were summarised and set in a wider context in Jukes-Browne and Hill's comprehensive memoir 'The Cretaceous Rocks of Britain' (1900–04); Jukes-Browne had mapped much of the Lincolnshire Wolds, mostly within this district. More refined biozonal schemes for the Chalk followed, using ammonoids and belemnoids (Bower and Farmery, 1910; Rowe, 1929). J R Farmery and the Reverend C R Bower were local amateur geologists who helped Rowe while he was in the area working on his zonal classification for the whole of the English and French Chalk. However, Rowe's own Lincolnshire work was not published until after his death. Research by the British Geological Survey in the region in the last two decades has instigated a revised stratigraphical classification (Wood and Smith, 1978), which is used in this account.

The Pleistocene deposits of the district have attracted comment since the early nineteenth century. The Kelsey Hill Gravels near Keyingham were noted by William Smith in his 1821 geological map of Yorkshire and were discussed by Phillips (1829). The first comprehensive review of the east Yorkshire and Lincolnshire drift deposits was made by Wood and Rome (1868). They recognised many of the Pleistocene lithostratigraphical divisions which have provoked scrutiny and debate to the present day, including the Basement, Purple and Hessle boulder clays and the 'Bridlington Crag' north of the Humber, and the Chalky and Purple boulder clays and the Kirmington interglacial beds on the south side. They correctly correlated all the surface till ('Boulder Clay') of the coastal plain south of the Humber with the late Pleistocene (Devensian) Purple and Hessle tills of the Holderness cliffs, and unequivocally recognised the Basement till of Holderness as the only older Pleistocene deposit east of the Wolds. Subsequent discussion has centred on the nature of the Kelsey Hill Gravels and the 'Bridlington Crag', on which interglacial is represented by the Kirmington beds, and on whether the Devensian tills are the products of one or more glacial advances. Meticulous descriptive work on the Holderness coast by Reid (1885), Lamplugh (1881) and especially by Bisat (1939, 1940) and Catt and Madgett (1981) facilitated subsequent studies of the tills by the Hull University-based geologists, L F Penny, J A Catt and P A Madgett. In two major papers (Catt and Penny, 1966; Madgett and Catt, 1978) they interpreted the Holderness cliffs succession as comprising contemporaneous late Devensian Withernsea (Purple) and Skipsea (Drab) tills locally separated by the Dimlington Silts from the underlying pre-Devensian Basement Till which incorporates 'rafts' of Hoxnian or even older 'Bridlington Crag'. This interpretation, based largely on petrographical analysis of the tills and a radiocarbon age for the silts, has become a cornerstone of Pleistocene studies in England (see Rose, 1985), but has been challenged on evidence from both geomorphology (Straw, 1979, and in discussion of Madgett and Catt, 1978) and sedimentology (Derbyshire et al., 1984). The shells in the Kelsey Hill Gravels were described by Prestwich (1861); most subsequent authors (for example Penny, 1974) have considered them to be an at least partly derived assemblage reworked during the late Devensian glaciation. A Hoxnian age for the Kirmington interglacial is now generally accepted, following work based on palynology (Watts, 1959; Harland and Downie, 1969), artefacts (Boylan, 1966) and sea-level criteria (Gaunt et al., 1992).

The postglacial depositional history has received less attention, partly because of a scarcity of data. The broad chronology has been established in this and neighbouring districts by radiocarbon dating and correlation of peats, within both shoreline sequences and lacustrine 'mere' infills (Swinnerton, 1931; Gaunt and Tooley, 1974; Beckett, 1981). The most recent deposits along the coast are better understood because they have topographical expression and their development has been documented. Coastal processes and changes have been described by Valentin (1971), A H W Robinson (1964), D N Robinson (1970), Pringle (1981) and de Boer (1964, 1981).

Deep boreholes and geophysical techniques have brought a greater understanding of the subsurface geology in recent years. Gravity and magnetic anomaly surveys have been interpreted to define basement structures (Bott et al., 1978), downhole geophysical logs have been used for Chalk lithostratigraphical correlation (Barker et al., 1984) and, in several syntheses of borehole, seismic and other geophysical evidence, the late Sir Peter Kent (e.g. 1966, 1974, 1980a) described the broad structures of the Palaeozoic and Mesozoic rocks in the region. He also did much to popularise the subject both as an active officer of local learned societies and as an author (1980b) or co-author (Swinnerton and Kent, 1976) of local geological guides.

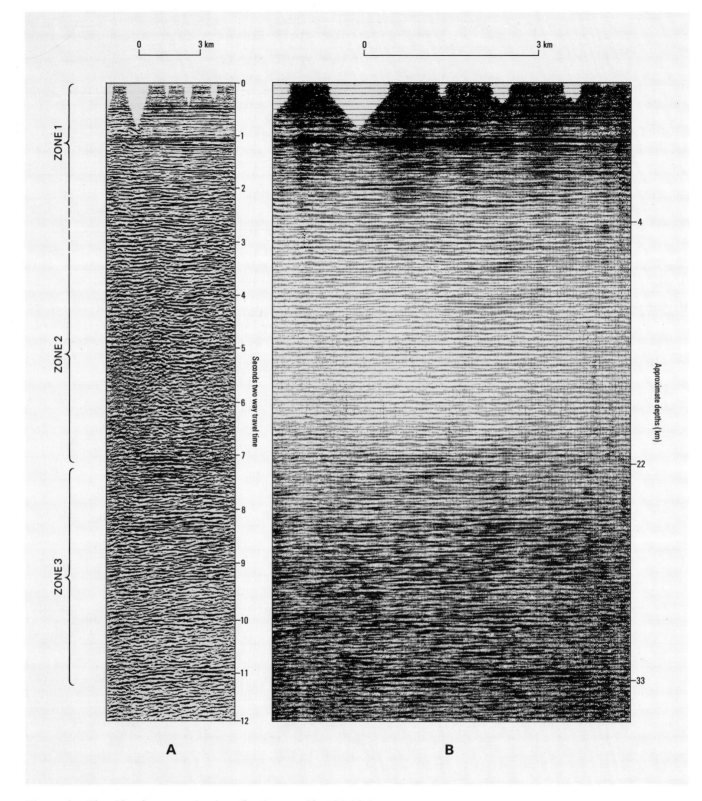

Figure 3   The Cleethorpes seismic reflection profile IGS-83-1.
A. Final Stack.
B. Stack with no Automatic Gain Control (AGC) scaling, showing approximate
true relative amplitudes. From Whittaker and Chadwick (1984) fig. 3.

TWO

Structure

Whereas the structure of the Cretaceous solid rocks of the district at outcrop is simple, with an average dip of less than 1° east in the Chalk and little recorded faulting, that of older strata is more complex. The following summarises the crustal setting of the district and its post-Caledonian tectonic history, the effects of which are illustrated with a series of stratum-contour maps. Pleistocene glaciotectonics are discussed elsewhere, in the context of syngenetic sediments.

Throughout much of northern England it has been shown by seismic reflection profiles, down to 12 seconds two-way travel time (s TWTT), that the Earth's crust can be divided into three zones (Whittaker and Chadwick, 1984; Whittaker et al., 1986; Chadwick et al., 1989). One of these profiles (Cleethorpes IGS-83-1) confirms this pattern in the present district (Figure 3).

The lowest unit (Zone 3) is characterised by strongly layered high-amplitude reflections seen on IGS-83-1 from around 7 to just below 11s TWTT (approximately 22 to 33 km) (Figure 3) and corresponds to the lower crust, with its base at or close to the Mohorovičić discontinuity (Whittaker and Chadwick, 1984). The overlying Zone 2 (2 to 7s TWTT) is characterised by ill-defined, incoherent, low-amplitude reflections (Figure 3b), including multiple reflections from the overlying Zone 1. Zone 2, although not penetrated by drilling, is believed to contain Lower Palaeozoic rocks which form part of a northwest–south-east–tending Caledonian orogenic belt (Turner, 1949; Kent, 1967; Whittaker et al., 1986; Pharaoh et al., 1987). Aeromagnetic data (Figure 9) indicate that two types of Lower Palaeozoic rock form the basement: an igneous or metamorphic 'magnetic' sequence lying at relatively shallow depths in the south-west of the district, overlain by a north-easterly thickening sequence of Lower Palaeozoic sediments. Zone 1 comprises subparallel, continuous reflections of varying strength and amplitude which have been correlated with the Mesozoic and Upper Palaeozoic sediments proved in deep boreholes (Figure 4). On seismic profile IGS-83-1, the base of this zone at around 2s TWTT (approximately 4 km) is indistinct (Figure 3), although more recent (post-1980) seismic data elsewhere in eastern England has shown it to be a well-defined unconformity. Maps of depth to the pre-Upper Palaeozoic 'basement' surface, based largely on seismic reflection and refraction surveys (Kent, 1967; Evans et al., 1988), indicate a general north-north-east-dipping surface from around 2.6 km in the extreme south-west of the district to 4 km at Grimsby.

Regional interpretations of subsurface data have been published for the Carboniferous (Holliday, 1986) and Permian and Mesozoic sequences (Gale et al., 1983; Whittaker, 1985). The main post-Lower Palaeozoic features of the region are summarised in Figure 5. Structural activity during Carboniferous times was characterised by the development of stable blocks (East Midlands Shelf) and syndepositional fault-bounded basins (Gainsborough Trough, Widmerpool Gulf) (Kent, 1966), during a period of north–south crustal extension possibly associated with subduction of the Variscan Fold-Belt to the south (Leeder, 1982; Bott et al., 1984; Fraser et al., 1990). Deformation and erosion of the Carboniferous rocks occurred as a consequence of late Carboniferous (Variscan) compression. Thereafter, until the end of the Cretaceous, an extensional stress field dominated the tectonic development of Britain. In early Permian times the region formed an area of low relief, the Eastern England Shelf, which lay on the western margin of the Southern North Sea Basin. During late Permian and Triassic times the shelf was dominated by subsidence related to peripheral flexuring associated with active rifting in the Southern North Sea (Chadwick, 1985b). Differentiation of the region into a stable southern shelf (Eastern England Shelf) and an unstable, rapidly subsiding northern basin (Cleveland Basin) began in Rhaetian times (Kent, 1955). The northern part of the Eastern England Shelf, the Market Weighton Block, which lies close to the north

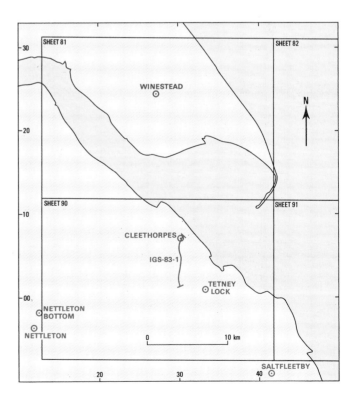

Figure 4   Location of deep boreholes and seismic profile IGS-83-1 (Cleethorpes).

of the district (Figure 5), was characterised by intermittent uplift from late Triassic to early Cretaceous times. Previously, the area of the block had been a depocentre for the Sherwood Sandstone (Holloway, 1985).

Pronounced gravity lows centred at Market Weighton [SE 85 40] and 8 to 12 km offshore [TA 25 45] from Hornsea have been interpreted as buried ?Caledonian granites (Bott et al., 1978; Bott, 1988; Cornwell and Walker, 1989; Donato and Megson, 1990) and are thought to have resulted in the relative 'buoyancy' of the block. The Vale of Pickering–Flamborough Head Fault zone forms the northern margin of the Market Weight Block; it can be traced offshore to intersect the Dowsing and Central fault zones (Figure 5) (Kirby and Swallow, 1987).

A gradual decrease in the rate of subsidence on the shelf from early to mid-Jurassic times was related to a decrease in active extension in the Southern North Sea and was followed by an increased rate in late Jurassic times due to renewed extension (Chadwick, 1985a). Cessation of active extension in early Cretaceous times led to hiatuses in sedimentation, with a complex sequence of regressions, erosional episodes and transgressions. A regional thermal subsidence, possibly in conjunction with global rise in sea level, began in Aptian times and had its major effect in this district at the beginning of the Albian, heralding deposition of the Chalk during later Cretaceous times (Chadwick, 1985b). A change in the tectonic regime in late Cretaceous to early Tertiary times from one of dominant crustal extension to one of dominant compression resulted in uplift, gentle easterly tilting and erosion of the region during the Tertiary.

The relatively simple structure of the Upper Palaeozoic and Mesozoic sequences is demonstrated by the top 2s TWTT of seismic reflection profile IGS-83-1 (Figure 6) and six structure contour maps of the district (Figures 7a–f). These maps are generalised from regional studies and they omit small-scale faults and folds. Two major regional unconformities divide the sequence structurally: the first at the base of the Permian (Figure 7b), and the second at the base of the Albian.

The basal-Permian unconformity separates folded, faulted and eroded Carboniferous strata from the largely undeformed Permian and Mesozoic sequence. Although there is little apparent discordance in dip between the subcropping Coal Measures and the overlying rocks on IGS-83-1 (Figure 6), a northerly increase in the depth of erosion can be demonstrated (p.5). Only limited data are available concerning the structure of the Dinantian

and Namurian sequences within the district. Structure contours on the top of Carboniferous Limestone indicate a general north-easterly dip from 2000 m in the south-west of the district to in excess of 3000 m beneath Cleethorpes (Figure 6). Structure contours on the Top Hard Coal (=Barnsley Coal, Wesphalian B; Figure 7a) show a regional dip of 2 to 3° to the east, trending more north-easterly in the south-east of the district. The Carboniferous sequence in the district is characterised by low-amplitude folding and a large number of minor faults. Displacement on these faults are generally of the order of tens of metres (Figure 6); they a form a conjugate set trending largely north-east and north-west, with a subordinate easterly trending set. Few of the faults are seen to penetrate the post-Carboniferous cover; where they do, they have much reduced throws (Figure 6). Similarly, few of the low-amplitude folds recognised in the Carboniferous strata affect later rocks.

Structure contour maps of the top surface of the Sherwood Sandstone Group, Mercia Mudstone Group and the Lias (Figures 7c–e) show gentle (1 to 2°) easterly dipping surfaces 'rippled' by numerous open folds, commonly associated with minor, dominantly normal faults, orientated north-east or north-west, with displacements typically less than 20 m.

The Albian unconformity separates eroded Upper Jurassic and Lower Cretaceous strata from the overstepping Carstone. Structure contours on the base of the Chalk (Figure 7f) show a largely undeformed gently dipping surface. The base of the Chalk crops out in the south-west of the district; it reaches depths of 550 m below OD beneath the Withernsea coast, and more than 750 m in the offshore part of the district (Whittaker, 1985). In the north of the district this surface dips mainly to the east-north-east, but towards the south the dip changes to north-east. This change takes place at the principal structure within the Chalk, the Caistor Monocline (Figure 7f; Versey, 1934; Berridge, 1985, 1986), an east–west-trending structure which can be traced eastwards from the Chalk outcrop using data from numerous water wells (Barker et al., 1984); it is also associated with minor irregularities in the aeromagnetic and Bouger gravity anomaly maps (Figures 8 and 9). In the west of the district, this structure has an effective northerly downthrow of c.90 m (Berridge, 1986). However, there appears to be no comparable structure at depth beneath the Chalk (Figure 7e) and it dies out towards the coast. Another minor east–west-trending fold is seen to the south of the Winestead Borehole (Figure 7f).

Figure 5   Sketch map of eastern England showing the post-Lower Palaeozoic structural context of the district. Carboniferous features in italics. (Adapted from Kirby et al., 1987).

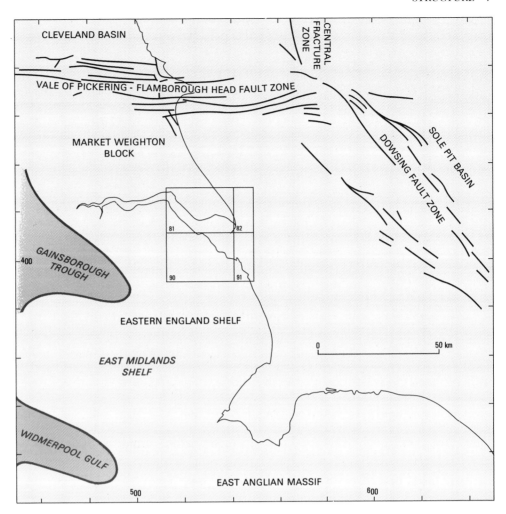

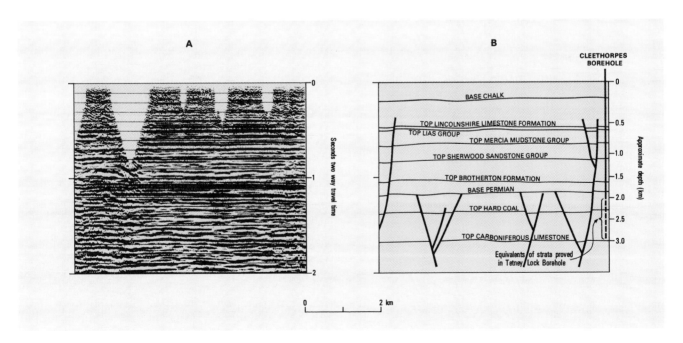

Figure 6   A. Upper part of Cleethorpes seismic reflection profile IGS-83-1
B. Simplified geological interpretation.

Figure 7   Generalised structure contour maps showing six stages in the structural evolution of the district.

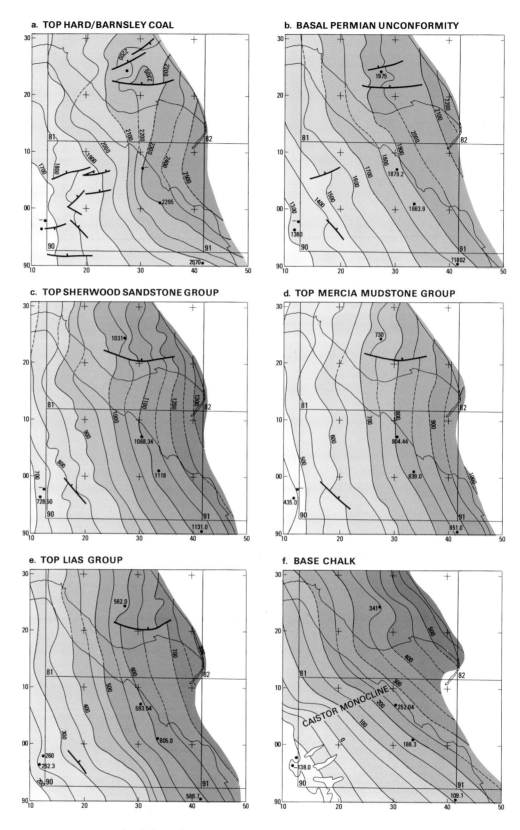

a. TOP HARD/BARNSLEY COAL

b. BASAL PERMIAN UNCONFORMITY

c. TOP SHERWOOD SANDSTONE GROUP

d. TOP MERCIA MUDSTONE GROUP

e. TOP LIAS GROUP

f. BASE CHALK

• Borehole proving contoured surface (see Figure 4 for borehole names)

0   10 km

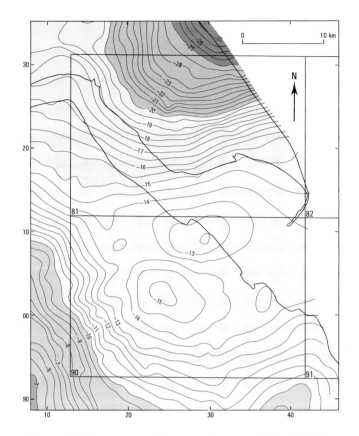

Figure 8 Bouger gravity anomaly map of the district.

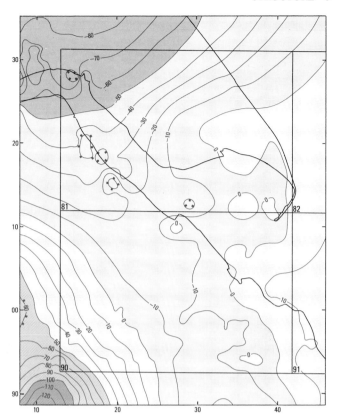

Figure 9 Aeromagnetic anomaly map of the district.

THREE
Concealed strata

The oldest rocks at surface within the district belong to the late Jurassic Kimmeridge Clay Formation. Below these, strata as old as Upper Carboniferous have been proved in the deep boreholes at Cleethorpes [3024 0709], Tetney Lock [3325 0900] and Winestead [2741 2433], and at Nettleton [1185 9642] just beyond the south-western margin of the district (Figure 4). Boreholes about 40 km to the south and south-west of Grimsby (Kent, 1967; Pharoah et al., 1987) have proved cleaved and highly deformed Precambrian (inferred) and Lower Palaeozoic basement rocks, which are thought to underlie the district. The Carboniferous Limestone, probably about 1000 m thick, which unconformably overlies the basement rocks, has been proved 2 km to the south of the district at Saltfleetby [4145 9088] and near Brigg [0377 0639], 30 km west of Grimsby (Gaunt et al., 1992); it probably underlies the whole of the district. In addition to the borehole data, there are numerous commercial seismic reflection profiles which reveal much about the geology of the concealed formations. However, apart from a short section (IGS-83-1) linking the Cleethorpes Borehole to the commercial seismic network, these data remain confidential. From such data, Fraser et al. (1990) have reviewed the Carboniferous rocks in the subsurface of eastern England, and general reviews of the concealed Permian and Mesozoic strata of the Lincolnshire and east Yorkshire region have been prepared by Gale et al. (1983) and Whittaker (1985).

CARBONIFEROUS

Namurian

Throughout much of eastern England, the Carboniferous Limestone was exposed and eroded in late Dinantian and early Namurian times. The succeeding Namurian and Westphalian rocks are commonly uncomformable on the eroded top of the limestone and such a relationship probably applies throughout much of the district. Seismic data suggest that the Namurian rocks thin towards the south of the district, a view confirmed by the Saltfleetby Borehole in which rocks of this age are absent. The Namurian rocks must, therefore, be overstepped between Tetney Lock and Saltfleetby, considerably farther north than shown in some recent reconstructions (e.g. Howitt and Brunstrom, 1966, fig. 5; Holliday, 1986, fig. 5.9b).

There is no direct evidence relating to the nature or age of the early Namurian rocks of the district. The seismic evidence suggests that Pendleian and Arnsbergian rocks can have only a limited development, and that they are onlapped by Westphalian strata near the southern margin of the district. The suggestion that there might be a major late Dinantian to early Namurian basin (Humber Basin) in the district, comparable to the Gainsborough, Edale and Widmerpool gulfs east of the Pennines (Kent 1966; Howitt and Brunstrom, 1966), is not supported by the present data.

The oldest rocks for which there is direct evidence within the district were penetrated in the Tetney Lock Borehole (Figure 10). There, an incomplete Namurian succession containing a variety of lithologies comparable to those of the late Namurian Millstone Grit of the Pennines was proved. Only limited core material is now available, and the sequence is largely based on the mud (rock cuttings) log and on interpretation of the wireline (geophysical) logs (Figure 10). A wide range of sandstone lithologies was recorded, including white to pale grey, very fine- to very coarse-grained and pebbly, friable to hard varieties; siderite, pyrite, carbonaceous matter and several kinds of mica were also present locally. Interbedded with these are grey siltstones and grey to dark grey mudstones and silty mudstones, and one thin coal seam. Although no detailed sedimentological review of these beds is available, the lithologies are consistent with the deltaic origin generally inferred for the Millstone Grit.

Stratigraphical division of these Namurian rocks (Figure 10) has been attempted using palynological methods (by Dr B Owens) and by comparison of wireline log signatures (by Dr D W Holliday, Dr G A Kirby and Mr K Smith). The limited faunas in the cores have been examined by Dr N J Riley. From these studies, the position of the Subcrenatum Marine Band, marking the Namurian/Westphalian boundary, seems firmly fixed, although no goniatites and only *Lingula mytilloides* J Sowerby were recovered from the core taken at this level. Below this, the value of the palynological work is uncertain as, with one exception, the results are based on cuttings samples which may include caved material. However, the presence of *Crassispora kosanke* (Pontonié and Kemp) Bharadwaj in significant numbers in a sample from the penultimate core at a depth of 2842 m suggests a late Namurian age and supports the view that the borehole did not penetrate strata older than of Kinderscoutian age (Figure 10).

Westphalian

A thickness of 740 m of Westphalian rocks was proved in the Tetney Lock Borehole (Figure 11). They are comparable in lithology and general character with the Coal Measures exposed to the west in the South Yorkshire/ Derbyshire/Nottinghamshire Coalfield, and are part of the concealed extension of that coalfield beneath Lincolnshire and Humberside (Howitt and Brunstom, 1966). The log signatures obtained at Tetney Lock are broadly similar to those of Coal Measures farther west (Howitt and Brunstrom, 1966; Downing and Howitt,

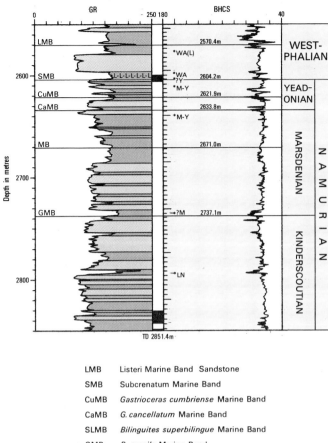

LMB   Listeri Marine Band Sandstone

SMB   Subcrenatum Marine Band

CuMB   *Gastrioceras cumbriense* Marine Band

CaMB   *G. cancellatum* Marine Band

SLMB   *Bilinguites superbilingue* Marine Band

GMB   *B. gracile* Marine Band

* Palynological age determination

WA   Westphalian A (L Lower)

LN   Late Namurian

Y   Yeadonian

M   Marsdenian

[ ] Sandstone

[ ] Siltstone and mudstone

L-L-L-L-L *Lingula* Band

[ ] Cored interval

GR   Gamma ray log in API units

BHCS   Borehole compensated sonic log in μsft⁻¹

Figure 10 Namurian strata proved in the Tetney Lock Borehole.

1969; Whittaker et al., 1985), and this has enabled the position of many of the marker beds and horizons of the outcrop area to be recognised or inferred at Tetney Lock (Figure 11). The dominant rock types are grey siltstones and grey to dark grey mudstones, associated with numerous coal seams, pale grey sandstones, seatearths and iron-stones. The sandstones exhibit considerable lithological variation, ranging from very fine to very coarse grained and pebbly, with variable amounts of carbonaceous mat-

ter, micas and other accessory minerals. The upper 180 m of strata are stained red, purple or green beneath the sub-Permian unconformity.

The boundaries between the Wesphalian A, B and C stages can be broadly located from the palynological studies of Dr Owens, and then refined by the geophysical log correlation of Dr Kirby and Dr Holliday (Figure 11). A fauna including *Euestheria* sp. and *Geisina arcuata* (Bean), identified by Dr Riley from core between 2442.51 and 2447.09 m, is believed to indicate the Low Estheria Band. The age of the beds above 1972 m is uncertain; Dr Owens has found no diagnostic palyno-morphs in these beds, but an unpublished study by Shell UK Exploration and Production Ltd has suggested that beds of Westphalian D age may be present above 1958 m.

Coal Measures were also proved in the Cleethorpes (208 m thick) and Winestead (20 m proved) boreholes. The partially reddened and stained sequence in the former has been described by Kirby (1985) but, due to borehole collapse, wireline logs are not available for most of the Westphalian sequence. However, there is sufficient biostratigraphical detail to establish that both Westphalian B and C strata were penetrated and that the top of the Coal Measures sequence there is close to the level of the Cambriense Marine Band. Only cuttings descriptions are available from the Winestead Borehole, where red, maroon, green and grey argillaceous silt-stones with coaly streaks were proved. These are believed to be Westphalian B in age (Smith, 1985).

About 540 m of Lower and Middle Coal Measures strata (Westphalian A to C) were proved just beyond the district boundary at Saltfleetby. There, Lower Coal Measures directly overlie the Carboniferous Limestone and, early Westphalian A rocks are apparently absent. It is likely that similar stratigraphical relationships occur over much of the southern margin of the district.

PERMIAN AND TRIASSIC

In late Carboniferous and early Permian times, the Carboniferous rocks of the district were gently uplifted, folded and faulted during the Variscan Orogeny. The extensive reddening, staining and erosion of the Westphalian rocks occurred at this time. Although there is generally only little apparent discordance in dip between the Coal Measures and the overlying rocks, there is a major unconformity at this level. Within the district, the basal Permian rocks gradually overstep the older Westphalian rocks towards the north and north-east. At Tetney Lock they rest on late Westphalian C or early Westphalian D strata; at Cleethorpes on mid-Westphalian C beds, at a level about 175 m stratigraphically lower; and at Winestead on Westphalian B rocks more than 300 m stratigraphically lower (Smith, 1985) (Figure 12). At Saltfleetby, Permian strata rest on Middle Coal Measures (beds high in mid-Westphalian C).

During Permian and Triassic times, the district lay towards the south-western margin of the Southern North Sea Basin. The regional setting and correlation of the Permo-Triassic rocks has been described by various

Figure 11
Westphalian
strata in the
Tetney Lock
Borehole.

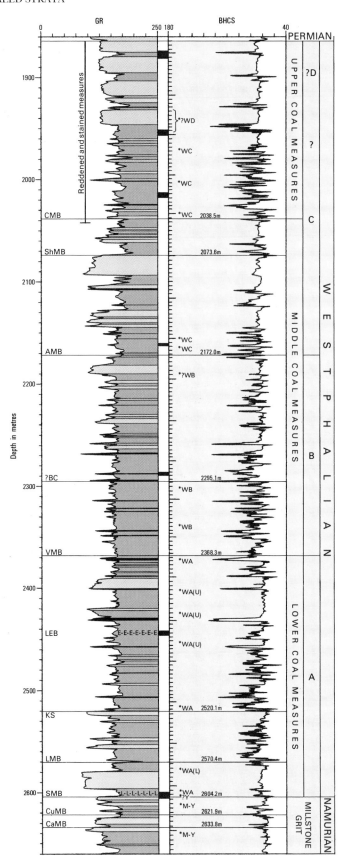

CMB	Cambriense Marine Band
ShMB	Shafton Marine Band
AMB	Aegiranum Marine Band
VMB	Vanderbeckei Marine Band
LMB	Listeri Marine Band
SMB	Subcrenatum Marine Band
LEB	Low *Estheria* Band
CuMB	*Gastrioceras cumbriense* Marine Band
CaMB	*G. cancellatum* Marine Band
?BC	Inferred position of Barnsley/Top Hard Coal
KS	Kilburn Sandstone

*	Palynological age determination
WD	Westphalian D
WC	Westphalian C
WB	Westphalian B
WA	Westphalian A (U Upper, L Lower)
Y	Yeadonian } Namurian
M	Marsdenian }

Sandstone

Siltstone and mudstone

— Coal

L-L-L-L-L *Lingula* Band

E-E-E-E-E *Euestheria* Band

▮ Cored interval

GR	Gamma ray log in API units
BHCS	Borehole compensated sonic log in μsft^{-1}

authors concentrating on special aspects of the subject (e.g. Smith, 1989; Smith et al., 1974; Warrington, 1974; Warrington et al., 1980; Gale et al., 1983; Glennie, 1986; Whittaker, 1985; Harwood and Smith, 1986; Taylor, 1986; Fisher, 1986). There is considerable lateral variation of thickness and facies across the basin, especially within the Permian rocks (Figure 13), but little of that variation is shown in the three deep boreholes within the district (Figure 12). There are, however, significant differences when these are compared with boreholes, such as that at Nettleton, just beyond the borders of the district (Figure 12). The Market Weighton Structure, which significantly influenced Jurassic and Lower Cretaceous sedimentation in eastern England (Kent, 1980a), appears to have had little noticeable effect on the Permo-Triassic rocks of the district.

Despite the great variety of lithologies and the wide range of depositional environments shown by the Permo-Triassic rocks of eastern England, they are unified by their common origin in a region with hot and arid climate (Smith et al., 1974). Much of the sequence is in a redbed facies, and those parts that are not (i.,e. the carbonate/evaporite sequences) are interbedded with, and pass laterally into redbeds, largely beyond the margins of the district. Evaporite minerals (notably gypsum, anhydrite and halite) occur abundantly throughout the Permian sequence as discrete, commonly thick beds, in nodules and veins, and more pervasively as cements. Dolomite is also common, replacing limestones in the Permian rocks, and is an important component of the late Triassic argillaceous rocks. Although sedimentation was not continuous throughout the period, breaks in deposition were few and did not give rise to unconformities of any significance within the district. The paucity of fossils in these redbeds means that the precise position of the boundary between the Permian and Triassic systems in eastern England is not known. It cannot be related with certainty to any basinwide lithological marker, but probably occurs within the Eskdale Group, just above the Littlebeck Anhydrite, though it may be as high as the basal part of the Sherwood Sandstone Group (Smith et al., 1974; Warrington et al., 1980).

The Permo-Triassic sequences proved in the boreholes of this district are shown in Figure 12. There is only limited core material available and the stratigraphical successions have been constructed mainly from integrated borehole, mud log and wireline log data. Few biostratigraphically significant data have been obtained from these boreholes; the stratigraphical nomenclature used here follows Smith et al. (1986) and Warrington et al. (1980). A detailed description of the sequence proved in the Cleethorpes Borehole has been published by Kirby (1985). Only minor variations from this have been found in the other deep boreholes (Figure 12).

Basal Permian Sands

The Basal Permian Sands thicken from north to south in the district, from 19.2 m at Winestead to 25.7 m at Cleethorpes and 40.5 m at Tetney Lock, as part of a regional thickening from eastern Yorkshire to central Lincolnshire. The rocks cored at Cleethorpes are wholly fluvial in character; they are dominantly composed of interbedded medium-grained sandstones and conglomerates, with a few mudstone partings (Kirby, 1985). Typically, the quartz grains are only moderately sorted and rounded. Porosity values range up to 20 per cent, and the maximum permeability is about 200 mD. Coarse, well-rounded and frosted, 'millet seed' quartz grains, indicative of aeolian deposition, are rare. At Tetney Lock, mudstone and siltstone partings, and (below 1856.8 m) conglomerates, are also present. This, and the general similarity of lithologies and geophysical log character to those proved at Cleethorpes, suggest a dominantly fluvial common origin. According to the composite log, 'millet seed' grains occur only 'occasionally'. The mud log for the Winestead Borehole is less detailed, but suggests that conglomeratic rocks are present there also, and that a fluvial origin for all or most of the beds present is likely. The occurrence of relatively small but significant numbers of 'millet seed' grains, at Winestead as well as Tetney Lock, suggests that aeolian strata are locally interbedded with those of fluvial origin and/or that, elsewhere in the basin, aeolian dunes were reworked by rivers which flowed periodically within the desert area. This evidence for widespread fluvial deposition within the district is apparently contrary to the commonly stated conclusion that the Basal Permian Sands of eastern England are dominantly aeolian in origin (Smith et al., 1974; Marie, 1975; Glennie, 1986).

Don Group

The continental Basal Permian Sands are succeeded by dominantly marine deposits of the late Permian Zechstein Sea. Within the district, and over much of the Southern North Sea Basin, these take the form of carbonate/evaporite cycles. Five major cycles have been recognised, namely English Zechstein (EZ) 1 to 5, although the upper two cycles are much thinner and less completely developed than the lower ones (Smith, 1989); the first two commonly can be subdivided into a number of subcycles. The cyclic nature of these beds is believed to result from periodic transgression and subsequent regression of the Zechstein Sea. The Don Group encompasses the deposits laid down during the first of these major transgressive (carbonate)/regressive (evaporite) sequences (EZ1).

The **Marl Slate** is taken as the basal bed of the Don Group, although locally the upper part of the Basal Permian Sands includes deposits reworked by the initial Zechstein marine transgression. It is a finely laminated, sapropelic, calcareous and dolomitic, pyritic siltstone, generally 2 to 3 m thick within the district, and is believed to have formed under anoxic conditions below wave base in the sea which drowned the pre-Zechstein topography. The Marl Slate is a thin but persistent marker, generally easily recognised on gamma-ray logs (Whittaker et al., 1985) (Figure 12).

In the three deep boreholes of the district, the succeeding **Cadeby Formation** is relatively thin (8 to 15 m). It comprises fine-grained dolomites ranging in colour between cream, brown and grey, with a varying, and commonly large, proportion of associated white anhydrite. It is regard-

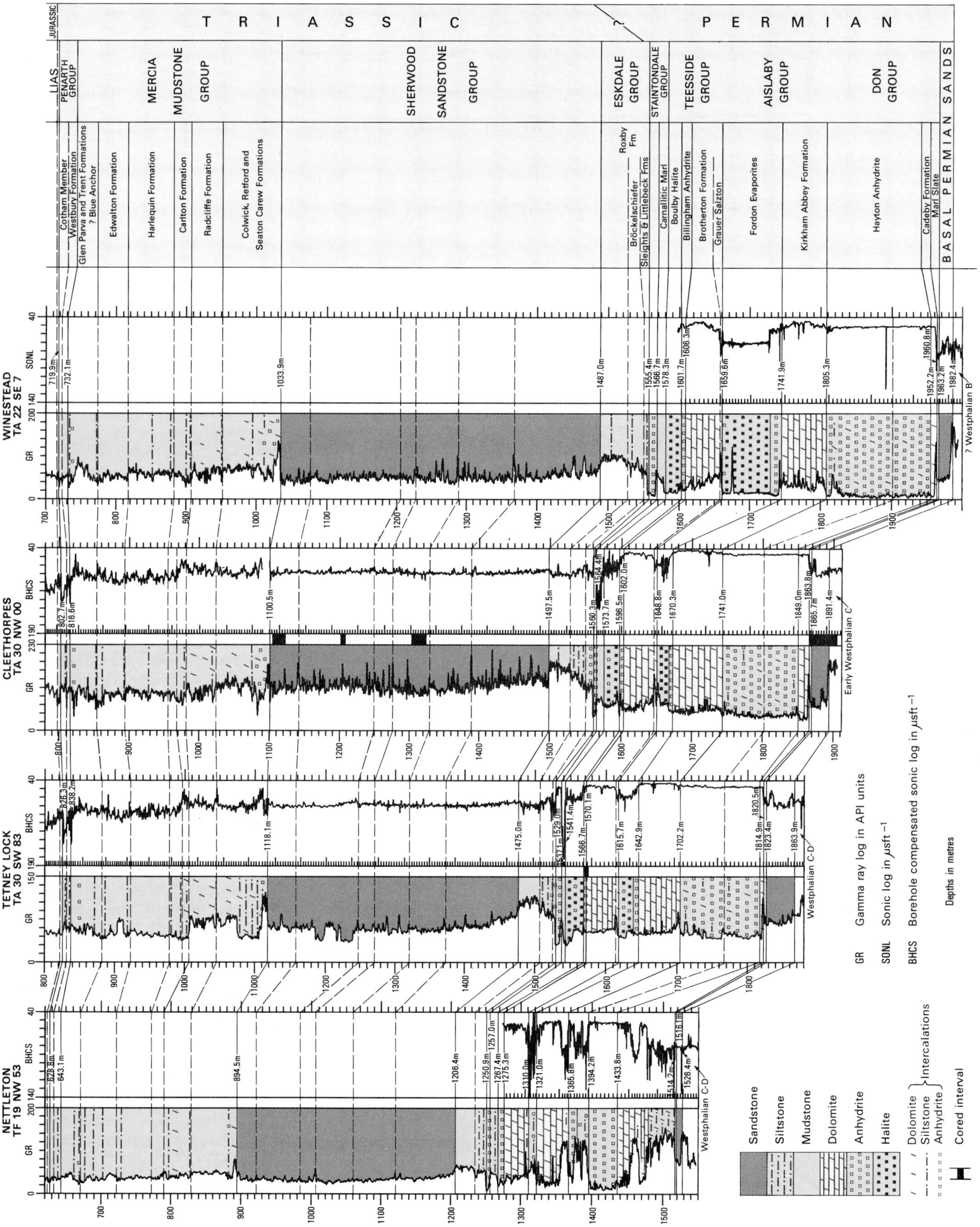

Figure 12   Correlation of Permo-Triassic strata proved in boreholes.

ed as being a basinal relatively deep-water facies and is probably consistent through much of the district. Towards the south-west, however, as evidenced by the Nettleton Borehole (Figure 12), the formation thickens to around 80 m. It is more silty and argillaceous (Lower Permian Marl) and is in part more calcareous and less dolomitic. There, the formation is probably of shelf and slope origin. Elsewhere at this time, major shelf-edge reef complexes developed around the margins of the Zechstein Sea (Figure 13). Reefs may be present in the south-west of the district, but this is currently unproved (Smith, 1989).

The geophysical log signatures suggest a fairly sharp lithological junction between the Cadeby Formation and overlying **Hayton Anhydrite** (Figure 12), but the distinction is commonly less clear from the study of rock cuttings. The dominant lithology in the three deep boreholes is white to grey, cryptocrystalline, sporadically silty anhydrite with varying amounts of grey to pale brown sugary dolomite, commonly forming an anastomosing intergrowth (nodular or chicken-wire anhydrite). Thicknesses range between 100 and 150 m. Over much of the

district these beds are probably of slope, passing up into shelf facies, but precise details are lacking. To the south-west (Nettleton Borehole), the beds are thinner (65 to 70 m) and probably wholly of shelf, largely subaerial origin. Mudstone and siltstone interbeds in the upper part of the formation in the Nettleton Borehole indicate a gradual transition into the largely clastic Edlington Formation of the basin margin (Figure 13).

Ailsaby Group

The Ailsaby Group comprises the sediments of the second Zechstein cycle (EZ2). Throughout much of the district the **Kirkham Abbey Formation** consists of 60 to 70 m of white to cream, hard dolomite which is commonly oolitic in the upper part. Gamma-ray logs (Figure 12) suggests that the basal beds of the formation are generally argillaceous. The oolitic rocks are shelf deposits, but the lower part of the formation may be a slope deposit, particularly towards the north-west. To the south-west (Nettleton), towards the basin margin, it thins to about 45 m. There, the lower part of the formation is very

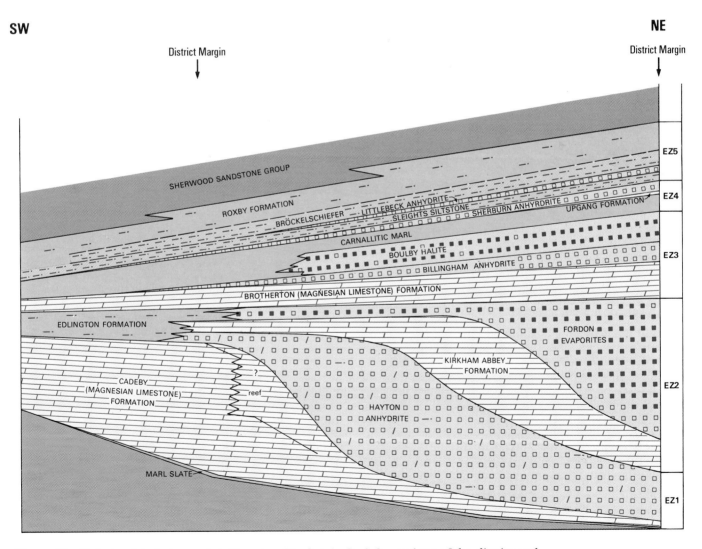

Figure 13 Relationship between late-Permian (Zechstein Sea) formations of the district and ground adjacent to the west (diagrammatic and not to scale).

argillaceous and includes redbeds, indicting passage into the marginal Edlington Formation (Figures 12 and 13), whereas higher parts of the formation contain ooliths and pellets, and are of shallow shelf origin.

The regressive part of the cycle, the **Fordon Evaporites**, comprises 20 to 80 m dominantly of halite with some associated and interbedded anhydrite. Few details are available of these beds, but they are likely to be largely of shelf origin. Towards the south-west of the district, the formation thins to about 10 to 15 m, and passes laterally into red mudstone and siltstone with relatively minor anhydrite, which perhaps more correctly should be assigned to the **Edlington Formation** (Figure 13).

TEESSIDE GROUP

The deposits of the third Zechstein cycle (EZ3) are collectively known as the Teesside Group. The lowest division, the **Brotherton Formation**, is a cream, pale grey or brown dolomite, commonly oolitic and 40 to 50 m thick. There is little lateral variation across the district, indicating the establishment of a widespread shallow shelf sea at this time. The basal part of the formation, the **Grauer Salzton** (Grey Salt Clay), is argillaceous and forms a widely recognised gamma-ray marker comparable to that of the Marl Slate.

The overlying **Billingham Anhydrite** is only 3 to 6 m thick and, as a result, is not always easily separated from the Brotherton Formation either by means of rock cuttings analysis or from the study of the geophysical logs. The formation is composed of white to grey anhydrite with associated grey dolomite and red mudstone, and is believed to have been deposited in very shallow marine or supratidal conditions.

The succeeding **Boulby Halite** is 20 to 25 m thick over much of the district. It is coarsely crystalline and commonly coloured red by finely dispersed hematitic clay. White anhydrite, grey dolomitic mudstone and red mudstone and siltstone partings are also locally present. The halite is believed to be displacive in origin, having formed in supratidal and continental sabkhas. The formation thins and dies out towards the south-west, passing into red mudstones and siltstones (Figure 13).

STAINTONDALE AND ESKDALE GROUPS

Within the district, the Staintondale and Eskdale groups, which form cycles EZ4 and EZ5 respectively, comprise red mudstones and siltstones, with evaporites, principally anhydrite, dispersed both within the clastic rocks and in well defined beds. The **Sherburn Anhydrite**, a 4 to 11 m-thick bed of white cryptocrystalline anhydrite, is especially easy to recognise in both rock cuttings and geophysical logs. A gamma-ray low a few metres above this bed indicates the presence of a thin marginal development of the **Littlebeck Anhydrite**. The recognition of these anhydrites allows the redbed sequence to be subdivided into three formations, the **Carnallitic Marl**, the **Sleights Siltstone** and the **Roxby Formation**. The first of these is notable because there is commonly extensive caving in boreholes at this level, probably due to the presence of soluble evaporite minerals. The last of the formations is very silty in its lower part, a division widely recognised

across the Southern North Sea Basin and known as the **Bröckelschiefer.**

In this region, the only carbonate-rich unit within these groups is the **Upgang Formation**. It underlies the Sherburn Anhydrite and is known only from cored sections, being too thin (commonly only a few centimetres thick) to be recognised from cuttings or from geophysical logs. Its presence within the district is likely, but unproved. This and the two anhydrite formations probably indicate some limited influence of the Zechstein Sea at this time within the basin, but the redbeds were probably deposited in continental playas and sabkhas.

SHERWOOD SANDSTONE GROUP

Regionally, the boundary between the Eskdale and Sherwood Sandstone groups, or their offshore equivalents, is markedly diachronous. However, the borehole evidence in the district (Figure 12) suggests that the junction is sharp and not significantly diachronous. The group, 300 to 450 m thick, dominantly comprises red to purplish hematite-brown, micaceous sandstone. The grain size ranges from fine to coarse, but is dominantly medium. The grains, which are hematite-coated, range from subangular to subrounded and are moderately well sorted. The main cements are dolomite and anhydrite. Porosity values are generally greater than 20 per cent; permeability is generally above 100 mD and commonly above 1 D. The cores taken in Cleethorpes Borehole suggest that most of the sandstones are massive, with lamination and cross-lamination only present locally; pebble-sized mudclasts occur at some levels. Thin interbeds of red and locally green laminated, micaceous mudstone and siltstone occur only rarely. They are more common in the basal c.100 m, in which the sandstone is somewhat finer grained (fine to medium grained only) and less well sorted (more argillaceous and silty material). The Sherwood Sandstone Group is thought to have been deposited by a large system of braided rivers.

No lithological subdivision of the group has proved possible within the district. Rare quartz pebbles have been noted near the top of the group, for example in the Tetney Lock and Cleethorpes boreholes, but nowhere in sufficient numbers to justify a separation of an upper pebbly division (equivalent of the Nottingham Castle Formation) from a lower pebble-free unit (Lenton Formation) such as is possible in Nottinghamshire and south Lincolnshire. An overall consistency of geophysical log signature is evident, from which some tentative correlations can be suggested (Figure 12). However, only the lowest c.100 m, noted above, can yet be linked to any significant lithological change.

MERCIA MUDSTONE GROUP

There is a sharp junction and sedimentary break between the Sherwood Sandstone and Mercia Mudstone groups throughout the region, which is probably related to a widespread unconformity, the 'Hardegsen Disconformity' of Germany. There is little evidence within the district to indicate either the magnitude of this break in deposition or the extent of any erosion that might have taken place at this time.

The Mercia Mudstone Group, 250 to 300 m thick in the district, is dominantly composed of red and red-brown mudstone, dolomitic in part, and siltstone, with minor amounts of green and grey mudstone and siltstone, very fine-grained sandstone and thin beds of anhydrite. These rocks are believed to have been deposited on an extensive coastal plan, which for the most part was slightly above sea level, but which was subject to periodic marine inundation. Regional palynological studies have established that the age of the group ranges from Scythian to Rhaetian.

Detailed study of the lithologies, their sequence, sedimentary structure and log signatures, and the use of sandstones as marker beds, has enabled Kirby (1985) to subdivide the Mercia Mudstone sequence of the Cleethorpes Borehole and relate it to the sequence at outcrop in south Nottinghamshire. He has identified correlatives of the **Retford, Colwick, Radcliffe, Carlton, Harlequin, Edwalton, Trent** and **Glen Parva formations.** The same subdivisions can be recognised in the other deep boreholes of the district (Figure 12). Additional divisions can also be identified: the gamma-ray high at the base of the group probably corresponds with the **Seaton Carew Formation** of North Yorkshire and Cleveland; the succeeding gamma-ray low and sonic velocity peak marks a widespread anhydrite development at the level of the **Esk (Rot) Halite**; and another anhydrite bed occurs close to the top of the group near the level of the **Newark Gypsum.** The presence of the highest formation of the group, the **Blue Anchor Formation** (Tea Green Marl) is uncertain. It is generally only a few metres thick and the mud logs are not sufficiently precise to confirm its presence.

The offshore nomenclature of the group (Rhys, 1974) which proposed a three-fold subdivision based on lithological and geophysical (particularly sonic) log data, provides an alternative lithostratigraphical scheme for the district. The lower unit, the **Dowsing Dolomitic Formation**, from the base of the group up to the middle part of the Carlton Formation, is characterised by dolomitic beds (low-interval transit times). The **Dudgeon Saliferous Formation** (with higher interval transit times) includes the upper part of the Carlton Formation, the Harlequin Formation and the lower part of the Edwalton Formation. These beds contain much halite in offshore areas, but this is lacking within the district. The upper part of the group (upper part of the Edwalton, Trent, Glen Parva and ?Blue Anchor formations), which generally has low interval transit times because the unit is markedly anhydritic, correlates with the **Triton Anhydritic Formation.**

PENARTH GROUP

The Penarth Group sequences in the Humber region and the adjacent offshore area have been summarised by Kent (1953, 1955), Gaunt et al (1980), Lott and Warrington (1988) and Gaunt et al. (1992). The group has been proved in the Tetney Lock, Cleethorpes (Kirby, 1985) and Winestead boreholes in the district, where it ranges from 12 to 15 m in thickness (Figures 12–14). It comprises two major formations of which the lower, the **Westbury Formation**, is composed of black, fissile shales interbedded with thin, sandy limestones containing phosphatic bone beds. The second unit, the **Cotham Member** of the **Lilstock Formation**, comprises red to reddish brown and green, weakly calcareous and dolomitic mudstones with angular fracture. No evidence of the succeeding **Langport Member** has been found in the district, but the lowest 0.5 m of the beds classified as **Lias** may be its lateral equivalent; a fauna of Rhaetian affinity has been found in corresponding strata in boreholes in the adjacent Brigg district (Gaunt et al., 1980, p.26; Lott and Warrington, 1988; Gaunt et al., 1992).

The lithologies itemised above are readily identified and correlated by their geophysical log signatures (Figure 12). It can thus be seen that the Westbury Formation thickens northwards as it is traced from Tetney Lock (6 m), via Cleethorpes (8 m) to Winestead (10 m), whereas the Cotham Member maintains an approximately constant thickness of 4.5 to 5.5 m, although it is somewhat thinner to the north. Similar changes were detected at outcrop by Kent (1953 fig. 2) and, together with the above observations, they indicate an east–west orientation of a Rhaetian Market Weighton High (Kent, 1955).

The basal few metres of the Lias in the district lie below the base of the Jurassic System as defined by Cope et al. (1980a) but, for convenience, they are described in the succeeding section.

JURASSIC

The stratigraphical units used here for the Jurassic follow broadly the divisions used by Cope et al.(1980a and b), but with revisions reflecting recent work in the adjacent Hull and Brigg (Gaunt et al., 1992) and Grantham (Brandon et al., 1990) districts. No Jurassic strata older than the Kimmeridge Clay is exposed in the present district, but they are proved in deep boreholes. The cored and geophysically logged Nettleton Bottom Borehole* [1249 9820], sited close to the south-western corner of Sheet 90, provides a reference section for the Jurassic down to its base within the lower part of the Lias. Three other boreholes, Tetney Lock [3325 0090], Cleethorpes [3023 0709] and Winestead [2741 2433], provide geophysical logs through the Jurassic, but chip samples only are available from the first two and there is no material from Winestead Borehole. Consequently, the following analyses of the strata is based on correlation of the geophysical signatures in these logs interpreted against data from Nettleton Bottom and other boreholes, mainly to the west of the district.

Lower Jurassic

LIAS GROUP

Lias Group strata in the region comprise pale to dark grey, more or less calcareous, fissile to blocky, commonly silty and shelly mudstones interbedded, in both small- and large-scale cycles, with thin, argillaceous limestones,

---

* Nettleton Bottom Borehole is distinct from Nettleton Borehole [1185 9642] referred to in other parts of the text.

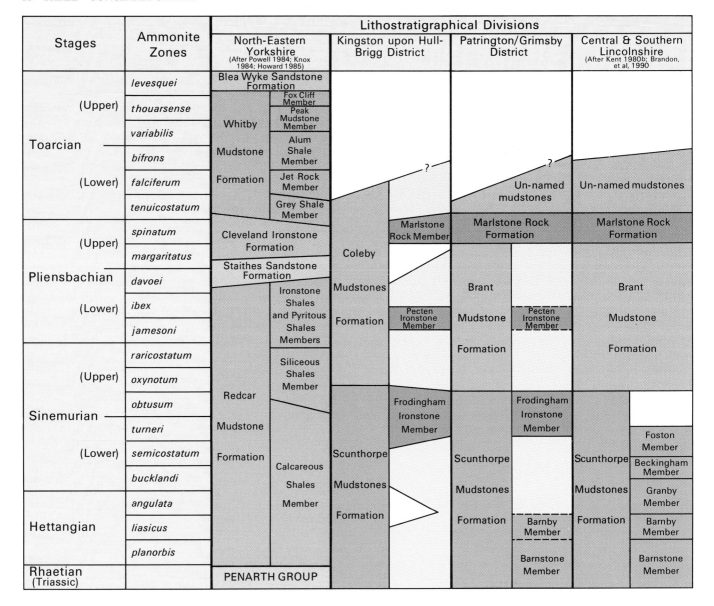

Figure 14   Relationship of Lias stratigraphy of the district to that of neighbouring regions.

more or less calcareous siltstones and fine-grained sandstones, each of which may be more or less shelly. Locally, the beds may be oolitic or organic-rich and are in places sufficiently ferruginous to have attracted ironstone exploration. As throughout most of England, the Lias is capable of fine biostratigraphical subdivision; Whittaker et al. (1985) have shown that its characteristic geophysical log signatures can be used for detailed correlation and subdivision within and between different sedimentary basins. The beds range in age from latest Rhaetian to early Toarcian (Figure 14).

In the adjacent Hull–Brigg district, these beds were classified into two formations, the Scunthorpe Mudstones and the overlying Coleby Mudstones (Figure 14). The former comprises calcareous mudstones and limestones capped by the Frodingham Ironstone. The term Coleby Mudstones Formation was applied to the remainder of the

Liassic mudstones, including two ironstones, the Pecten and Marlstone Rock members. More recent work farther south in Lincolnshire (Brandon et al., 1990) has proved the succession shown in the right-hand column of Figure 14. There, the lower part of the Coleby Mudstones is separated off as the Brant Mudstone Formation, comprising the upper part of what was formerly known as the Lower Lias and the Middle Lias up to the base of the Marlstone Rock. In the district, the overlying mudstones are un-named (see p.21). These units can be traced in the geophysical logs from the biostratigraphically controlled Nettleton Bottom Borehole onto the flank of the Market Weighton Structure.

Scunthorpe Mudstones Formation

These beds comprise a sequence of alternating mudstones, siltstones and limestones with, at the top, the distinctive Frodingham Ironstone. The mudtones are grey to dark grey, fissile, calcareous, silty, sporadically micaceous and shelly. The siltstones are medium grey to white, calcareous and argillaceous medium to coarse grained (locally grading to a very fine-grained sandstone) with accessory mica, berthierine ('chamosite') and goethite. The limestones are grey to cream and brown, and range from calcilutites to calcarenites with sporadic goethite ooliths.

The rapidly alternating limestone/siltstone and mudstone sequence gives rise to deeply serrated geophysical log signatures in which low gamma-ray values and high sonic velocity characterise the hard beds, and opposite values the interbedded mudstones. This pattern of rapid alternations in log values is superimposed upon larger-scale fluctuations which define alternating limestone-rich and limestone-poor subdivisions of the sequence (Figure 15). Thus the basal Lias is characterised by the dominance of thin limestones (the Barnstone Member of Lincolnshire). Overlying these alternating limestones and mudstones is a limestone-poor sequence in which the mudstones are typically dark grey to brown, laminated and fissile. These correspond to the Barnby Member and are in turn overlain by an alternating limestone/mudstone sequence, the Granby Member (Brandon et al., 1990). The Scunthorpe Mudstones, including the Frodingham Ironstone, thin northwards from 90 m at Tetney Lock to 80 m at Cleethorpes, and to 70 m at Winestead (Figure 15). It is possible that in the extreme north of the district they show more rapid attenuation, because they attain only 45 m in the Cockle Pits Borehole [SE 9323 2865] which is situated to the west, along the inferred depositional strike (Gaunt et al., 1980; Brandon et al., 1990, fig. 7). The northward attentuation appears to be by northward depositional thinning coupled with the development of non-sequences.

Detailed correlation by means of geophysical log signature allows the horizons of the zonal boundaries determined in reference sections such as the Cockle Pits Borehole (Gaunt et al., 1980) and the Nettleton Bottom Borehole [TF 1249 9820] (Figure 4, Gaunt et al., 1992) to be traced throughout the district. The base of the Jurassic System (*sensu* Cope et al., 1980a) (i.e. the lowest record of *Psiloceras*) in Cockle Pits Borehole is at the top of the Barnstone Member but in the Grantham district *P. planorbis* has been found within that member.

The top of the Scunthorpe Mudstones comprises the distinctive **Frodingham Ironstone** which has been extensively worked near Scunthorpe, to the west of the district, where it has recently been described by Gaunt et al. (1992). These authors selected the 9.4 m-thick cored succession of the Roxton Wood No. 11 Borehole [TA 1651 1180], which lies within the district, as the type sequence. The ironstone has been cored in a number of other boreholes (see p.00) drilled to prove the resource, and in the Nettleton Bottom Borehole (Bradshaw and Penney, 1982). Lithological variations within it can be traced from Nettleton Bottom, via the Tetney Lock and Cleethorpes boreholes to the Winestead Borehole. In the area of the ironstone provings around Brocklesby, at the western edge of the district, it generally comprises a lower, cal-

citic, oncolitic and shelly, berthierine-oolith grainstone, which passes upwards into a sideritised, locally shelly, berthierine-mudstone, commonly capped by alternating grainstones and mudstones. This fining-upwards sequence is composed of many similar, but sporadically developed, smaller-scale cycles, typically half a metre or less in thickness. In the Nettleton Bottom Borehole, southwest of the district, the coarser phases of the cycles are represented by grey, fine-grained, micaceous siltstones with very subordinate oolitic, calcitic and ferruginous material as the succession becomes more arenaceous and less calcitic and iron-rich (Bradshaw and Penney, 1982; Gaunt et al., 1990). At Cleethorpes (Kirby 1985), the Frodingham Ironstone comprises hard, white to medium brown calcilutite or calcarenite packstones with 'goethite' ooliths and shell fragments, which are interbedded with grey, locally argillaceous siltstones; the latter sporadically grade into grey fine-grained sandstones.

The characteristic log profile, indicating cyclic repetition of relatively fine- and coarse-grained variants with a general upward-fining (Figure 15), allows the thickness of the Frodingham Ironstone to be determined in the uncored boreholes. In association with cored borehole data, the log profiles thus show the following range of thickness when traced from south to north across the district: Nettleton Bottom, 9 m; Tetney Lock, 6.5 m; Cleethorpes, 6 m; Brocklesby, 12 m; Kirmington, 9 m; Roxton Wood, 9.4 m; Carr Leys Wood, 10 m; Harbrough, 9 m; Ulceby, 6.2 m; Winestead, 8 m. There is thus no obvious pattern of thickness variation within the district. Gaunt et al. (1992) show that the bulk of the Frodingham Ironstone to the west of the district lies within the *turneri* and *obtusum* zones. Ammonites indicative of the *semicostatum* Zone locally occur in the basal beds, but these may be derived (reworked). Ammonites from the highest part of the ironstone show the upper boundary to lie locally within the *oxynotum* Zone. It is likely that the Frodingham Ironstone occupies a similar zonal range within the Lower Humber district.

Brant Mudstone Formation

Correlation of the Lias sequence between the Frodingham Ironstone and the Marlstone Rock Formation has been facilitated by recent work in central Lincolnshire, where the name Brant Mudstone Formation was introduced (Brandon et al., 1990). Details of its lithology and biostratigraphy are known from the cored succession in Nettleton Bottom Borehole (Gaunt et al., 1992). The strata comprise pale to dark grey, more or less calcareous and silty, laminated or blocky mudstones which may exhibit small-scale sedimentary cycles. They are commonly burrowed and may contain thin shelly layers. Interbedded with the mudstones, particularly in the lowest 30 m, are thin, commonly burrowed siltstones, some of which grade into very fine-grained, more or less calcareous and shelly, sporadically oolitic sandstones. At some levels thin, calcitic, goethite-oolith packstones occur and, in the **Pecten Ironstone**, calcite, oolitic, shelly grainstones are interbedded with pale grey, olive-green and brown, shelly, goethite-berthierine-oolitic, sideritic wackestones. Ironstone nodules are common immediately above the Pecten Ironstone.

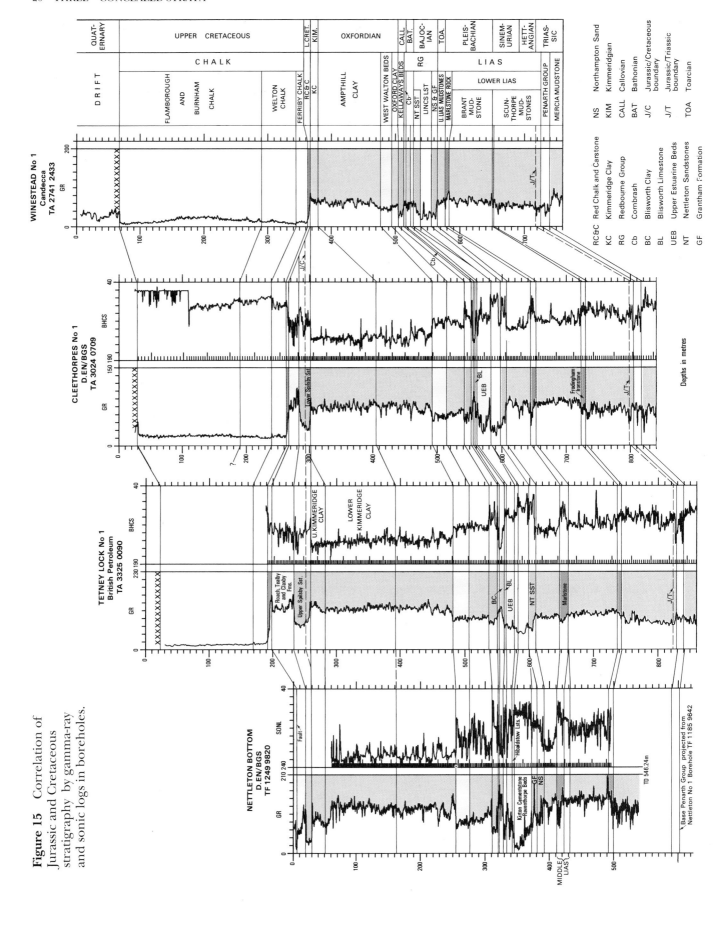

Figure 15 Correlation of Jurassic and Cretaceous stratigraphy by gamma-ray and sonic logs in boreholes.

Gamma-ray and sonic signatures (Figure 15) show a lower siltstone-dominated unit overlain by a mudstone-dominated unit; both contain thin hard siltstone, sandstone and limestone beds, which are more numerous in the siltstone-rich unit but more conspicuous in the mudstone unit where they may provide equivalents to the 'marker beds' identified in the Midlands (Horton and Poole, 1977; Ambrose and Ivimey-Cook, 1982; Brandon et al., 1990).

In the upper part of the formation, the sequence coarsens upwards, becoming more silty, with siltstones and fine sandstones (the Middle Lias Silts and Clays) before passing into sandy limestones and calcareous, commonly glauconitic and ferruginous sandstones which form the Marlstone Rock. The lower part of the Middle Lias (*margaritatus* Zone) is proved only in Nettleton Bottom Borehole, though it probably extends into the south-western part of the district. It contains burrowed silty, finely micaceous mudstone with numerous pyritised, glauconitic layers as well as a prominent phosphatised pebble bed and scattered berthierine ooliths (Gaunt et al., 1992).

The regional consistency of the geophysical log characters enables the beds to be traced across the district in some detail. They show that the Brant Mudstone Formation thins from 79 m at Tetney to 70 m at Cleethorpes and Winestead, principally by attenuation, mainly in the lower silty levels (Figure 5). Biostratigraphical work on samples from Nettleton Bottom Borehole shows all the zones of the Upper Sinemurian and Pliensbachian are present there. Northward correlation (see below and also Gaunt et al., 1992), however, indicates that the *margaritatus* Zone is cut out within the district. The geophysical signature in the borehole shows a marked increase in sonic velocity at about the top of the Lower Lias, which is seen elsewhere in England (Whittaker et al., 1985).

Marlstone Rock Bed

This formation comprises burrowed, sideritic or calcitic very fine- to fine-grained, moderately to well-sorted, glauconitic, greenish grey to white sandstones, commonly with berthierine grains in a ferroan calcite cement. These are interbedded with olive-green, silty mudstones with goethite ooliths. These lithologies give rise to much lower average gamma-ray values and a higher 'spikey' sonic trace sharply demarcated from the underlying beds (Figure 15).

When traced from north to south the Marlstone thickens from 3 m at Winestead to 9 m at Cleethorpes and 11 m at Tetney Lock. In these boreholes the Marlstone rests nonsequentially on older Lias of Lower Pliensbachian age; at Nettleton Bottom, some 8 m of Marlstone overlie 7 m of *margaritatus* Zone Lias.

Mudstones above Marlstone Rock Bed

Mudstones overlying the Marlstone Rock have traditionally been known as the Upper Lias, but this name is now deemed inappropriate. In the absence of a reference section within the district, they remain for the present unnamed.

The rocks comprise dominantly of distinctive laminated and fissile more or less bituminous, locally shelly, micaceous mudstones; the succession is laterally persistent over much of eastern England. At outcrop in north-east Yorkshire, north of the Market Weighton Structure, the sequence corresponding to that in the district comprises the Grey Shales, Jet Rock and Alum Shales. South of the structure, in Humberside and north Lincolnshire, outcrops are very restricted and the succession is less well known, though a useful exposure was described by Howarth and Rawson (1965) at Kirton in Lindsey. The lithostratigraphy and biostratigraphy are proved in Nettleton Bottom Borehole and other BGS boreholes in the Humber estuary area (Gaunt et al., 1980; Gaunt et al., 1992).

Three units can be recognised in the district. The lowest consists of dark grey, fissile, laminated mudstones interbedded with wispy-bedded siltstones, and contains sideritic and calcitic nodules. These beds become more micaceous upwards and contain distinct bituminous layers. They pass up into a unit of finely laminated, bituminous mudstones and shales with thin, quartz-rich layers. Thin, shelly, lignitic layers with phosphatic and fish debris are common, and bands of calcareous, silty concretions and cementstones commonly yield ammonites (see Howarth and Rawson, 1965; Gaunt et al., 1992). The uppermost unit consists of medium grey, calcareous and silty, but similarly fissile and laminated mudstones, with thin shell-fragmental layers.

The laminated and argillaceous nature of the sequence gives rise to a charactertistic, finely serrated geophysical log signature mainly of high gamma-ray values and low sonic velocity (Figure 14). A distinctive decrease in gamma-ray values and interval transit time marks the well-developed bituminous levels, giving rise to correspondingly thin, pencil-like, sonic 'spikes'. Broader, more prominent spikes reflect the presence of silty, concretionary limestones, which are best developed at the level of the most bituminous beds.

The stratigraphical detail reflected in the geophysical log characters enables thin beds to be correlated throughout the East Midlands. In the district, the limits of the Lower Toarcian zones can be identified in the geophysical logs of deep boreholes by comparing them with the logs of Nettleton Bottom Borehole (Gaunt et al., 1992), which has been calibrated by ammonites recovered from the cores. This shows the sub-bituminous basal beds to lie there within the *tenuicostatum* Zone and the bituminous (middle) levels to lie within the *falciferum* Zone.

The succession is some 13 m thick at Winestead, 35 m thick at Cleethorpes, 38 m thick at Tetney Lock and only 23 m thick in the Nettleton Bottom Borehole, where the highest beds are known to be of *falciferum* Subzone (*falciferum* Zone) age. In the Hull–Brigg district, the late Toarcian erosion cut down through beds of *falciferum* Subzone age into those of the *exaratum* Subzone (*Falciferum* Zone) at Cockle Pits Borehole [SE 9323 2865] and into those of the *tenuicostatum* Zone at South Cave Borehole [SE 9366 3230]. The northward reduction in thickness in the district differs in that the Upper Lias is significantly thicker in Tetney Lock and Cleethorpes boreholes, with a probability that beds of *bifrons* Zone age are present; the thinner sequence at Winestead could well be capped by beds of the *falciferum* Zone. The south-westward decrease in thickness from Cleethorpes Borehole to Nettleton Bottom may be due in part to pre-Middle Jurassic channelling, because the overlying Middle Jurassic is complementarily thickened in the Nettleton Bottom Borehole.

Middle Jurassic (excluding Callovian)

The Middle Jurassic of the district, as traditionally understood by BGS, comprises the strata between the base of the Northampton Sand and the base of the Upper Cornbrash. They approximately correspond to the Redbourne Group (Gaunt et al., 1992) or to the Inferior Oolite and Great Oolite groups of central and southern England. For convenience, the Upper Cornbrash, the highest member of the Great Oolite Group, is included in this account, although it belongs to the Upper Jurassic chronologically.

Both the Inferior Oolite and the Great Oolite attain their thickest development in the carbonate shelf facies of midland and southern England. They occur in thinner, mostly lagoonal facies across the East Midlands where they are bounded by mainly minor unconformities and non-sequences. Most of the Middle Jurassic succession in this district can be correlated with parts of the Inferior and Great Oolite groups, but the sequence also contains tongues of more arenaceous rocks that correlate with the Ravenscar Group of northern England. The Middle Jurassic rocks of the Grimsby–Patrington district are therefore transitional between those of the midlands and those of northern England. Since the beds more closely resemble the former, the terms Inferior Oolite and Great Oolite are retained here. In the Kingston-upon-Hull–Brigg district, where these beds are poorly exposed, both groups are referred to the 'Redbourne Group' (Gaunt et al., 1992). To the east of the district, beneath the North Sea, Middle Jurassic strata are referred to the West Sole Group (Rhys, 1974).

Inferior Oolite Group

The Inferior Oolite Group comprises sandstones, limestones, mudstones and shales of Bajocian (including Aalenian) age, and is separated from both underlying and overlying strata by major stratigraphical breaks. Over the whole of the East Midlands and south and central Yorkshire, rocks representing the Upper Toarcian and part of the Middle Toarcian substages are missing beneath these Middle Jurassic strata. Similarly, at the top of the Inferior Oolite, representatives of most of the Upper Bajocian Substage are missing. Even larger breaks occur locally over the Market Weighton Structure (Gaunt et al., 1980).

In this district and adjacent areas the Inferior Oolite includes three formations, in ascending order the Northampton Sand, the Grantham Formation and the Lincolnshire Limestone, the last being the thickest. It also includes part of a fourth formation, the Thorncroft Sands, which will also be discussed here (Gaunt et al., 1980; Bradshaw and Penney, 1982; Gaunt et al., 1992). Terrigenous interbeds occur in the Lincolnshire Limestone as it thins northwards from this district towards the Market Weighton Structure: these pass laterally into the Cloughton, Scarborough and Scalby formations of the Cleveland Basin of northern Yorkshire. Tongues of some of these Yorkshire terrigenous beds crop out in the Hull–Brigg district (Gaunt et al., 1992) where they have been termed the Raventhorpe Beds (included in the Lincolnshire Limestone) and the Thorncroft Sands. The latter comprise a lower unit of Bajocian age, which rests on the Lincolnshire Limestone, overlain non-sequentially by an upper unit of Bathonian age. The distinction between the two is readily made by means of geophysical log signatures.

Although the various formations have been identified in the Winestead, Cleethorpes and Tetney Lock boreholes, the most comprehensive record relates to the Nettleton Bottom Borehole, which is thus used as the main reference despite being marginally outside the district.

Northampton Sand and Grantham formations

The fully cored Northampton Sand sequence in Nettleton Bottom Borehole proved 10.13 m of dark green, cross-bedded, burrowed, berthierinitic, oolitic, shelly medium-grained sandstones interbedded with berthierinitic mudstones and siltstones, which commonly contain carbonaceous layers. They are overlain by 6.81 m of pale brown to white, very fine- to fine-grained, micaceous, commonly laminated sandstones of the Grantham Formation, which are poorly consolidated in part and locally rich in terrestial plant material. These sandstones are interbedded with dark grey, silty, micaceous mudstones which locally contain abundant carbonaceous and coaly fragments. Beds of the Grantham Formation are known at outcrop to be channelled into underlying Middle and Lower Jurassic strata (Gaunt et al., 1992).

Within the district, the two formations are hard to separate by means of available geophysical logs (Figure 15); they are, therefore, considered together. The formations are known to lie within the Aalenian Stage at outcrop (Gaunt et al., 1992) and are probably of the same age throughout the district.. Northwards from Nettleton Bottom, they thin to 10 m at Tetney Lock and maintain this thickness to Winestead (Figure 15). The occurrence of berthierinitic sandstone at Tetney Lock and goethite ooliths in the basal beds at Cleethorpes (Kirby, 1985) indicates that the Northampton Sand lithology is still identifiable. Since both formations disappear beneath overlapping Lincolnshire Limestone at outcrop towards the Market Weighton area, (Gaunt et al., 1992), they may well also be absent in the far north of the district.

Lincolnshire Limestone

Four main subdivisions of the Lincolnshire Limestone can be traced throughout all parts of the district where data is available; their northward facies variation is comparable to that of the adjacent Hull–Brigg district (Gaunt et al., 1992). Following the nomenclature of these authors, the subdivisions in ascending order are: Raventhorpe Beds with Santon Oolite, Kirton Cementstones and Hibaldstow Limestones; as discussed above, the Thorncroft Sands are also described in this context.

The **Raventhorpe Beds** typically consist of interbedded, pale grey, burrowed, more or less calcareous, micaceous mudstones and siltstones with thin layers of shell grit. Discrete, thin, argillaceous, micritic, bioturbated, procellanous limestones with sporadic peloids and, less commonly, finely fragmented shall debris also occur. At Nettleton Bottom the sediments are coarser than at outcrop and comprise pale grey, fine-grained, calcareous, wispy-bedded sandstones with carbonaceous debris, which are poorly consolidated in part. At the top of this lowest subdivision are thin, grey, fine- to medium-grained, shell-fragmental oolites with argillaceous lenses, the **Santon Oolite**. The succeeding **Kirton Cementstones** comprise interbedded, thin, hard, pale grey, argillaceous, more or less peloidal, micritic, porcellanous limestones and dark grey, highly calcareous mudstones. Locally, shelly mudstone, the **Kirton Cement Shale**, may be developed within the limestone sequence. The **Hibaldstow Limestones** comprise white to buff, fine- to coarse-grained, shell-fragmental, generally poorly cemented oolitic limestones with sporadic shelly, silty and carbonaceous layers. The **Thorncroft Sands** dominantly comprise pale to dark grey, fine-grained, micaceous sandstones, of which some of the darker grey beds are laminated and contain carbonaceous and coaly streaks. Interbedded sandstones are calcareous, wispy bedded and shelly. In addition to the sandstones, there are also thin, pale grey, sandy limestones with shell concentrations (including the **Nettleton Limestone** of Gaunt et al., 1992), medium grey, silty limestones, and dark grey and black, laminated, silty and shelly mudstones, locally rich in plant debris. Gaunt et al. (1992) draw attention to the irregular base of this formation, which they attribute to channelling into the solution-hollow infill of the Lincolnshire Limestone surface.

The geophysical log signatures of the various members of the Lincolnshire Limestone (Figure 15) are sufficiently diagnostic to be recognisable from borehole to borehole. This is also true of the Thorncroft Sands, in which an upward increase in clay content of the lower (Bajocian) division is reflected in higher gamma-ray values.

The availability of both geophysical log profiles and a cored section in Nettleton Bottom Borehole allow the beds to be correlated with the Winestead, Cleethorpes and Tetney Lock boreholes, and also with those described to the west, in the Hull–Brigg district by Gaunt et al. (1980, 1991) and with those to the south described by Ashton (1980). According to the authors quoted above and Cope et al. (1980a), the Raventhorpe Beds, including the Santon Oolite, together with the Kirton Cementstones, lie within the *discites* Zone of the Bajocian, and the Hibaldstow Limestones within the *laeviuscula* and possibly higher zones. The Thorncroft Sands (lower division) in the Nettleton Bottom Borehole lie, at least in part, within the *humphriesianum* Zone (Bradshaw and Bate, 1982).

Borehole geophysical log correlation within the district shows that the beds which approximate to the *discites* Zone (Raventhorpe Beds to Kirton Cementstone) thin from 13 m at Nettleton Bottom to 9 m at Tetney Lock, and to 5 m at Cleethorpes and Winestead (Figure 15). Similarly, the Hibaldstow Limestones thin from 13.5 m at Nettleton Bottom to 8.5 m at Tetney Lock and Cleethorpes, and to 7 m at Winestead. This thinning may reflect a northward passage of the highest beds into the basal Thorncroft Sands. If so, these beds are equivalent to the **Lebberston Member** of the **Cloughton Formation** (cf. Gaunt et al., 1980, figs. 11 and 14). The lower (Bajocian) division of the Thorncroft Sands thickens from 5 m at Nettleton Bottom to 8.5 m at Tetney Lock, and to 10 m at Winestead. At Cleethorpes, however, beds assigned to the Great Oolite Group (Bathonian) rest directly upon Hibaldstow Limestones. As already noted, Gaunt et al. (1992) attribute large variations in Thorncroft Sands thickness to irregularities on its limestone floor; Cleethorpes may thus have been either a contemporary 'high' or a site of later erosion of the missing Thorncroft Sands. The latter explanation is more likely because the overlying Upper Estuarine Series is anomalously thick here, suggesting the presence of a channel infill.

GREAT OOLITE GROUP

The well-established stratigraphical subdivisions of the Great Oolite Group of midland England are readily traceable in the three deep boreholes of the district. In ascending order these are the Upper Estuarine 'Series' the Blisworth Limestone, the Blisworth Clay and the Cornbrash. In the adjacent Hull–Brigg district (Gaunt et al., 1992), the Upper Estuarine 'Series' and Blisworth Limestone are named Priestland Clay and Snitterby Limestone respectively, and are regarded as members, along with the Blisworth Clay, of the Glentham Formation. The Nettleton Bottom Borehole core is again used here as the lithological reference.

The **Upper Estuarine 'Series'** comprises sandstones overlain by mudstones. The sandstones are, in the main, white to grey and fawn coloured, fine grained, well sorted, non-shelly, sporadically wispy bedded and commonly weakly cemented. Thin-bedded, laminated sandstones associated with seatearths and coals are locally present. Both types of sandstone may contain pyritised or limonitised rootlets and be interbedded with black and green, rootlet- and lignite-bearing mudstones. The overlying mudstones are variously brown to green with black carbonaceous layers, purple to grey, with a brackish to lagoonal shell fauna, and thin grey and greyish green limestone beds. These thin interbeds are arranged in cycles, each showing evidence of decreasingly saline conditions of deposition. The cycles commence with a shelly layers, locally a limestone, containing brackish/lagoonal faunal elements, and culminates in a rootlet-bearing bed or, locally, a diagenetic limestone (calcrete). The tops of the cycles are usually sharply defined and represent breaks in the sequence. The **Blisworth Limestone** rests on one of these breaks in the Nettleton Bottom Borehole. It comprises two beds of grey, hard, sandy, sporadically argillaceous and oolitic, oyster-rich limestone each of which is underlain by grey, calcareous, silty, locally laminated mudstone containing thin calcareous and shelly beds. The limestones and most of the mudstones carry an abundant marine macrofauna, but at some levels there are laminated brown mudstones which contain a brackish-water fauna. The **Blisworth Clay** is mostly mudstones that ranges in colour from dark grey to olive-green, green, and even pink; it is laminated in part. It also contains thin, laminated siltstones, and lenses, laminae and interbeds of white sandstone. Carbonaceous debris is common, and brackish-water faunal elements occur at some levels. The overlying **Cornbrash** is a brown, sandy, well-cemented, shelly limestone with fine- to coarse-grained carbonate particles including ooliths. Upper and lower divisions of the Cornbrash are locally recognised in the adjacent Hull–Brigg district but only the Upper Cornbrash is thought to be present in the district.

In this sequence, as elsewhere, the interaction of sonic and gamma-ray log curves reflects subtle changes in lithology and allows correlation of the Nettleton Bottom strata with deep borehole records of the district. The Blisworth Limestone, for example, gives a characteristic twin-peaked 'spike' corresponding to its two-fold lithological division. In combination with palaeontological evidence, the geophysical logs also help in chronostratigraphical correlation.

So far as is known, beds of early, middle and late Bathonian age are present within the district, albeit with numerous non-sequences, implied by stratigraphical breaks and northward thinning. The Upper Estuarine beds are assigned to the early and middle Bathonian following general East Midlands practice (Sylvester-Bradley and Ford, 1968; Horton et al., 1974; Cope et al., 1980b). As elsewhere in the region, at outcrop the arenaceous lower beds are unfossiliferous, but the overlying mudstones yield diverse macro- and microfaunas. The thickness is 7 m at Tetney Lock and 9 m at Winestead, but is 20 m at Cleethorpes, coincident with the absence of Thorncroft Sands below. Cleethorpes Borehole may thus be on the site of a downcutting channel of early Bathonian age. The Blisworth Limestone, of the middle and late Bathonian ages, thins northward from 4 m at Nettleton Bottom and to 2 m at Tetney Lock and Cleethorpes, and to only 1.4 m at Winestead, where only a single leaf is resolvable from the gamma-ray log. The Blisworth Clay is of late Bathonian age and thins from 8 to 10 m in the south and south-west, through 5.5 m at Cleethorpes to 2 m at Winestead. The Cornbrash likewise thins from 2 m at Nettleton Bottom to 1.5 m at Tetney Lock and Cleethorpes, and to only 1 m at Winestead. These changes are summarised in Figure 15.

Upper Jurassic (including Callovian)

'Ancholme Clay Group'

The 'Ancholme Clay Group' is a clay-dominated sequence which, apart from the Kellaways Beds and Brantingham and Elsham Sandstone formations, is undivided in the Hull–Brigg district (Gaunt et al., 1992). However, in the present district the traditional East Midlands succession to the south is recognised, i.e. Kellaways Beds, Oxford Clay, West Walton Beds, Ampthill Clay and Kimmeridge Clay.

The stratigraphy of the concealed Upper Jurassic (including Callovian) onshore part of the Eastern England Shelf has been described by Penn et al. (1986), who showed that all the formations recognised at outcrop in eastern England occur in their typical facies in the district and are readily identifiable in boreholes (Figure 15). By combining lithological, faunal and geophysical-log information from numerous cored boreholes in the region, it has been possible to identify a complete sequence of chronostratigraphical units, mostly 2 to 3 m thick, for the Callovian, Oxfordian and Kimmeridgian stages. This account, summarises the variation discovered within the district, referring to the previously quoted Winestead, Cleethorpes, Tetney Lock and Nettleton Bottom boreholes in the context of the regional study of Penn et al. (1986).

The **Kellaways Beds** comprise basal, shelly mudstones, the **Kellaways Clay**, overlain by more or less well-cemented, calcareous, shelly sandstones, the **Kellaways Sands and Rock**. Together, they attain a maximum thickness of about 12 m at Tetney Lock within a north-easterly trending depocentre, but thin rapidly to the south-east and less rapidly to the north-west and south-west; they are 8 m thick at Nettleton Bottom, 11.5 m at Cleethorpes and 10.2 m at Winestead. The Kellaways Clay, thins to the north-west and shows a regional variation in thickness which is complementary to that of the Kellaways Sand and Rock, suggesting that the sandy beds prograde south and south-eastwards within the district (Penn et al., 1986), figs. 6–8).

The **Oxford Clay** is divided into three members. The Lower Oxford Clay consists of partly bituminous, shelly mudstones which thin northwards from about 5 m in the southern part of the district and which are absent in the north-east. This thinning is mainly caused by overstep by the calcareous, locally silty mudstones and fine-grained argillaceous limestones of the Middle Oxford Clay which rest on progressively older zones within the Lower Oxford Clay as it is traced north-eastwards.: at Winestead, the Middle Oxford Clay rests on Kellaways Beds. The Middle Oxford Clay maintains a constant thickness of about 23 m in the south and south-west of the district, but thins north of the Humber, to 13 m at Winestead, where it is overstepped by younger Oxfordian strata. The Upper Oxford Clay comprises grey, mudstones overlain by thinly interbedded mudstones and calcareous mudstones. It thins northwards from around 10 m thick in the southern part of the district to 9 m thick at Cleethorpes, and is absent at Winestead, being progressively overstepped by the overlying West Walton Beds (Penn et al., 1986, figs. 5, 9 and 10).

The **West Walton Beds** comprise more or less shelly, calcareous silty mudstones and argillaceous siltstones which locally become sandy. Sixteen stratigraphical subdivisions have been identified in eastern England (Gallois 1979, pp.71–72); all of these can be recognised in the geophysical logs of deep boreholes in the district. The formation thins from 20 m to 24 m in the south-west to about 14 m at Winestead in the north-east (Penn et al., 1986, fig. 11). The succeeding **Ampthill Clay** comprises interbedded, more or less calcareous or silty mudstones, with thin bituminous beds and concentrations of shell debris. Most of the 42 stratigraphical subdivisions of the Ampthill Clay of eastern England (AmC 1–42 of Gallois and Cox, 1977) have been traced in geophysical logs throughout the district as far north as Winestead. The formation appears to thicken to the north and north-east; it is 87 to 88 m thick at Cleethorpes and Tetney Lock, 91 m at Nettleton Bottom and 97 m at Winestead. This thickening occurs principally by the expansion of the lower beds (Penn et al., 1986, figs. 12–14).

The **Kimmeridge Clay** comprises rhythmically interbedded, more or less shelly, mudstones, calcareous mudstones, muddy siltstones, silty mudstones, muddy limestones, oil shales and rare phosphatic pebble-beds. Within the district, most of the 48 stratigraphical subdivisions (KC 1–48 of Gallois and Cox, 1976; Gallois, 1979; Cox and Gallois, 1981) have been recognised by Penn et al. (1986). In the southern part of the district, the Kimmeridge Clay is 130 to 135 m thick. The youngest bed proved beneath the unconformity at the base of the Spilsby Sandstone is KC 44, which lies within the Hudlestoni Zone. The formation thins northwards to just over 100 m at Cleethorpes where KC 37, at the base of the Scitulus Zone, is overlain by Spilsby Sandstone. At Winestead, only 15 m of Kimmeridge Clay are present, with KC 6 (in the Cymodoce Zone) at the top, and the Carstone directly above. Borehole DG 1 [1498 1908] near Killingholme, some 13 km south-west of Winestead and 19 km north-west of Cleethorpes, similarly entered the Cymodoce Zone directly beneath Carstone. There is thus a strong possibility that much of the thinning of Kimmeridge Clay north of Cleethorpes is due to post-Jurassic erosion, because the Spilsby Sandstone and most of the Lower Cretaceous are missing at North Killingholme. The **Elsham Sandstone** member, locally occurring in the Mutabilis Zone at and near outcrop in the Hull–Brigg district, has not been proved in this district but may occur at its western margin around the 81–90 sheet junction.

The oldest strata which crop out in the district, comprising the topmost c.35 m of the Kimmeridge Clay, occur on the lower slopes of the Wolds escarpment in the extreme south-west. Blown sand and alluvium cover most of the outcrop, but 1.5 m of bluish grey to black shale are visible in stream-bank sections around Normanby Mill [130 929].

Over the central and southern parts of the district, the Kimmeridge Clay is unconformably overlain by the **Spilsby Sandstone**, the lower part of which is Jurassic in age. The formation is dominantly a grey, coarse- to medium-grained, moderately sorted, generally poorly consolidated, glauconitic sandstone, but is fine grained and more homogeneous towards the base. Interbeds of green clay and glauconitic siltstone are locally present and phosphatic nodules and pebble beds are widespread at some stratigraphical levels. The most pronounced nodule bed, characterised by a high velocity 'spike' on sonic logs, lies at the base of the formation, but the highest of the basal cluster of such spikes is usually the Mid-Spilsby Nodule Bed which marks the top of the Volgian Lower Spilsby Sandstone and the base of the Cretaceous System (Casey, 1973).

As noted earlier, the Spilsby Sandstone is overstepped by the Carstone (Albian) at Killingholme and at Winestead. Only 7 km to the south of the Killingholme site, however, it is c.18 m thick beneath Carstone in the Roxton Wood No. 11 Borehole [1651 1180]; the thickness implies that both lower and upper members are present. It is of comparable thickness (21 m) at Cleethorpes where the basal 8 m is assigned to the Lower Spilsby Sandstone, but somewhat thicker at Tetney Lock (29 m) where the lower member is c.9 m thick. At outcrop, just to the west of the district, the formation first appears beneath overstepping Carstone at Clixby [TA 103 044] and then thickens southwards; some 10 m are present in the Nettleton Bottom Borehole (Casey 1973; Kelly and Rawson, 1979; Gaunt et al., 1992). South of Clixby, a progressively increasing sequence of Lower Cretaceous rocks separates the Spilsby Sandstone from the Carstone. The authors named above proved that at outcrop very little Upper Spilsby Sandstone is preserved. Their observations probably also apply to the Spilsby Sandstone at outcrop in the south-west of the district which is, however, not well exposed because of slippage across it of overlying strata. The thickness at outcrop in the district is c.12 m.

FOUR
Cretaceous

Lower Cretaceous

In Lincolnshire, the greater part of the Lower Cretaceous was characterised by alternate phases of marine shelf sedimentation and differential uplift with concomitant erosion, associated with the Market Weighton Structure. This structure (Figure 5) lies a short distance to the north of the district and most Lower Cretaceous formations lens out towards it. The stratigraphical succession is summarised in Figure 16, which is reproduced from Gaunt et al. (1991, fig. 27); the same reference provides details of petrology and palaeontology relevant to the district. Local details are given in the appropriate Technical Reports for 1:10 000 sheet areas.

The sub-Chalk Lower Cretaceous (the Chalk group is described separately below) crops out only in the southwest corner of the district, on the Wolds scarp and as inliers within deep Wolds valleys, but it probably underlies the remainder of the district to the north and east, at least as far north as the River Humber. Apart from the Spilsby Sandstone (described in Chapter three) and the Carstone, the succession near outcrop is dominantly argillaceous and contains varying proportions of ferruginous ooliths. The coverage of subsurface data is adequate near the outcrop because of the economic value of the Claxby Ironstone, but elsewhere it is sparse, especially to the north of the Humber.

Claxby Ironstone

This formation consists of a sequence of mainly argillaceous limonite (goethite in part), berthierine and siderite oolitic mudstones and wackestones; it is split into two members, the Lower and Upper Claxby Ironstone, by a non-sequence beneath a conglomeratic bed at the base of the latter. A full description is provided in Gaunt et al. (1992).

The Claxby Ironstone crops out on the Wolds scarp in the extreme south-west of the district, where it was mined commercially until 1969. There are no surface sections available within the district and borehole data are rare beyond the limits of prospecting boreholes adjacent to the ironstone workings. The eastern limit of these borings is effectively the Caistor–Horncastle scarp-top road, known as High Street.

In the prospected 'ironfield' area, the formation is thickest, 7 to 8.5 m, at or close to its outcrop, from the southern margin of the district to about National Grid line 955N. Beyond this it thins rapidly and tapers out at outcrop at Audleby in the adjacent Brigg district [111 040]. To the south-east of the ironfield, the Claxby Ironstone thins to about 5 m at Kirmond le Mire (beyond the district margin). It is absent from the record of a borehole at Rothwell [1594 9855], only 3 km east of the abandoned workings, but it has been proved to the east and south of Rothwell, where 6 m were recorded at Thoresway [1646 9632] and around 4 m at Croxby [1918 9814] and Binbrook [2174 9382]; the iron content is possibly lower in this area. The sparse underground data of the remainder of this district includes evidence of the absence of Claxby Ironstone at Brocklesby, Immingham, Killingholme and Ottringham (Winestead Borehole), but also the presence of 4 m at Cleethorpes and 9.75 m, the thickest occurrence of all, at Tetney Lock.

Tealby Formation

At its outcrop in the south-west of this district, the Tealby Formation consists of grey silty mudstone with subordinate beds of impure limestone, all accompanied by minor proportions of ferruginous ooliths. The limestone beds are concentrated in the Tealby Limestone member, which separates the Upper and Lower Tealby clays. These subdivisions cannot be maintained far to the north or east because of the facies and thickness variations indicated by the sparse borehole data.

The Tealby Formation is absent in the Winestead Borehole, the only record available on North Humberside, and also north of Cabourne, at the western margin of the district. However, 9 m are preserved at Cleethorpes and 17 m at Tetney Lock, where arenaceous lithologies are dominant over mudstone. It is probable that this development of sandstone in the Tealby sequence is widespread across the district, but there is insufficient borehole data to prove this. The first sandstone below the Carstone has hitherto been equated with the Spilsby Sandstone; however, the Tetney Lock and Cleethorpes data show that this is at best a rash assumption. Evidence of a substantial sand content in the Tealby Formation occurs as close to the outcrop area as Croxby [1918 9814], where 20 m of sandy strata separate the Chalk from Claxby Ironstone, and Binbrook [1990 9559], where at least 24 m of dominantly sandy strata are present beneath the Carstone. East of the Wolds, boreholes at Utterby [3067 9320] and Little Grimsby [3306 9264] sustain this trend by proving sandstone-dominated sequences for at least 24 m below the Chalk. The Carstone probably accounts for about the top 8 m of this; the quality of the records precludes differentiation of the Roach and Tealby formations in the remainder.

Description of members of the Tealby Formation relates only to the outcrop area in the south-western corner of the district.

The **Lower Tealby Clay** is composed of silty mudstone, olive-grey at outcrop but bluish grey where fresh, containing ferruginous (mainly limonite) ooliths superficially similar to those of the underlying Claxby Ironstone. The thickness in the Claxby Ironfield area varies between 10 m and 13 m, but it is 14 m near Rothwell and Bin

Figure 16 Lower Cretaceous stratigraphy (reproduced from Gaunt et al., 1991)

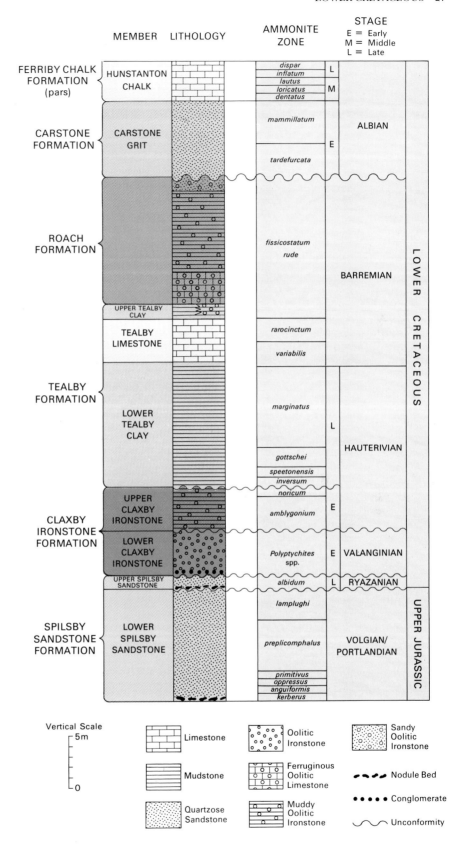

brook. The outcrop on the Wolds escarpment occupies a steep slope beneath a shelf formed by the Tealby Limestone. A small inlier has been identified within the Wolds, in the floor of the valley at Dales Bottom, 1.5 km west of Stainton le Vale.

The **Tealby Limestone** consists of a sequence of flaggy, fine-grained, buff-weathering, bluish grey limestones and calcareous silty sandstones with mudstone partings and sporadic ferruginous ooliths. The thickness in the Claxby Ironfield is commonly about 3 m but ranges from 1.5 to 5.5 m. It is 2.5 m thick in the Thoresway Borehole [1646 9632] but cannot with certainty be identified farther north-eastward because of the general increase in arenaceous content of the Tealby Formation. At outcrop on the Wolds scarp, the limestone tends to form a cambered bench, giving an outcrop area disproportionate to its thickness. Within the Wolds, the presence of inliers is signalled by characteristic slabs of limestone in the valley-bottom soil at Thoresway [16 96] and between Stainton le Vale and Kirmond le Mire [18 93]. In the latter area, the limestone is clearly raised to the surface in a series of isolated domes, presumably caused by valley bulging, involving the upward flowage of the mainly argillaceous Lower Cretaceous strata under load from the Chalk-capped interfluves (Fletcher, 1988).

The **Upper Tealby Clay** is lithologically similar to the Lower Tealby Clay and differs from the overlying Roach Formation in containing only minor proportions of ferruginous ooliths. In the type area to the south of the district, the Roach is younger than the Upper Tealby Clay, but here the iron-rich Roach facies may, at least in part, be contemporaneous with the Upper Tealby Clay. Certainly the Upper Tealby Clay facies is dramatically reduced in thickness in this district, a maximum of only 2.7 m being recorded 0.5 km north of Otby Top, near the Wolds scarp; only 0.52 m is recorded at Thoresway. There may, however, be as much as 12.5 m at Rothwell, where a borehole record of 'blue clay' between Carstone and Tealby Limestone suggests Tealby Clay rather than Roach, but this would be a grossly anomalous thickness if true.

To summarise, the Tealby Formation in this district extends northwards and eastwards from its outcrop in the extreme south-west to a feather edge running from just north of Cabourne, conjecturally eastwards through Laceby into the Humber Estuary north of Grimsby. Throughout most of its subcrop, it is probably dominantly arenaceous, but it rapidly grades to the mudstone-limestone-mudstone sequence of the type area in and around the Claxby Ironfield.

Roach Formation

The Roach is essentially a very low-grade sedimentary ironstone. In its type area, to the south of the district, it consists of three members: the Lower Roach, heterogeneous but dominantly argillaceous; the Roach Stone, calcareous and/or arenaceous; and the Upper Roach, argillaceous. All three, with the exception of parts of the Roach Stone, are highly ferruginous and mainly oolitic. In the Claxby Ironfield, the only area in this district where sufficient outcrop and borehole data allow detailed study, only two main divisions are present; a lower hard, porous, calcareous bed, which is relatively poor in ooliths and 2 to 3 m thick, and an upper argillaceous, highly ferruginous member. Lithologically, these two divisions match elements of the type Roach Stone and Upper Roach members respectively, but it is not known whether they are in continuity with them (the intervening ground has not been recently mapped). If they are, then the members are probably highly diachronous, because the only available macrofossil evidence suggests that the upper member in the district is coeval with the Lower Roach of the type area and that the lower member equates with part of the type Upper Tealby Clay.

The Roach is poorly exposed, commonly occupying debris-covered slopes below the Carstone on the Wolds scarp face, and the drift-covered floors of valleys within the Wolds around Thoresway and Stainton le Vale. Where drift-free, the outcrop is characterised by bright orange-brown, clayey soils in which ferruginous ooliths are common. The best exposure is at Lud's Well [1761 9380], Stainton le Vale (Fletcher, 1988), where a stream section shows about 4 m of strata at the top of the Roach in contact with the Carstone (formerly excavated here for aggregate). The beds are argillaceous and rich in ooliths, typical of the upper member in this district.

The greatest thickness of the Roach in the Claxby Ironfield is about 11 m, but as little as 6 m are present in places; some, but not all of the variation is related to a northward tapering towards the Market Weighton Structure. The thickness is 12.2 m at Thoresway, 10.97 m at Tetney Lock and 2.7 m at Cleethorpes; it is absent at Killingholme and Winestead. In the neighbouring Brigg district the formation has not been recorded on the Wolds scarp north of Nettleton. It seems probable that the northern limit of the Roach is approximately parallel to and a few kilometres south of that of the underlying Tealby formation (see above).

Carstone

The Carstone is typically a coarse, friable, relatively poorly sorted sandstone that, despite minor variations in facies, remains identifiable over a large area of Britain. It was deposited in a transgressive sea during Aptian times following a period of uplift and erosion that was particularly marked over the Market Weighton Structure; the Carstone is itself severely reduced in thickness in that area.

In the district, the Carstone is a greenish brown, coarse-grained to conglomeratic, clayey, ferruginous sandstone at outcrop, containing abundant subrounded, polished grains of quartzite and some of black chalcedonic 'lydite'. It also commonly contains rounded lumps of pale phosphatic material and sundry lithic and bioclastic debris, mainly from preceding Cretaceous formations. Where fresh, the sandstone is greenish grey and pyritous, grading to reddish brown where influenced by the overlying Red Chalk. Boreholes prove that the sandstone is sporadically interbedded with mudstone; it is not possible, however, to distinguish an upper 'Carstone Grit' from a lower 'sands-and-clays' (Swinnerton, 1935) as in south Lincolnshire. The presence of mudstone in the Carstone, and of sandstone in the underlying Cretaceous formations throughout much of the district, makes differentiation of the two formations in borehole records difficult. The upper boundary of Carstone with the Red Chalk is commonly transitional, and is thus difficult to determine in borehole logs, for example that of Cleethorpes Borehole.

The Carstone crops out on the main Wolds scarp face in the extreme south-west of the district and as inliers in the heads of valleys within the Wolds. Its status as the main local aquifer is emphasised by a spring line at the base of the formation (Fletcher, 1988). The best exposures in the district are at Lud's Well [1761 9380], Stainton le Vale, where a spring at the foot of a 7 m-high face of the formerly quarried sandstone provides an exposure of a basal fossiliferous conglomerate with phosphatic pebbles, resting on the Roach Formation. Similar spring-line exposures at the base of sandstone cliffs occur at and near Thoresway [1653 9653; 1779 9728]. Mudstones have not been seen at outcrop.

In the well-drilled Claxby Ironfield area, the thickness of the Carstone is generally 7 to 8 m, but ranges from 5 to 10 m. Nearby, to the east and north-east, it is 7 m thick at Stainton le Vale, 6 m at Thoresway and only 1.5 m thick at Rothwell. At and near Cabourne, to the north of Rothwell, mudstone is a major component in the formation, which is between 3.5 m and 6 m thick. The occurrence of mudstone interbeds can be inferred from borehole data to the south-east at Beelsby, Croxby, Swinhope, Wold Newton and Utterby, where the formation is about 10 m thick; it is possible that the lower part of this sequence belongs to an underlying formation, but the quality of data is inadequate to prove it. About 10 m of Carstone without mudstone occur at Swallow, and 10.97 m near Laceby, but a thickness of 14.6 m of sandstone beneath the Chalk at Riby suggests overstep of the Carstone onto the Spilsby Sandstone. To the north, 4 to 8 m are recorded in the Brocklesby area, probably overlying the Ancholme Clay Group. At North Killingholme [1498 1908] 4.2 m of very coarse Carstone rest on fossiliferous, dark grey Kimmeridge Clay. Data is very sparse in the areas of thick drift cover, but northward thinning is indicated by the records of 5.79 m at Tetney Lock and 3.1 m at Cleethorpes (including Red Chalk with the Carstone). Although not identified from available samples in the Winestead Borehole, the geophysical log traces suggest the presence of a very thin Carstone there. The likelihood is that the basal Chalk at Winestead will include arenaceous material that could be attributed to the Carstone.

A full account of the petrology and palaeontology of the Carstone is given by Gaunt et al. (1992), to which the reader is referred.

Upper Cretaceous: The Chalk Group

At its base, the Chalk Group in Northern England includes the Hunstanton Chalk Member, which is of Lower Cretaceous age (Middle and Late Albian sub-stages); however, it is described in this section for convenience.

The constituent formations of the group in this Northern Province were defined by Wood and Smith (1978),

and the stratigraphy was further elaborated by Wood (in Gaunt et al., 1992). Much of the detail given in the latter is directly applicable to the district because the stratigraphy of the Chalk is remarkably consistent in this region. Within the Patrington (81) sheet, higher parts of the Chalk succession occur, but most of them are deeply buried beneath drift and have not been investigated.

The most characteristic Chalk lithology is a dazzling white, soft, porous, micritic limestone, formed dominantly of coccolith microfossils. It is modified by variations in degree of recrystallisation and by varying proportions of 'impurities' such as clay, iron oxide, macrofossil debris, clastic limestone grains and, most prominently, chert segregations generally known as flints. The variations from 'standard' white chalk are generally stratigraphically consistent over large areas (Wood and Smith, 1978) and, except in the basal Ferriby Chalk Formation, tend to be confined to thin units which constitute thin marker beds. Much of the Northern Province chalk is more pervasively affected by diagenetic alteration (usually causing hardening of the rock) than its southern counterpart. The markers may be correlated from section to section according to their individual characteristics or, more reliably, by comparing discrete groups of markers; in this context, even the spacing of bedding-plane partings and stylolites (load-induced solution planes) can be of value. The chief markers, namely clay-rich 'marl' bands and horizons of continuous or discontinuous flint segregation, show up well on downhole geophysical records; detailed sonic and resistivity logs are particularly valuable, and natural gamma traces can also be used. Suitable logs permit detailed stratigraphical correlation where other data are inadequate or absent (Gray, 1958; Murray, 1982, 1986; Barker et al., 1984; Mortimore and Wood, 1986; Gaunt et al., 1992); in the district, good correlation has been achieved in the Wolds and the adjacent Lincolnshire Marsh areas (see the Chalk correlation diagram on the 1:50 000 Grimsby–Saltfleet (90/91) Sheet).

At and near outcrop, the chalk forms the Wolds, a dry upland bounded by a scarp face in the south-west and a former marine cliff in the north-east. It is drained mainly by deep north-east-trending valleys in some of which there are inliers of Lower Cretaceous rocks. A planar, hilltop surface on the Chalk outcrop, effectively a dip slope, is inclined gently to the north-east (see p.38 and diagram on the 1:50 000 sheet); where the Chalk is partially masked by Devensian till, a similar surface grading northwards, but not a dipslope, can be recognised. Lithological variations within the Chalk have comparatively little influence on the topography of the Wolds, but in places the abundant flint bands near the base of the Burnham Chalk produce a subsidiary escarpment. 'Slack' features related to the presence of marl bands are rare in this district. East of the concealed cliff-line feature, the buried Chalk surface seems, according to available borehole evidence, to be a remarkably even, gently seaward-inclined wave-cut platform (Figure 20).

Tabulated and graphical summaries of the regional Chalk stratigraphy are provided in Wood and Smith (1978) and Gaunt et al. (1992). The succession comprises, in ascending sequence, the Ferriby Chalk, the Welton Chalk, the Burnham Chalk and the Flamborough Chalk.

Ferriby Chalk

The lowest Chalk formation is also the thinnest, softest and most distinctive lithologically. Like the other formations it has a consistent internal stratigraphy with characteristic geophysical log 'signatures' (Figure 17, Barker et al., 1984, fig. 3); it differs from them in containing a generally high and widely disseminated clay content, and more clastic limestone and ferruginous material. Most significantly, it entirely lacks flint.

Outcrops are commonly distinguished by the presence of particularly pale, 'bleached'-looking derived soils, possibly because the soft weathered greyish white chalk tends to integrate with its dark residuum, whereas the 'brash' of harder white chalk of higher formations stands out against its dark matrix. The distinctive brick-red colour of the Red Chalk in soil brash makes its outcrops conspicuous.

The Ferriby Chalk crops out along the upper slopes of the Wolds escarpment in the extreme south-west of the district and along valley sides and bottoms within the Wolds. It subcrops beneath thick drift at the foot of the Pre-Devensian cliff around Utterby. Boreholes (mainly water wells) provide evidence of distribution beneath the remainder of the Wolds and parts of Lincolnshire Marsh, but there is scant information north of the Humber. There are no measurable exposures of the Ferriby Chalk in the district and borehole cores have been obtained only at Killingholme. The recognition and correlation of marker beds, other than of colour bands (see diagrammatic section on the Grimsby (90) Sheet), has been made possible only by comparison of geophysical log 'signatures' (Figure 17).

The total thickness throughout the Wolds and the adjoining parts of the marsh is generally within a range of 24 to 26 m, but it is only 22 m around Great Limber and between 19 and 21 m around Killingholme. Reduced thicknesses are also recorded at Keelby and Laceby, but the quality of the data is suspect. The northward thinning implied by these figures contrasts with a thickening to the east and south. Thus, the Ferriby Chalk is 25 m thick at Cleethorpes, 27 m at Wold Newton and 32 m at Fulstow. The thickness of 30 m at Beelsby is anomalously large in its geographical context, but the geophysical log shows that the extra thickness is entirely accommodated at the base, presumably infilling a shallow depression on an otherwise remarkably level Carstone surface (see diagrammatic section on the Grimsby (90) Sheet). North of the Humber, the only available record is of the Winestead Borehole [2741 2433], the gamma log of which suggests that the Ferriby Chalk, resting directly on Kimmeridge Clay, is 20 m thick, much the same as at Killingholme: this is the only record in the district of Chalk resting on anything other than Carstone. and its validity is doubtful (see previous page).

Although most units of the Ferriby Chalk are recognisable in this district only by their geophysical log signatures, there are abundant references in written logs to colour bands, and every borehole bottoming the Chalk refers to the basal Red Chalk.

In this district, the term **Red Chalk** is used lithostratigraphically to describe the brick-red coloured beds at the base of the Ferriby Chalk, which form a mappable unit. Such beds are in some areas equivalent to the Red Chalk *sensu* Jeans (1973, 1980), which is synonymous with the Hunstanton Chalk Member of Wood and Smith (1978) and Gaunt et al. (1992), but may locally correspond to either more than or, more commonly, only part of that member. Emphasis has already been laid on the consistency of the Chalk lithostratigraphy of the Northern Province and the persistence of marker beds. Thus, the pigmentation of the Red Chalk *sensu* Jeans, and also of the two 'pink bands' higher in the Chalk succession, may also once have been regionally persistent, but it has suffered from differential secondary reduction, causing, in extreme instances, the total bleaching out of red colouring, for example at and near the scarp face between Barnetby and Searby on the adjacent Brigg (89) Sheet. So far as is known, the process has not gone to completion anywhere in the district, but the 'pink bands' are commonly not recorded in borehole logs and the Red Chalk is notably thin in places.

The minimum recorded thickness of the Red Chalk is 0.6 m near the Chalk scarp face south of Caistor, in an area where it is generally less than 2 m. Elsewhere, the thickness is commonly around 3 m, but exceeds 4 m at Thoresway and Covenham. To the north, around Killingholme, thicknesses range from 1.9 to 3.5 m; the record of 12.8 m at Winestead is highly suspect (judged on chippings, but not closely related to the gamma log signature). The base of the Red Chalk is not always sharply defined; where clay interbeds occur in either or both the basal Chalk and the underlying Carstone, the only criterion for distinguishing them may be colour: red for Chalk, green for Carstone.

The eponymous colour of the pink bands, which is absent in adjacent parts of the Brigg Sheet (Gaunt et al., 1992), continues to be lacking as far east as Riby, Swallow and Wold Newton, but is retained at Cleethorpes, Beelsby, North Ormsby, Fulstow and Covenham.

Welton Chalk

The basal few metres of the Welton Chalk are lithologically similar to the Ferriby Chalk, being soft, argillaceous and devoid of flint; but thereupon, the sequence consists of harder, pure white, 'standard' chalk, sparsely interspersed with thin (commonly 1 cm or less) volcanigenic bentonitic marl beds (Pacey, 1984) and courses of nodular flints; the abundance, form and size of flints is very variable from course to course.

The Welton Chalk forms the high Wolds plateau southwards from Cabourne Woods and westwards from Riby, Irby, Beelsby and Binbrook. East of its outcrop, it subcrops in the floor of a drift-filled valley between Ravendale and Wold Newton, and more extensively in a south-east-widening wedge along the eastern margin of the Wolds from Laceby to the district margin between North Ormsby and Yarburgh. Derived soils of the Welton Chalk at outcrop tend to be heavy brown loams, rich in a brash of flint and chalk fragments, the former in en-

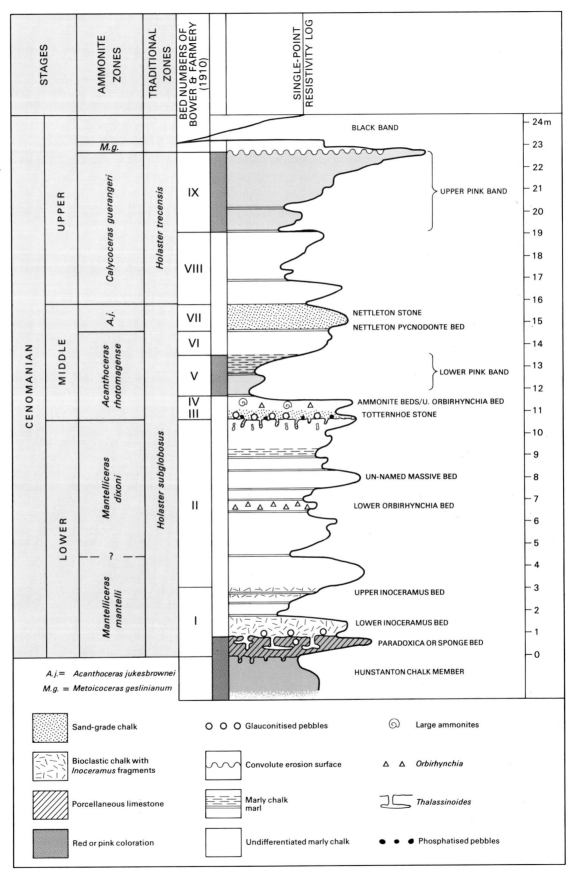

Figure 17
Cenomanian stratigraphy. A diagrammatic representation of stratigraphy applicable to this district, with mean thicknessess. (Reproduced from Gaunt et al., 1991).

hanced proportions relative to the host rock because of differential solution.

The stratigraphy of the Welton Chalk is summarised in Figure 18, which is modified from fig. 31 of Gaunt et al. (1992); a more detailed lithostratigraphy is shown in fig. 33 of that memoir. South of the River Humber, there are sufficient surface outcrops and boreholes to demonstrate the consistency of the stratigraphical sequence; however, the Winestead Borehole is the only source of information north of the Humber. Over a wide area including Cleethorpes, Covenham and Swallow, the total thickness of Welton Chalk is in the range of 52 to 53 m, but there is some thinning to the south-west, with less than 50 m at Ravendale and North Ormsby, and also to the north-east where about 48 m is present in the Killingholme district and less than 47 m at Winestead.

At the time of the survey, only two major quarry sections in the Welton Chalk, at Swallow Vale [174 043] and Irby Dale [1923 0518], remained clear, but small degraded exposures are fairly common. In particular, a roadside exposure [1618 9951] near Rothwell gave a clear view of the distinctive **Black Band**, which is the thickest (up to 0.3 m) of the Chalk marls and is thought to be in part equivalent to the Plenus Marls of southern England. The base of the Welton Chalk is taken at a glauconitised convolute hardground at the first parting below the Black Band; it is commonly 0.3 m below. The beds immediately above the Black Band up to and including the First Main Flint were exposed in a small roadside quarry [1749 0094] at Cuxwold. A small quarry [1731 0304] at Swallow showed the basal flint-bearing beds. At Swallow Vale, cited above, the quarry face gives an 11 m sequence, including the Croxton Marl 4 m above the base: this section is of special structural interest because it lies on or close to the axis of the Caistor Monocline (see p.6). The main Irby Dale section (there is a smaller face nearby across the valley) reveals the topmost 13 m of the Welton sequence together with the rather poorly exposed basal beds of the Burnham Chalk. The Welton Chalk here includes the Deepdale Flint, the only semitablular flint band beneath the Burnham Chalk, and also some sporadically developed 'injection' flints — thin, planar, sill-like sheets that do not strictly follow bedding planes. The boundary between the Welton and Burnham formations is also exposed at the foot of quarry sections at West Ravendale [227 000], Ludborough [282 944] (Plates 1 and 2) and North Ormsby [288 935]. Formerly, there were excellent sections of these parts of the Chalk sequence in quarries at Riby [173 063] and Irby Dales Farm [194 044], but these have been obscured by landscaping and landfill processes. There are also a number of small sections in old abandoned quarries, particularly in the Irby Dale area, which repeat parts of the succession seen in the sites quoted above.

An extensive, uninterrupted, clean, 13 m-thick section was provided by the excavation of a liquified-gas storage cavern at South Killingholme [174 172]. It showed a sequence from the lowest Barton Marl in the roof to a level 1.5 m below the Grasby Marl in the deepest cutting. The section gave an exceptionally clear view (The Quarterly Journal of Engineering Geology, 1985) of flint horizons,

marl bands and stylolites, and was particularly useful in correlating the Croxton Marl with the remainder of the succession at Swallow Vale pit [174 043], and at Melton Ross [081 113], to the west of this district.

Burnham Chalk

This formation is distinguished by the presence of tabular flint bands, i.e. continuous or semicontinuous layers of flint, which may be either solid or careous, the latter being intermixed with chalk (Gaunt et al., 1992, fig. 34). The chalk matrix, as seen at outcrop in the lower third of the formation, is distinctly harder than that of contiguous formations. As in the Welton Chalk, the main rock fabric is white throughout, but includes pale greenish grey volcanigenic marl bands (Plate 3) which provide strict control of stratigraphical correlation.

The Burnham Chalk caps the Wolds to the east of the Welton Chalk outcrop and subcrops beneath drift deposits throughout most of the Lincolnshire Marsh. As already mentioned, the thick tabular flints near the base of the formation tend to coincide with a subsidiary scarp feature. Soils are commonly characterised by a brash of angular, hard, white chalk and fragments of tabular flint, both solid and careous.

A detailed lithostratigraphical graphic section of the lower half of the Burnham Chalk is provided by fig. 34 of the Hull–Brigg memoir (Gaunt et al., 1992), supplementing the generalised data of Figure 18. The base is defined as the first bedding-plane parting beneath the prominent Ravendale Flint. Available evidence indicates that the Burnham Chalk is about 130 m thick in the district but only about 50 m of this crop out. Widespread stratigraphical data are available only for the basal 15 m or so of the Burnham Chalk; they indicate slight thickening towards the southern margin of the district.

Excluding boreholes, the best available sections at the time of survey were the disused quarries at North Ormsby [288 935], Ludborough [282 944] and West Ravendale [227 000], all of which showed sequences from the topmost Welton Chalk to just above the Wootton Marls. Smaller disused pits, with the Wootton Marls low in the sections, occur at The Valley, Wold Newton [2480 9603], Beelsby [206 019] and Oaklands, Laceby [206 055]. A degraded old pit at Waterdell House, Barnoldby le Beck [227 024], combined with a nearby pit at Hatcliffe Top [2274 0215] provided a complete section from below the Wootton Marls to just above the Enthorpe Marls. The stratigraphically highest sections at outcrop include an old quarry at Cadeby Top Farm[2601 9577], which contain the three Kiplingcotes Marls, and at the Ashby Hill quarry [240 005] which formerly exposed 13 m of strata with the topmost Kiplingcote Marl near its base. It also featured a giant 'paramoudra' flint, an irregular sub-vertical cylindrical pillar, 0.5 to 1.0 m in diameter and about 2.5 m high, which has been illustrated in the literature (Bromley et al., 1975, pl. 1c; Hancock, 1975, plate 1d; Clayton, 1986). There are numerous smaller sections available in the Wolds and these have been noted in appropriate 1:10 000 sheet reports (Berridge, 1985, 1986, 1987a and b). They repeat parts of the sequences shown in those exposures cited above.

Figure 18 Stratigraphy of the Welton and Burnham Chalk (partly after Gaunt et al., 1991).

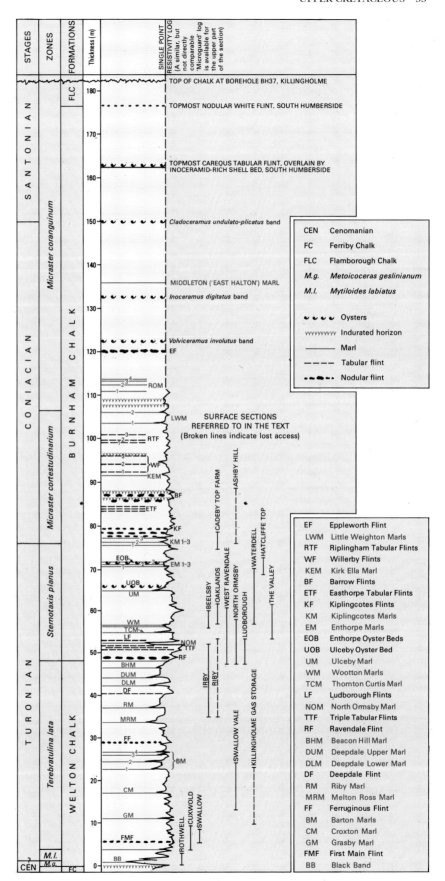

Plate 1 Ludborough Quarry, North Ormsby [2817 9441].

General view of part of the quarry face, looking north-westwards, showing the junction between the Welton and Burnham chalk formations.

The Ludborough Flint, thick white and tabular, is prominent at the top of the clean vertical face and in the grass at the left of the picture. The North Ormsby Marl and Triple Tabular Flints occur in downward sequence on the vertical face, with the Ravendale Flint, discontinuous and bifurcating, visible towards the foot of the face. The Welton–Burnham boundary shows as a prominent bedding-plane parting, with a change in the chalk texture, less than a metre below the Ravendale Flint (see below).

Plate 2 Ludborough Quarry, North Ormsby [2817 9441].

A closer view of the foot of the face seen in Plate 1, showing the relatively massive nature of the Burnham Chalk compared with the softer, more rubbly Welton Chalk. The boundary is the most prominent bedding-plane parting on the face, passing behind the lower end of the hammer shaft. This boundary is also the junction between the *Terebratulina lata* and *Sternotaxis planus* zones and is approximately equivalent to the Middle Chalk–Upper Chalk boundary of southern England. Note the prominent semitabular, bifurcating Ravendale Flint in the Burnham Chalk and the contrasting nodular flints in the Welton Chalk. The semitabular flint near the base of the section is part of a secondary 'injection' flint horizon.

As in other Chalk formations, detailed correlation and stratigraphical variation between boreholes have been immeasurably improved by the use of electrical resistivity logs and, to a lesser extent, by natural gamma-ray logs. To date, such data are not available for much of the area, particularly in Holderness, but recent industrial activity in the Killingholme area has provided useful information, from both core material and geophysical logs, to correlate otherwise cryptic records from older boreholes in the district. The material from Killingholme and neighbouring areas has not as yet been exhaustively studied, but preliminary correlation work has been carried out by Mr C J Wood, whose conclusions are summarised below. This information extends the de-

tailed knowledge of Chalk stratigraphy higher into the Burnham Chalk than was covered in the Hull–Brigg memoir (Gaunt et al., 1992). It identifies marker beds which provisionally define the local junction between the Burnham and Flamborough Chalk formations (Figure 19).

Borehole data now available from Killingholme, the Humber estuary and Sunk Island provide an overlapping composite section down to the base of the Chalk, including some 120 m of Flamborough Chalk. The key boreholes are NIREX South Killingholme DG1 [1498 1908] and BH37 [1732 1905], CEGB M7 [1460 2414] in the Humber estuary, and BGS Humberside No. 3 [2756 1677] on Sunk Island. The Killingholme boreholes

Plate 3 Ludborough Quarry, North Ormsby [2822 9441].

Part of the upper face of the quarry, with the uppermost Triple Tabular Flint near the bottom of the picture, the North Orsmby Marl near the centre and the Ludborough Flint at the top. Weathering has etched out a platey fabric in the chalk, verging on fissile just above the marl band, apparently related to undulose thin partings of marly granular material separating more massive chalk 'flags'. The fabric is particularly well shown to the left of the ruler.

(Central Electricity Generating Board and UK NIREX Limited, 1987) together provide a complete section from below the base of the Chalk to approximately 105 m above the Kiplingcotes Marl No. 3; marker beds enable the overlapping part of the sequence to be correlated precisely. In BH37 (Figure 18) a white flint (or porcellanous silicified chalk) occurs near the top of the cored sequence, above all occurrences of 'normal' grey flint and, specifically, 14 m above a careous tabular flint band, which is overlain by chalk with *Inoceramus* shell debris. Almost exactly similar relationships occur in borehole M7, some 6 km to the north-west. The careous tabular flint is 26 m above the Middleton Marl and 40 m above the more uniformly developed Little Weighton

No. 2 Marl in BH37. In Humberside No. 3 Borehole, a white flint occurs at a structurally analogous depth to equate with that of M7 and BH37, and there are no grey flints above it; however, there is no record of careous tabular flint 14 m below. The core is fragmental, however, and it may be disrupted by faulting at this level. The 120 m of core above the white flint marker contain some small white flints between 70 m and 75 m above it, and also marl bands and partings at numerous levels, commonly in confined zones (see following section). Correlation of these Humberside sections with the type Flamborough Chalk basal beds of Flamborough Head can only be tentative without additional study, but it seems reasonable, as a working hypothesis, to treat the white

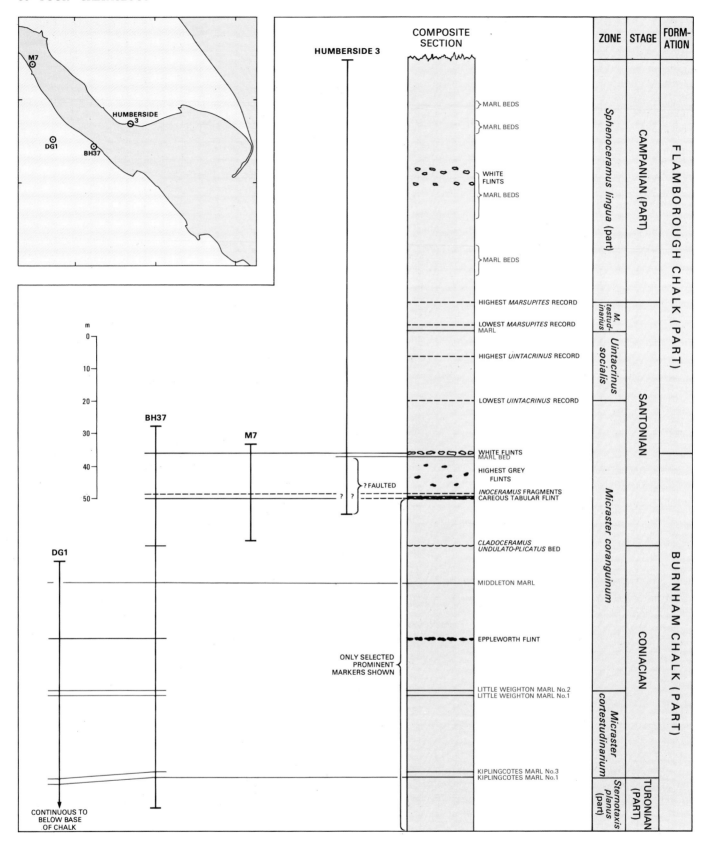

Figure 19 A summary of evidence for the proposed Burnham Chalk–Flamborough Chalk
boundary at the Humber estuary, showing stratigraphical correlation of key boreholes.

flint marker of boreholes BH37, M7 and Humberside No. 3 as the local top of the Burnham Chalk. This determines a total thickness of about 130 m of Burnham Chalk in the Killingholme area. Figure 18 summarises the interrelationships discussed above and includes biostratigraphical information supplied by Mr Wood and Mr A A Morter.

Flamborough Chalk

The Flamborough Chalk is typically less indurated than the Welton and Burnham Chalk formations, and is lithologically similar to 'standard' Southern Province white chalk (Wood and Smith, 1978). Although originally defined as flintless (Wood and Smith, 1978), sporadic bands of white flints do occur, but the grey flint marker beds that typify the underlying formations are absent. Marl bands continue to characterise the sequence. The formation subcrops over the whole of the district north of the Humber and also beneath parts of the Humber southern shore, including urban Grimsby. It is not exposed at the surface in this or any other recently surveyed area and hence its stratigraphy is less well known than those of underlying formations.

About 340 m of Flamborough Chalk are present beneath rockhead on land in the district. This estimate is based on geophysical evidence for the position of the base of the Chalk and limited borehole evidence for depth to rockhead. There are no detailed stratigraphical or palaeontological records for strata above the basal 120 m because of inadequate logging of the few available boreholes; the total thickness of Flamborough Chalk is unknown.

Data for the basal 120 m is primarily from the BGS Humberside No. 3 Borehole on Sunk Island [2756 1677] (Figure 19), which was lithologically logged in the field and later in part studied biostratigraphically by C J Wood and A A Morter. Sufficient macrofaunal data was obtained to prove a Santonian–Campanian age, including the *Micraster coranguinum–Uintacrinus socialis* zone boundary at a shelly horizon 14.86 m above the white flint basal marker and the *Marsupites testudinarius–Sphenoceramus lingua* (base of Campanian) boundary 45.67 m above the same datum. The intervening *socialis–testudinarius* boundary may be at or near a marl horizon 36.48 m above the datum. This marl is only one of a large number of partings, streaks and bands, individual-

ly up to 25 mm thick, which are present in this borehole sequence, notably in the Campanian from about 55 to 64 m, 73 to 87 m, 100 to 103 m and 107 to 108.5 m above the basal white flint. There are also prominent marl partings about 2 m below the basal marker and at about 10, 18 and 33 m above it. It is possible that the topmost 10 m of the chalk in this borehole, reduced to a 'putty' consistency by weathering, also contain marls. The Campanian (*lingua* Zone) core also included small white flints at 81.03, 85.50 and 86.21 m above the assumed base of the Flamborough Chalk. It is recognised that the *socialis* and *testudinarius* zones are abnormally condensed in the regional context.

The Winestead Borehole [2741 2433], near Ottringham, offers little additional evidence because logging was generalised and only the gamma-ray trace is of any stratigraphical value. It suggests that only about 100 m of Flamborough Chalk are present, based on the matching of marl signatures upwards from the base of the Chalk. On such an interpretation, a note of 'marly chalk between depths of 500 and 700 ft' covers the top 43 m of the Burnham Chalk and the basal 18 m of the Flamborough Chalk. It cannot match up with the marl-rich Campanian in the Humberside No. 3 borehole without the intervention of a major fault cutting out some 100 m of Burnham Chalk. The presence of only 100 m of Flamborough Chalk at Ottringham would be anomalous on a broad, regional, structural prediction, but geophysical data (see Figure 7f) indicates that a local upwarp affects the Chalk in this area.

Other boreholes in the Chalk of Holderness are of minimal use because they either lack sufficient penetration for identification purposes or predate the introduction of geophysical logging techniques. Of these, a borehole [4171 1617] at Kilnsea Fort proved 265 m of chalk beneath almost 40 m of drift and was originally reported by Lamplugh (1919, p. 63) to be flint-free throughout. However, a graphic log in BGS records (from a War Department source) indicates 'small beds of flint' at a depth of 95.10 m. It must be assumed that the whole of this borehole was within Flamborough Chalk. Similarly, a borehole [3382 2543] at Hollym, near Withernsea, penetrated 42 m into chalk beneath 40 m of drift and the record refers to 'only a little flint'. The available borehole data thus confirm that the Flamborough Chalk cannot be regarded as totally flintless.

FIVE

Quaternary

In the district there are no known deposits related to the time interval between the Upper Cretaceous and the Quaternary. Claims have been made (Straw, 1961) that the planar tops of the Wolds interfluves represent several marine planation surfaces, the highest produced by a Pliocene incursion, but the evidence is, at best, inconclusive. In this resurvey no consistent back features were identified. It is likely that a single Wolds-top planar surface results from rejuvenation of a subaerial peneplain, as contoured in the diagram in the margin of the Grimsby (90) sheet. Whatever the origin of the surface, it is clear that substantial volumes of post-Campanian sedimentary rocks have been removed by erosion during and after post-Cretaceous tilting and uplift.

As is common in Great Britain, the distribution of Quaternary deposits is strongly influenced by pre-existing topography and, therefore, they generally lack continuity of cover across the district. Distinction of mappable units is based largely on lithology and mode of origin. Fluviatile, lacustrine, glacial and aeolian deposition, and also erosion, occurred penecontemporaneously in different parts of the district on many occasions; thus the relative ages of deposits are difficult to determine. Despite this, an assessment of local stratigraphical relationships, together with various chemical and palaeoclimatic age determinations, has allowed the setting up of a general stratigraphical framework. Figure 20 summarises the inferred age relationships of the main units in the district, including those which have not been depicted on the face of the published maps because lack of exposure or weathering makes them difficult to map. For example, the various tills of the district, most of which are readily divisible where fresh, cannot be distinguished where they are weathered and/or reworked at the surface without intensive analysis at close intervals. The terminology used here is that of British rather than North European convention, e.g. 'Devensian' rather than 'Weichselian' (e.g. Bowen et al., 1986b).

Most of the district was covered by ice of the late Devensian (Dimlington) stadial (Rose, 1985) and thus older Quaternary deposits are relatively poorly represented because of either removal or burial. Some post-Dimlingtonian deposits are not readily assigned to the Pleistocene and Holocene because their generative processes have been continuous throughout both.

There is little doubt that depositional remnants of the Anglian glaciation are preserved in this district and a strong probability that succeeding Hoxnian interglacial sediments also occur. It is now commonly considered, however, that the post-Hoxnian, pre-Ipswichian ('Wolstonian') glaciation was not as extensive as previously thought; thus, the age of the Basement Till of Holderness, which has been ascribed to this glaciation, is a matter of critical reappraisal. Ipswichian sediments have not been identified in situ but are assumed to have contributed to the spectrum of fossil debris in the Kelsey Hill Beds (of Devensian age); they may also be locally preserved in small pockets on the concealed chalk platform extending under much of Holderness and Lincolnshire Marsh, east of the buried Ipswichian sea cliff.

ANGLIAN

Remnants of till that are here tentatively correlated with the Lowestoft Till ('Chalky Boulder Clay') (Bowen et al., 1986b) occur extensively in the Vale of Ancholme, to the west of the district, with extensions eastwards across the Wolds to the south of this district. An isolated relic of this Wolds-top cover occurs on the south-western margin around [146 927], near Walesby Top Farm. Resting on Ferriby Chalk, it forms a sandy clay soil rich in pebbles, cobbles and boulders mainly derived from the Lower Cretaceous formations, such as those which crop out along the scarp face to the west: it thus approximates in composition to the Belmont Till of Straw (1969). Some 10 to 12 km to the east, on the Wolds summit between Binbrook and North Ormsby, there is a thin almost continuous cover of till with enclaves of sand and gravel. This spread of drift, at about 100 m and more above sea level, is in continuity with the westernmost cover of Devensian till. It was, however, classified in the primary geological survey as 'Older Drift' (Jukes-Browne, 1885) and is therefore probably also continuous with the presumed Anglian Wolds-top till (Calcethorpe Till of Straw, 1969) in the area west of Louth. Differentiation of the Devensian and older tills in the field, if indeed both are present, did not prove possible (see p.48); this may be because the older till was reworked by the Devensian ice. Furthermore, all glacial deposits have since been affected by periglacial processes as well as by later pedogenesis and agriculture, and much of the mapped till cover on the Chalk is probably only about one metre in thickness around Kelstern Airfield. As described above, almost continuous interfluvial relics of an old Wolds-top planar surface extend from the southern margin of the district to about 2 km north of Caistor and Swallow (see inset map on the published Grimsby 1:50 000 sheet). No mappable till was identified on this surface (beyond the limits of the Devensian cover in the east and the Kelstern area described above), but the clay soil cover is commonly rich in pebbles and cobbles of distant origin: Caledonoid igneous and metamorphic rocks, Upper Palaeozoic sandstones and dolerite resembling that of the Whin Sill are particularly prominent. This erratic-rich clay soil may well be the residuum of a formerly more extensive Anglian till cover. An isolated patch of clean sand containing rounded chalk pebbles occurs at Cabourne Vale farm

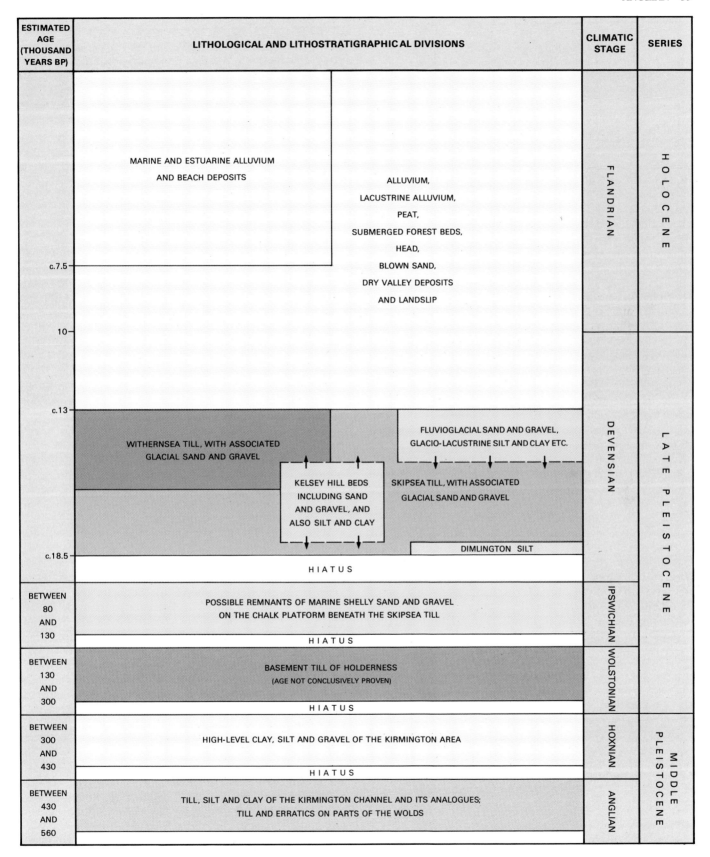

Figure 20 The probable time and space relationships of Quaternary deposits in the district.

Note that divisions listed do not necessarily correspond to mapped units on the face of the map; there are some generalisations and some conjectural additions here. Devensian and Flandrian ages are discussed in the text. Pre-Devensian ages are generalised from Bowen et al., 1986a.

[132 014], near Caistor; this pebbly sand was probably associated with the inferred Anglian till.

Evidence of the Anglian glaciation is not preserved at the surface farther to the north in the district, but a buried channel, the Kirmington Channel (Figure 21) (otherwise known as the Kirmington Buried Channel, Kirmington Fjord or Immingham Channel), traverses the district from Brocklesby to Immingham, and probably extends across the Humber; it and possible unproved analogues beneath Holderness are of probable Anglian age. The proved Kirmington Channel (see Williamson, 1983) is an almost straight, east-north-east-trending incision carved into the Chalk; it is about 8 km in length, 2 km across and up to 50 m deep, and its floor grades from about sea-level near Kirmington and Brocklesby to 75 m below OD at Immingham Docks (see Figure 21). The floor of the channel is more steeply graded in its upper and lower parts (where proved) than along the middle course between Haborough and Immingham. The channel is infilled mainly by silt and clay, interlaminated in part, but locally contains interbeds of sand, gravel and till. These deposits are considered to be Anglian in age because they are overlain by estuarine silty clays and marine gravels of presumed Hoxnian age around Kirmington (Gaunt et al., 1992). By analogy with numerous structures of similar form occurring across north-west Europe (see Wingfield, 1989, 1990 and references therein), the Kirmington Channel is inferred to be part of a 'tunnel valley' produced by catastrophic localised escape of meltwater under great hydrostatic pressure near the periphery of an ice sheet: most, if not all, of the infill would have been deposited immediately after excavation of the valley. The direction of continuation of the Kirmington Channel towards the north-east is conjectural.

There are comparatively few borehole records or suitable geophysical interpretations from which the Chalk surface of Holderness can be defined. However, some borehole data indicate possible channel infills below a conjectural Ipswichian wave-cut platform (e.g. the Winestead Borehole near Ottringham, where 17.3 m of laminated silt and clay overlie Chalk at 61.07 m below OD), but their relationship to the Kirmington Structure is uncertain. Tunnel valleys ('incisions' of Wingfield, references cited) are typically simple in form and therefore a possible analogous structure detected by boreholes at Salt End [around 16 28] near Hull may be a separate entity rather than a tributary of the Kirmington Channel. At Salt End, up to 12 m of finely laminated silt and clay (overlain by possibly much later sand, gravel and peat) rest on a probable west–east-trending valley floor at 36 m below OD. There is as yet no proof that this channel is coeval with that of the Kirmington Channel, but available evidence indicates close similarity.

HOXNIAN

Gaunt et al. (1992) ascribe a Hoxnian age to high-level sediments overlying the Kirmington Channel infill around the village of Kirmington. Most of these deposits are in the Brigg and Hull districts (sheets 89 and 80) but there is a slight overlap into district near Brocklesby. The deposits are described in detail in Gaunt et al. (1992) but, in brief, they consist of estuarine silt and clay overlain by marine 'cannon shot' gravel. The Hoxnian age was inferred mainly from the height of the deposits, which indicates a sea level of about 22 m above OD, coupled with a flora and fauna characteristic of a climate similar to that of today. The combination of high sea level and mild climate (eliminating the possibility of local isostatic depression by an adjacent ice sheet) precludes an age younger than Hoxnian: the Ipswichian sea level in the district is well established by palaeontological and morphological evidence at 1 to 3 m above OD.

'WOLSTONIAN' the Basement Till of Holderness

'Wolstonian' is used here to describe the glacial maximum or maxima between the Hoxnian and Ipswichian interstadials, although the term may be invalid as applied to the deposits of its type locality. In this district too, there is some doubt about the age of the till that is ascribed to this stadial, but published evidence so far tends to favour this interpretation.

The Basement Till (Madgett and Catt, 1978 and references therein) is exposed at the surface only in cliff foot (up to 4 m seen at the time of survey) and foreshore outcrops between Easington and Holmpton, although it is also seen in the Bridlington area 40 km to the north. Boreholes on the foreshore at Easington prove that it is at least 30 m thick there, but it has not been positively identified elsewhere. Any particular coastal exposure is ephemeral because of the 2 to 3 m annual retreat of the Holderness cliffs and the migration of beach ridges from north to south over the foreshore.

Where exposed, the Basement Till commonly consists of dark olive-grey (Munsell colour 5Y 4/2 moist, 5Y 6/2 dry), chalk-bearing, gritty, silty clay containing up to 10 per cent of pebbles and cobbles: in practice, it has a greenish appearance relative to the brown or reddish brown of overlying tills. The fabric appears to be rubbly (Plate 4), chaotic or, where colour variations are available to show it, contorted. The top surface is smooth but undulating, and locally shows a 0.75 m-thick partial oxidation zone (see Plate 4), suggesting pedogenesis or solifluxion. Locally, this top surface is conformably overlain by Dimlington Silt (Plate 5). Particle size analysis (Madgett and Catt, 1978; Catt and Digby, 1988) indicates that the Basement Till is consistently more clay-rich (up to 50 per cent) than overlying tills, and geotechnical tests (Bell and Forster, 1991) indicate a significantly greater compactness than the Skipsea and Withernsea tills, which are similar in this property. Pebbles and cobbles include Caledonoid igneous rocks (including Scandinavian types), Magnesian Limestone, black flint and Chalk, the last of which tends to be concentrated in the less coarse-grained fractions. The till also contains marine fossils including 'Tellina balthica' (i.e. Macoma balthica (Linné)) and 'Cyprina sp.' (now Arctica sp.) (Bisat, 1939). Hiatella arctica (Linné) has been collected from a brownish grey clay lying on contorted blue-grey clay at [3850 2268] on

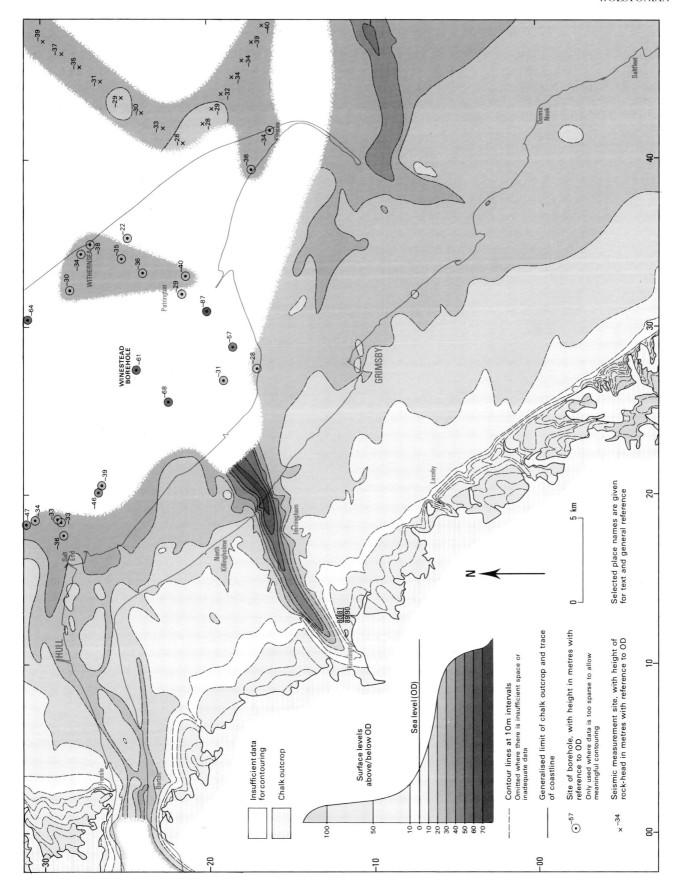

Figure 21 Generalised rockhead contour map to show the dominant buried physiographic features on solid rock, where known. Isolated data points are shown elsewhere.

Plate 4   Sea cliff, Dimlington High Land [3897 2189].

A part of the cliff on 17 August 1988 showing Basement, Skipsea and Withernsea tills in upward sequence. The observer stands on a 0.5 m-thick modified (weathered or soliflucted) top of the dark, rubbly textured Basement Till. The overlying Skipsea Till has a conspicuous layered structure: a 3 m- to 4 m-thick basal unit with planar foliation well marked in the lower 2 m; a 1.5 m-thick unit containing fewer pebbles; a 0.5 m to 1.0 m unit of silt, sand and gravel; and a 1.0 m unit of structureless silt or almost stone-free till. The upper boundary with relatively bland Withernsea Till is likely to be at least partly a recent slip plane.

the foreshore, 250 m north of Cliff Farm, Out Newton, 25 September 1985; sample number MPA 25063. It was accompanied by an extensive microfauna as follows (sample number PH 7195):

Foraminifera	No. of specimens
Bolivina sp.	1
Cassidulina reniforme Nørvang	75
C. teretis Tappan	2
Elphidium clavatum Cushman	207
Islandiella norcrossi (Cushman)	1
Miliolinella subrotunda (Montagu)	1
Nonion labradoricum (Dawson)	1
Nonionella auricula Heron-Allen & Earland	1
Polymorphinidae	3
Haynesina orbiculare (Brady)	5
Quinqueloculina stalkeri Loeblich & Toppan	1
Q. sp.	1
Trifarina cf. *angulosa* (Williamson)	1

Ostracoda	
Acanthocythereis dunelmensis (Norman)	9
Cytheropteron latissimum (Norman)	2
Elofsonella concinna (Jones)	28
Eucytheridea macrolaminata (Elofson)	1
Hemicythere villosa (Sars)	1

This assemblage (identified by Miss D M Gregory) indicates a shallow-water (c.20 m) glaciomarine environment.

According to Catt and Digby (1988), the lithological composition of the Basement Till remains fairly constant through the thickness of 30 m penetrated at the Easington gas terminal [395 200], but it seems possible that the fossil content of the matrix may be limited to the top of the sequence. Bisat (1939) records the presence of enclaves of bluish grey highly fossiliferous clay, his 'Sub-Basement Clay', within or below (as exposed in the beach) the 'Basement Clay' proper. This clay contained few erratics, most of which were of Scandinavian origin; fossils identified included 'Cyprina islandica' (i.e. Arctica islandica (Linné)) and 'Dentalium'. Similar enclaves of bluish grey fossiliferous clay ('Bridlington Crag') had been recorded in the 'Basement Clay' of the Bridlington district (Lamplugh, 1891).

It is possible that the upper parts of the Basement Till are a mélange of pre-existing till and glaciomarine sediments emplaced by an advancing ice sheet. This would explain the occurrence of apparent enclaves of bluish grey clay and of contorted structure. The top few metres of the Basement Till may thus be, locally at least, a zone of remobilisation attributable to the emplacement of the overlying Skipsea Till. If so, the fossil content of the till could reflect a range of dates right up to the Dimlingtonian, even though the bulk of the till had been deposited by an earlier glaciation. The petrological and physical properties of this till are consistently different from those of the overlying Skipsea and Withernsea tills, suggesting a pre-Dimlingtonian age (Madgett and Catt, 1978; Catt and Digby, 1988; Bell and Forster, 1991). Alabaster and Straw (1976) identified probable Hoxnian artefacts in gravels underlying till of Basement Till lithology at Welton-le-Wold, near Louth; if the till is correctly identified, a post-Anglian age is proved. Catt and Penny (1966) suggested that Ipswichian beach gravels resting on the Chalk wave-cut platform at Sewerby, near Bridlington, probably correspond to a 'calcreted beach deposit' overlying Basement Till nearby: if so, the till would be of pre-Ipswichian age. The inference is that the Basement Till is 'Wolstonian' in age.

A contrary view, that the Basement Till is what is now known as Early Devensian, was taken by Bisat (1939), mainly on faunal evidence and a lack of what he considered to be sufficient stratigraphical discordance with overlying tills. A similar conclusion was reached by Derbyshire et al. (1984), mainly on the basis of structural evidence. They drew attention to the occurrence of Basement Till at higher levels than the known Ipswichian marine planation surface without, in their view, sufficient tectonic evidence to explain a supposed subsequent push-moraine uplift.

Conclusive proof of the age of the Basement Till requires the dating of material from below any mélange containing glaciomarine sediments, or a site where it is overlain by undisturbed Dimlington Silt (age 18 000 to 18 500 years). In addition, the equivalence of Ipswichian beach gravels at Sewerby with similar deposits overlying Basement Till needs to be established with certainty.

IPSWICHIAN

There is no firm evidence for the preservation of Ipswichian sediments in situ in this district, although they may well contribute as source material to the Kelsey Hill Beds and analogous sands and gravels on South Humberside. They may also be locally preserved in pockets on the Chalk surface of Holderness and Lincolnshire Marsh.

As noted above, beach deposits dated as Ipswichian by mammalian and other fossils have been recorded at the foot of an exhumed cliff on the present-day shoreline at Sewerby, near Bridlington. The trace of the ancient cliff, the foot of which is at 1 to 3 m above OD, can be followed throughout the length of the Yorkshire and Lincolnshire Wolds; it is particularly prominent in this district between Laceby and North Ormsby. Borehole evidence to the south of the Humber shows that an Ipswichian wave-cut platform of remarkably consistent planar form grades gently seawards from the foot of the cliff (Figure 21). A similar platform may underlie Holderness, although the distortion of Basement Till and overlying Dimlington Silts at the coast suggest that Devensian ice may have buckled it.

DEVENSIAN

The possibility of the occurrence of relatively early Devensian sediments in Humberside has already been discussed. There is, however, no doubt that this district lies across the path of a major tongue of the late Devensian ice sheet which thrust southwards along the site of the present east coast of northern England, splaying out at its margins wherever topography allowed (Figure 22). In a brief period of around 5000 years, the ice sheet and its melt waters deposited vast quantities of detritus, mostly 20 to 30 m thick, over three quarters of the district. Although the ice had begun to build up in the mountains of North Wales and the Scottish Highlands 30 000 years ago, it did not arrive in Holderness until after 18 500 years BP; it had retreated by 13 000 years BP. The district includes some of the best available exposures of Late Devensian sediments, and the importance of the Holderness shore sections is recognised by the naming of the glacial maximum as the Dimlington Stadial (Rose, 1985). The drift blanket is commonly thickest where stacked up against the barrier of the pre-Devensian cliff south of the Humber; it reaches a maximum thickness of about 36 m around Barnoldby le Beck. A belt of thick drift extends from there north-eastwards to Cleethorpes. North of the Humber a thickness of 30 m is commonplace. In general, the relative proportions of till to sand and gravel have comparatively little effect on the total Devensian thicknesses.

The earliest confirmed Late-Devensian deposits are the Dimlington Silts, which are locally exposed along the North Sea shore of Holderness. They are succeeded by two lithologically distinct tills: the Skipsea Till, which is heterogeneous and widespread, overlain by the Withernsea Till, which is relatively uniform and confined to eastern Holderness. Both are closely associated with gravel, sand, silt and clay deposited mainly from melt-out waters, but in part possibly from mechanical incorporation of pre-existing sediments. The waterlaid deposits comprise dominantly englacial Glacial Sand and Gravel, and

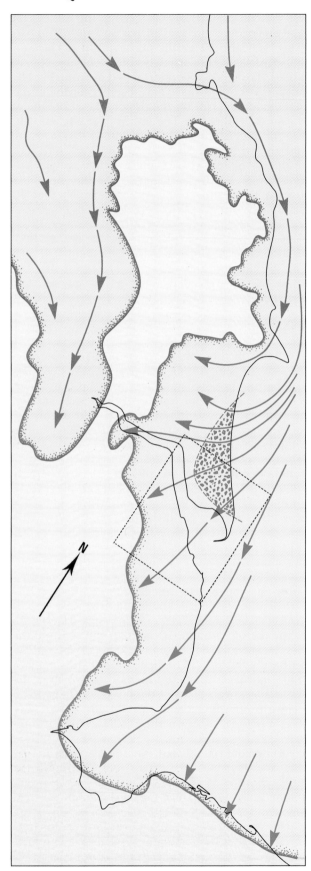

Figure 22 Generalised limits and flow of the Dimlingtonian ice sheet in eastern England showing the known extent of Withernsea Till (ornamented). The district is outlined by a dotted line. (largely after Madgett and Catt, 1978).

proglacial Fluvioglacial Sand and Gravel, both associated with supposedly lacustrine silt and clay, which have been mapped separately where possible. Some of the sand and gravel is also of lacustrine origin, related to ice-damned finger lakes in the Wolds, but in the coarser grades it was not considered generally feasible to differentiate them from fluviatile sediments. Historically, the Kelsey Hill Beds of Holderness, with distinctive lithological, faunal and structural attributes, have been regarded as a distinct group of deposits. They are treated as such here, although they are closely associated with other Devensian deposits and have fairly close analogues among the gravels of South Humberside.

Dimlington Silts

The Dimlington Silts occur sporadically between the Skipsea and Basement tills along the coast section between Easington and Out Newton. The sporadic occurrence is at least partly due to the fact that the silts, along with the Basement Till upon which they rest, have apparently been buckled up (Plate 5) and partly truncated by the oncoming and then overriding ice sheet that deposited the Skipsea Till. Outcrops occur in the intertidal zone of the slumping, rapidly eroding coastline; thus any individual exposure tends to be ephemeral. Catt and Penny (1966) give a full description, including a diagram showing recorded occurrences between 1941 (first discovery by Bisat and Dell) and 1962. They record thicknesses up to 3.66 m of strata consisting of silt passing upward to sand through a varied alternation of the two. Ostracod, foraminifer and moss debris prove a cold, freshwater origin and secondary derivation from the underlying Basement Till. Most significantly, the moss yielded ^{14}C dates of 18 240 ± 250 and 18 500 ± 400 years BP (Penny et al., 1969), the cornerstone upon which the interpretation of the Pleistocene stratigraphy of this area is built.

At the time of survey (1985) a small pocket of up to 1 m of presumed Dimlington Silts was seen beneath Skipsea Till at the cliff foot [3886 2210], 450 m south-east of Cliff Farm, Out Newton. The silt was greenish grey in colour, similar to that of the underlying Basement Till. Immediately north of Cliff Farm, Basement Till was directly overlain by flat-lying sands and gravels up to 6 m thick, but beyond this to the north-west [3836 2276 and 3841 2267] similar flat-lying sediments truncated 1 to 3 m of distorted silt, clay, sand and gravel resting on Basement Till. In 1988 there were exposures of gently folded, laminated silt resting on Basement Till in an 'ord' on the foreshore [4037 1970] (Plate 5) and [4046 1959], farther south towards Easington. These disturbed sediments are interpreted as local representatives of the Dimlington Silts.

The lateral extent of the Dimlington Silts is unknown. They are inferred to be the infilling of one or more shallow

Plate 5 Foreshore, north of Easington [4037 1790].

In the foreground, an 'Ord' channel has exposed the junction between undulating laminated Dimlington Silts overlying Basement Till: the hammer head rests on till and its shaft leans on the silts. Note the typical presence of 'lag' boulders from the eroded Devensian tills and the multiple slippage of these tills in the cliffs in the background. Date: 17 August 1988.

freshwater lakes on the surface of the former Ipswichian wave-cut platform. Elsewhere in this region, this platform is relatively even, except where crossed by pre-existing glacially scoured depressions such as the 'Kirmington Channel'.

Skipsea Till

Skipsea Till is the term defined by Madgett and Catt (1978) for the Drab Till of earlier workers in Holderness. Madgett and Catt extended the field of study of Devensian (Dimlingtonian) tills from the Holderness coast inland to the Wolds and southwards through Lincolnshire Marsh to Norfolk. Their detailed petrological studies established that the Skipsea and Withernsea tills each have distinctive characteristics. The former occurs throughout this district and comprises most of the Dimlingtonian till; the latter overlies it in part of Holderness (Figure 22). They have not been differentiated on the published 1:50 000 Sheet 82.

The Skipsea Till, as seen in temporary sections such as trenches, consists predominantly of brown to reddish brown silty clay with minor proportions of sand, sporadic pebbles and cobbles, and rare boulders. Locally the deposit is sandier and/or richer in pebbles and cobbles; these variants have been mapped as Glacial Sand and Gravel where practicable. Inland exposures rarely penetrate below the weathered zone, which extends to several metres depth and involves oxidation and at least partial leaching. This surface zone was misidentified by some early workers as a separate Hessle Till.

Sections through significant thicknesses of fresh till are limited to the Holderness North Sea coastal cliffs, sparse deep excavations such as those at Keyingham gravel pits and a few clusters of site-investigation boreholes. Of these, the cliff sections provide the most widespread, continuous and accessible data and they have been the subject of detailed geological study by many workers, notably W S Bisat, L F Penny and J A Catt. Bisat produced numerous papers, but in addition an excellent compilation of his detailed measurements of the cliffs over many years was published by Catt and Madgett (1981). The cliff sections show that despite the common petrological characteristics proved by Madgett and Catt (1978), the Skipsea Till is markedly heterogeneous, with a well-marked subhorizontal layering. Bisat was able to divide the till into five impersistent stratigraphical units, each with local subdivisions. The divisions are based primarily on the distribution of erratic lithologies, matrix colour and sediment type; for example, the fourth unit is composed of waterlaid sediments, here classified as Glacial Sand and Gravel (Plate 6). General features that emerged from the Bisat studies, supported by the analyses of Madgett and Catt, include an upward increase in the proportion of Liassic and Triassic erratics, and a complementary decrease in Scandinavian types, of which Larvikite and amygdaloidal porphyrite are notable examples. Another general trend is that Chalk with black flints (from higher in the Cretaceous than any northern England mainland outcrop) and Scandinavian lithologies are proportionally more abundant in the south than the north of Holderness. Subsequent workers have been unable to monitor the landward changes in Bisat's subdivisions because, although the rapidly eroding shoreline exposes fresh sections, a high proportion of the cliff face is obscured by slipped material at any given time. Figure 23 provides a generalised view of the changes that have occurred in the half century between Bisat's measurements and the recent survey.

Plate 6   Sea cliff, Dimlington High Land [3910 2169].

A southward view of a spur in the cliff on 17 August 1988 showing faulted Skipsea Till with integral Glacial Sand and Gravel. A normal fault, associated with wedges of blue-green-tinged mélange, strikes north-west and dips 70° south-west with a displacement of 0.75 m. Four layers of strata are recognisable: 1. chalk-rich till at the base;   2. crudely foliated till with sparse pebbles and cobbles (from foot to chest level of the observer);   3. till with moderately abundant large clasts, including some chalk blocks; and   4. water-lain laminated sand passing upwards to silt. Slipped Withernsea Till truncates the Skipsea sequences.

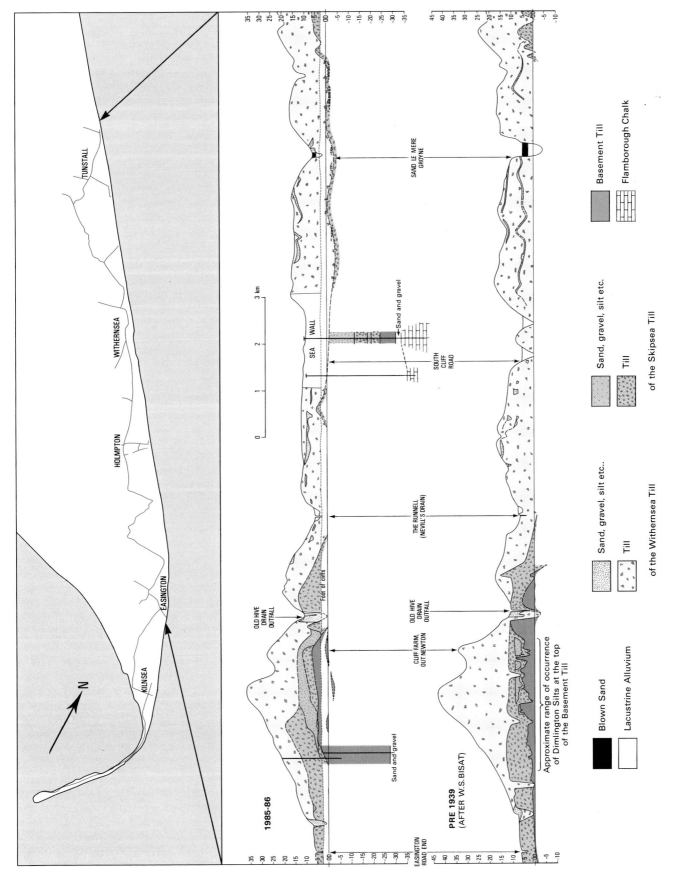

Figure 23 Cliff sections between Easington and Tunstall.

Madgett and Catt (1978) showed that both of the Dimlingtonian tills of Holderness differ from the Basement Till in having a higher silt-to-clay ratio in the matrix. The Skipsea Till has a lower silt and a higher sand content than the overlying Withernsea Till; the contrast is maintained by different heavy-mineral and clast-lithology ratios and highlighted by their distinctive matrix colours. Though varying slightly in depth of colour, the Skipsea Till matrix, where fresh, is consistently dark greyish brown (Munsell Colour 10YR 3/2 is typical of moist till), paler and 'warmer' than the underlying Basement Till but less 'warm' than the overlying Withernsea Till. In the field, the abundance of chalk 'grit' (angular fragments in the coarse sand to fine pebble range) in the matrix of unleached Skipsea Till generally distinguishes it from the other tills, in which chalk is normally sparsely distributed in south Holderness.

The sedimentology, and in particular the fabrics, of the Holderness tills were studied by Derbyshire et al. (1984). They drew attention to the variety of fabrics found in close proximity to one another and concluded that lodgement, remoulding and flow processes had all been active. The common subhorizontal planar fabric seen in elements of the Skipsea Till, associated with crushed and streaked out bodies of chalk (see Plates 4, 6, 7 and 8), is almost certainly a lodgement product from the sole of the ice sheet.

Beyond the Holderness coast section, exposures of Skipsea till are restricted to sections in drains, sporadic site excavations and gravel or chalk pit overburden sections. In addition, south of the Humber, the scattered boreholes enable thicknesses to be assessed and relationships with glacial sand and gravel to be established (Figure 24). There is some indication of a two-part layer structure south of the Humber (Central Electricity Generating Board and UK NIREX Limited, 1987), but any relationship between these layers and the five recognised by Bisat on the Holderness coast would be difficult to establish. Despite the effects of leaching, chalk 'grit' is commonly preserved in the matrix of till seen in dyke sections and even in ploughed-up subsoil throughout the Skipsea Till outcrop area. It was noted to the south of Patrington [e.g. 3150 2155], close to the supposed margin of overlap by Withernsea Till.

Although chalk grit is a common component of Skipsea Till matrix in this district, it is paradoxically the relative poverty of chalk and flint in derived soils which distinguishes areas of till cover on the Wolds. The eastern third of the Wolds is mantled by a partial coating of this till, which tapers to a feather edge at its western margin, close to the presumed limit of the ice sheet. The ice must have extended a short distance beyond the present (eroded) limit of till because subglacial channels, identifiable by undulating thalwegs, occur west of the till limit, for example at Ash Holt [190 010]. The till cover on the Wolds also thins southwards, so that increasing proportions of chalk outcrop reach the eastern cliff towards the south. Near the southern borders of this district, the western boundary of the Devensian till becomes obscure in the Wolds because there may be a thin remnant of earlier Anglian till present (see p.38). In the primary geological survey, a distinct break in the till mantle was identified immediately south of Wold Newton and a till-free area of Wolds was shown separating 'Hessle Clay' (Skipsea Till) from 'Chalky Clay' (Anglian Till) (Jukes-Browne, 1885, p.115). The recent survey failed to identify any such break and did not reveal any sudden increase in chalk content to identify the earlier till lithologically. There is therefore at least a possibility that the thin coating of till over the Wolds top at and around the former Kelstern airfield may be Devensian rather than Anglian as hitherto supposed.

Withernsea Till

The approximate outcrop of Withernsea Till (formerly the Purple Till of Bisat and other workers) is indicated on Figure 22 (p.44). Its distribution in Holderness roughly corresponds with an area of more vigorous topography than that formed on the Skipsea Till. Land forms throughout are a product of ice-melt, with little modification by subsequent erosion, although depressions have been infilled with peat and alluvium. So far as is known, the Withernsea Till forms a continuous mantle of variable thickness on the Skipsea Till, but locally there may be 'windows' of Skipsea Till. The two tills are distinct where fresh but are difficult to differentiate in the weathered zone.

Withernsea Till is typically a less stony and less variable silty clay than the underlying Skipsea Till and commonly lacks a prominent chalk content. Where fresh, the matrix colour is dark brown (Munsell Colour 7 5YR 3/2 when moist), but there is rapid oxidation, even in sea-cliff exposures (Plate 5), to lighter, redder colours of 5YR 4/4 (moist) to 5YR 6/4 (dry), which correspond to former descriptions of 'Hessle Till'. Madgett and Catt's (1978) quantitative analyses indicate consistently high proportions of silt and the dominance of Jurassic, Triassic and Carboniferous source rocks, with only minor Cretaceous chalk and flint.

Apart from soil and drainage-channel sections, exposure is probably limited to the Holderness cliffs and temporary excavations. The cliff sections prove the general lack of diversity in composition of the till, but also show that, like the Skipsea Till, it contains generally flat-lying structural elements. These are defined by wide-spaced partings associated with thin layers of sand and gravel, in some places passing laterally into 'pans' of iron-manganese oxide precipitation. These partings are traceable over distances of several kilometres (Figure 23); they may also be present in high cliff areas (especially near Dimlington), unseen because the Withernsea Till of the upper cliffs is largely inaccessible and/or disrupted by slippage. Madgett and Catt (1978) claimed that the base of the Withernsea Till is conformable on the Skipsea Till, but this was denied by Derbyshire et al. (1984), who particularly mention the occurrence of gravel at the interface. The recent survey suggests that sand and gravel partings are more common within both tills than at their interface, and that some of the lithological boundaries within the Skipsea Till are probably more sharply defined than its boundary with the Withernsea Till.

Plate 7 Foreshore, north-west of Holmpton [370 244].

This midtidal photograph shows the partial flooding of an 'Ord' channel with its beach bar beyond. Skipsea Till exposed in the foreground wave-cut platform shows a good development of a planar cataclastic fabric of chalk in a clay-dominant matrix. The planes dip away from the camera, shallowly to the north (beneath the observer) and north-east (right middle ground). Note the vertical jointing in the till and also the presence of lag boulders on the surface. Date: 20 June 1988.

Plate 8 Foreshore, north-west of Holmpton [370 244].

Close-up of part of the chalk-clay cataclasis structure shown above. The flint in the chalk beside the hammer head appears to be in situ (with reference to the chalk) but even the whitest of the chalk may be reworked, i.e. analogous to the 'putty chalk' commonly occurring at chalk rockhead beneath drift.

The observed thickness of Withernsea Till varies widely in the cliff section, ranging from 0 to c.30 m (Figure 23). The probable gap in its otherwise continuous coastal outcrop that occurs at Old Hive [3802 2312] is unlikely to be unique. The occurrence of stony chalk-rich till in settlement-lagoon excavations at North Carr Dales [3372 2592] near Hollym suggests that Withernsea Till is locally absent there.

Glacial Sand and Gravel

This is a pragmatic lithological division of mainly Devensian sediments, including englacial waterlaid deposits, but also containing glacially reworked material that may therefore be genetically till. The mapped division includes the genetic associates of both Skipsea and Withernsea tills. Distinction from tills on the one hand and Fluvioglacial Sand and Gravel on the other has necessarily been arbitrary in marginal cases because there are transitional relationships to both.

Since these sediments were laid down mainly by meltwater from the Dimlingtonian ice sheet, it is not surprising that the mineral content resembles that of the tills. Both sorting and rounding of the clasts are poor for the most part, although local lenses of clean sand do occur. Even these commonly contain laminae rich in 'grit'-grade clastic coal. Commercial quality as aggregate is therefore normally rather poor.

The Holderness cliff section (Figure 23) shows that most of the visible englacial sand and gravel is distributed in widespread thin sheets. Scattered inland outcrops of more compact bodies also occur in the same region, possibly related to drainage channels such as those transected by the coast at Old Hive [380 231] (Plate 9) and Easington [405 193]; the deposits of both channels appear to be associated with the Withernsea Till. The relatively thick and continuous sand and gravel in the Skipsea Till at Dimlington (probably subdivision 4 of Bisat's Drab Till; see Plates 7 and 8) may have counterparts in the drift south of the Humber estuary where there are no extensive sections available, but where the borehole coverage is much more comprehensive.

Figure 24 shows the sites of recorded boreholes reaching the Chalk in the Lincolnshire Marsh area of this district, together with the inferred distribution of sand and gravel occurring at the base of the drift sequence, excluding the supposed pre-Devensian Kirmington Channel deposits. It cannot, of course, be assumed that all of this 'basal' sand and gravel is of glacial origin or even of Devensian age. It rests on the Ipswichian marine, wave-cut platform and may therefore include Ipswichian beach deposits, possible early Devensian sediments and late Devensian analogues of the Dimlington Silts, as well as truly englacial Dimlingtonian deposits. Locally, the sand and gravel comprises the whole drift sequence, particularly adjacent to the foot of the Pre-Devensian (Ipswichian) cliff line north-westwards from Laceby. Where this occurs, there is a probability that the upper parts of the sequence are fluvioglacial rather than glacial in origin. In compiling Figure 23, an effort was made to ex-

clude 'Chalk Bearings' from gravel at the Chalk-drift interface. The term is traditional driller's parlance for fragmental chalk-rich material commonly found at rockhead in this district. Recent detailed site investigation work (Central Electricity Generating Board and UK NIREX Limited, 1987) around Killingholme [TA 11] suggests that this material is probably weathered Chalk with or without an overlying transitional mixed sequence involving silt, sand, clay or gravel. It may be a mainly Devensian periglacial deposit akin to head, but the term could also cover genuine Glacial Sand and Gravel containing high proportions of clastic chalk. Distinction between 'Chalk Bearings' and 'Gravel' is therefore a somewhat subjective decision when interpreting most old records.

Despite the limitations outlined above and the lack of data in some areas, several general conclusions can be drawn from the distribution of 'basal' sand and gravel shown in Figure 24. Firstly, about half of the drift-covered area has a layer of sand and gravel separating till from underlying rocks; initially there may have been a complete gravel cover prior to the disruptive arrival of the Dimlingtonian ice sheet. This seems particularly probable south-eastwards from Ludborough and Tetney, where there is a widespread and persistent thin layer of sand and gravel at the base of the drift. Secondly, the thickest deposits tend to occur adjacent to the confining western marginal Ipswichian sea cliff. Nevertheless, the most widespread and continuous development of thick deposits is between Laceby and Brocklesby, where the cliff barrier is least well developed. There, it is more likely to reflect a concentration of marginal englacial drainage channels of the ice sheet, which were precursors of rivers that later laid down fluvioglacial deposits (cf. diagram on 1:50 000 Geological Sheet 90) in the same vicinity. The origin and distribution of the 'Kelsey Hill Beds' (p.56) is also relevant in this context.

The till overlying the basal sand and gravel described above commonly contains additional thin leaves of waterlaid sediments in the Lincolnshire Marsh area and in Holderness; conversely, in areas where sand and gravel dominate the drift sequence, such as around Laceby, there are sporadic thin layers of till.

The mapped surface distribution of Glacial Sand and Gravel (Figure 25) appears to show a preferred concentration of large bodies in an arcuate belt running from Brocklesby Park, via Riby and Barnoldby le Beck, to Waltham, roughly parallel to topographical depressions to both north and south, and roughly normal to the presumed direction of ice advance; an association with an ice-sheet still-stand is implied. Less marked concentrations occur around North Thoresby and on the Wolds west of North Ormsby.

Some of the thick sands and gravels in the Laceby area contain a Quaternary marine molluscan fossil fauna, notably at a pit at The Grange, Keelby [151 100], where Read (in Ussher, 1890, p.180) recorded 18 species. The beds are essentially flat-lying and are overlain by till, but a mid-Dimlingtonian marine incursion at this level (at least 15 m above O D) was surely not possi-

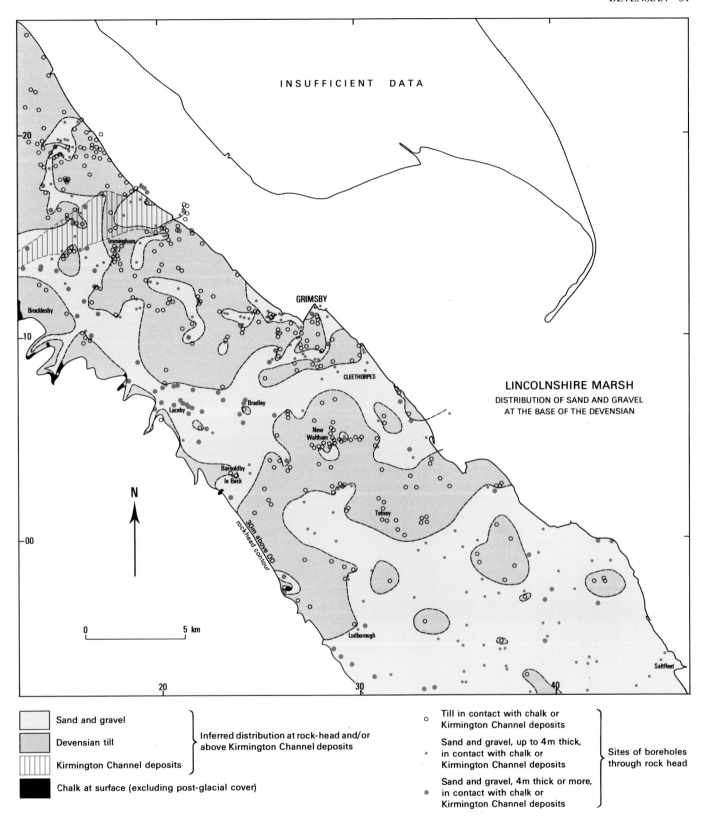

LINCOLNSHIRE MARSH
DISTRIBUTION OF SAND AND GRAVEL
AT THE BASE OF THE DEVENSIAN

Sand and gravel

Devensian till

Kirmington Channel deposits

} Inferred distribution at rock-head and/or above Kirmington Channel deposits

Chalk at surface (excluding post-glacial cover)

○ Till in contact with chalk or Kirmington Channel deposits

· Sand and gravel, up to 4m thick, in contact with chalk or Kirmington Channel deposits

● Sand and gravel, 4m thick or more, in contact with chalk or Kirmington Channel deposits

} Sites of boreholes through rock head

Figure 24 Distribution of sand and gravel deposits at the base of the Devensian in Lincolnshire Marsh.

Figure 25 Distribution of Dimlingtonian sand and gravel deposits (with associated silt and clay) at outcrop around the middle Humber estuary.

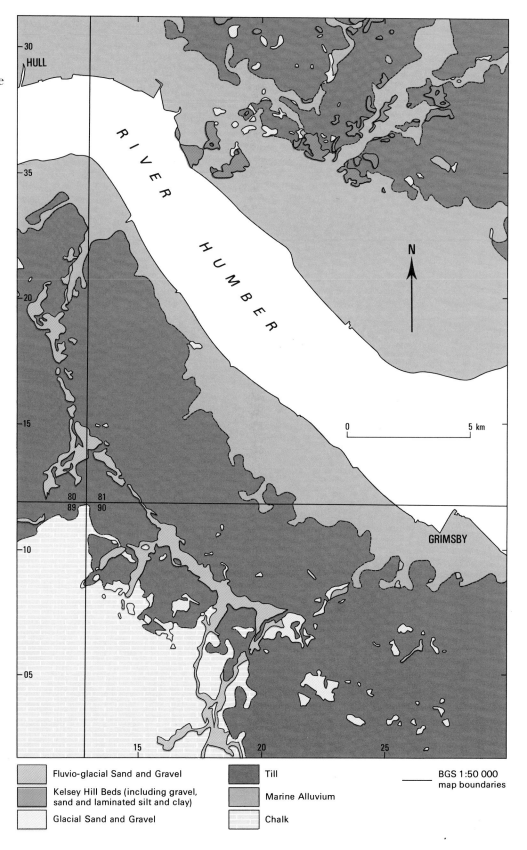

Fluvio-glacial Sand and Gravel		Till	
Kelsey Hill Beds (including gravel, sand and laminated silt and clay)		Marine Alluvium	
Glacial Sand and Gravel		Chalk	

BGS 1:50 000 map boundaries

Plate 9   Old Hive, Out Newton [3806 2306].

Part of a section through Glacial Sand and Gravel in the wall of the drainage cut where it intersected the sea cliff on 20 June 1988. Note the extremely poor sorting of much of the 'gravel', which may be clay-bound in part, although there are interbeds of relatively well-sorted laminated silty sand showing cross-bedding. A discontinuous sheet of apparent Skipsea Till (possibly an engulfed slice from the channel's bank) occurs near the base of the section.

ble here and the deposits must therefore be a translocated raft or, more probably, reworked Hoxnian or Ipswichian sediments. The Keelby deposits appear to be correlatives of the Kelsey Hill Beds (see p.56) of Holderness.

Geomorphological traces of some of the englacial drainage channels associated with the deposition of glacial and fluvioglacial sediments are most clearly preserved in two disparate areas, the Wolds (Plate 9) and the Withernsea Till outcrop in Holderness. After their formation, the channel features in the Wolds, which form a polygenetic lattice cut into the Chalk surface (see inset diagram on 1:50 000 Sheet 90) , were mantled by melt-out till from the former ice cover. There is some suggestion that there was a prevailing north-westward flow parallel to the ice margin, towards the thick sand and gravel deposits of the Laceby–Keelby area. Traces of probably contemporaneous gravel occur locally along the channels. In Holderness there is also a lattice of channels (Berridge, 1988, fig. 2), here preserved on the till surface, in which certain trends predominate. One of these is likewise parallel to the presumed ice front, but another trend suggests funnelling into pre-existing major valleys aligned normal to the ice front, which are now mainly infilled with alluvium. A rectilinear pattern of channels is common locally (Berridge, 1988, fig. 2), e.g. south-west of Hollym, suggesting the local influence of ice-crevasses on their orientation.

Glacial Silt and Clay

Fine-grained waterlaid englacial deposits are probably less common than their coarser equivalents. However, outcrops of silty clay may have passed unrecognised, because even in well-exposed cliff sections it is not always possible to distinguish some of the poorly sorted silty clays from neighbouring till.

Silt and clay have been recognised in parts of the Skipsea Till sequences in the cliffs from Holmpton to

Easington, where they are interbedded with sand and gravel. In some borehole logs from the Lincolnshire Marsh area (e.g. at [2104 0686]) there are references to thin beds of 'red clay' which are regarded as waterlaid, as distinct from the usual 'marl clay' (till). An isolated outcrop of varved clay situated on the Wolds at Great Limber, deposited near the western margin of the ice-sheet, has been almost wholly worked out for brick manufacture; here, a 1904 record shows that 3.05 m of blue clay separated the Chalk from overlying sand and gravel.

Proglacial deposits

Proglacial deposits are defined as those generated mainly by glacial meltwater, but which show by their distribution and/or topographical expression that they were laid down mainly above or beyond contemporary ice. Much of this sediment may be lacustrine, related in particular to finger lakes impounded in Wolds valleys by the ice front, but it is only locally practicable to distinguish them from fluviatile valley deposits (T P Fletcher was able to do so in the Binbrook–Kirmond le Mire–Stainton le Vale area). It was decided, as a generalisation, to classify predominantly coarse-grained deposits as Fluvioglacial Sand and Gravel and fine-grained deposits as Glaciolacustrine Silt and Clay.

FLUVIOGLACIAL SAND AND GRAVEL

In composition these deposits resemble the genetically related Glacial Sand and Gravel in containing clastic material akin to that of the Devensian tills, but the grading and rounding of particles tends to be better and the content of local chalk and flint is typically greater, becoming dominant within the area of the Wolds. In the most westerly occurrences in the Wolds, for example at Rothwell [156 998], the effects of weathering and erosion have reduced the remnants of these deposits to little more than rounded pebbles in hillside soils.

The distribution of these deposits (Figure 25) is strongly controlled by topography. They occupy the

Plate 10   Irby Dales, Irby upon Humber [1950 0500].
A subglacial valley cut through Burnham and Welton Chalk, as seen from Irby village looking north-west.
The Welton–Burnham Chalk boundary contours the steep slope on the right from the camera position to
just below the top of the gorge in the middle distance. A thin layer of Dry Valley Deposits covers the valley
floor.

Plate 11　Keyingham Gravel Pit, general view [238 253].
View looking north over the western parts of the workings in 1985. The worked mineral in this part of the
pit is mostly flat-lying gravel of the Kelsey Hill Beds, overlain by till on the left of the picture: The
underlying till is generally below water level. The yellow-flowered rape in the background is on the
alluvium of Keyingham Drain.

floors and lower slopes of valleys draining the Wolds
north-eastwards to the former ice front, and occur in
linking spillways across interfluves near that ice front.
Northwards from Irby, the valley deposits continue
downstream across the line of the former ice front to
coalesce in an arcuate vale running along the eastern
Wolds front from Thornton Abbey [12 19] (west of this
district) south-eastwards to Laceby. North of Thornton
Abbey and east of Laceby, the vale swings towards the
Humber shoreline where it is buried beneath estuarine
alluvium. Along the north-eastern Wolds-front vale the
Fluvioglacial Sand and Gravel forms level terrace-like
surfaces over wide areas, but their differentiation from
more unevenly distributed deposits of possible
englacial origin is not always obvious, notably at Keelby. Gaunt and Smith (1978) report that at Ulceby Skitter [12 15] the deposits 'appear to pass under as well as
to overlie boulder clay'. This again emphasises the
transitional relationship between glacial and fluvioglacial deposits.

The origin of the fluvioglacial deposits, which map
out as an integral continuous body of sand and gravel,
is clearly polygenetic. At the time of the glacial maximum, finger lakes dammed by ice in the Wolds valleys
would have tended to fill with debris from glacial meltwater en route to 'Lake Humber' (G D Gaunt in Kent,
1980b). As the ice decayed, these lakes would have mi-
grated eastwards and their levels fallen, and earlier deposits would have been eroded and redistributed. The
present-day distribution within the arcuate lowland vale
probably mainly relates to a stillstand of ice, now defined by a moraine of till bounding the north-east side
of the vale. The fluvioglacial deposits are interpreted as
deposits laid down, or at least reworked, by a north-
wards-flowing proglacial drainage system with a suggestion of englacial deposition at both the north and south
ends.

Within the Wolds valleys there is only one locality, at
Gunnerby [212 986] between Hatcliffe and Thornganby,

where a remnant flat top surface of Fluvioglacial Sand and Gravel marks an early contemporary water level. It is at 75 m above OD and occurs where fluvioglacial sediments are thickest in the Wolds. Exact thicknesses are difficult to determine because the buried chalk surface in the Wolds valleys is very variable and because, beyond the Wolds, fluvioglacial sediments commonly overlie lithologically similar glacial sand and gravel. However, in the Laceby area the common thickness is probably between 5 and 7 m, with a possible 12 m maximum at Aylesby.

North of the Humber, the main criterion distinguishing fluvioglacial from glacial deposits, namely topographical expression, is, with the possible exception of the Kelsey Hill deposits, largely absent; Fluvioglacial Sand and Gravel have not been mapped in this area.

GLACIOLACUSTRINE SILT AND CLAY

Glaciolacustrine Silt and Clay, as a mapped unit, is genetically and spacially related to the Fluvioglacial Sand and Gravel described above, from which it is distinguished by particle size alone. The sediments occur in the Wolds valleys upstream from Hatcliffe, south-westwards to Croxby Pond with an outlier south-west of Croxby, and also southwards via Gunnerby, Thornganby and Swinhope to Orford, near Binbrook. They also occur farther upstream from Orford towards Stainton le Vale and Kirmond le Mire, but are here fully masked, except in stream sections, by overlying sand and gravel. Between Thorganby and Hatcliffe there is also a partial irregular cover of sand and gravel.

The deposit is generally a rich reddish brown, plastic, silty clay with a little interbedded silt, although at its thickest and widest development between Gunnerby and Hatcliffe the proportion of silt is higher, with also some sand and more pebbles than elsewhere, suggesting transition to Fluvioglacial Sand and Gravel. A borehole in this area [2156 9907] records 18 m of clay beneath 6 m of sand, but this exceptional thickness is probably quite local; Chalk is at outcrop only 150 m away. The common thickness of silt and clay is likely to be only a few metres at most. Varves, a common feature of glacial lake clays, are present in the deposit around Kirmond le Mire, but were not identified elsewhere. The Kirmond le Mire deposit is also distinctive in showing surface cryoturbation and channel fills of the overlying sand and gravel, reflecting a sharp change from quiet to vigorous sedimentation hereabouts (Fletcher, 1988).

Kelsey Hill Beds

The term 'Kelsey Hill Gravel' has been in use since it was employed by Prestwich (1861) and Wood and Rome (1868), although the deposits to which it refers were remarked upon even earlier by both William Smith (1821) and Phillips (1829). The main distinction of the Kelsey Hill Beds, as they are termed here, is that they contain an abundant and diverse fauna of well-preserved marine molluscan shells despite being closely associated with late Devensian tills, ostensibly implying deposition contemporaneously with the tills at a time when sea-level is generally thought to have been more than 100 m below OD. However, they have also yielded freshwater shells, notably *Corbicula fluminalis*, a species no longer extant in Britain but a common constituent of Ipswichian faunas, and also remains of several vertebrates including both warm climate (elephant, rhinoceras) and cold climate animals (mammoth, reindeer and bison). The varied origins of the fauna point to it being partly or wholly derived, but the abundance and good preservation of its fossils, both shells and bones, are difficult to explain.

The Kelsey Hill Beds are in many ways similar to the Fluvioglacial Sands and Gravels mapped on Lincolnshire Marsh, with the presence of marine fossils common to both; together they were called 'Marine Gravels' by Reid (1885). However, the Kelsey Hill Beds are structurally complex, suggesting glaciotectonic disturbance, and the Fluvioglacial Sands and Gravels of Lincolnshire Marsh are integral with valley deposits in the Wolds.

Gravels and sands are the most widespread (Plate 12), constituents of the Kelsey Hill Beds but they are commonly interbedded with well-sorted silts and clays (Plate 13), which in clean sections can be seen to be laminated. In some places, silt and clay are sufficiently abundant and distinct to be mapped separately. As noted above, the Kelsey Hill Beds also contain zones of structural complexity (Plate 13) that have not been recognised elsewhere.

The more north-easterly outcrops in the district (Figure 25) have a linear distribution along the courses of the Keyingham Drain and Burstwick Drain valleys. Along the former, the Kelsey Hill Beds outcrop lies close to the western limits of the Withernsea Till, and in some sections they appear to form a 4 to 6m-thick unit between that till and the underlying Skipsea Till, but the identity of the upper till has not been confirmed by full analysis at this locality. The best exposures visible at the time of resurvey were in the large working gravel pit just west of Keyingham village (Plate 11). The generally horizontally bedded sequence in the face near its centre [2375 2535] was recorded as:

	Thickness m
Clay, reddish brown, chalky, silty and pebbly (?Withernsea Till)	3.0
KELSEY HILL BEDS	
Sand and gravel, brown, coarse-grained	2.2
Silt, brown, laminated	2.0
Sand and gravel, dark brown	1.0
Clay, dark greyish brown, with chalk pebbles (Skipsea Till)	1.0

The sand and gravel, which locally contains lensoid bodies of greyish brown till, display cross-bedding (Plate 12) with a preferred orientation from the north-east. Faces 500 to 600 m to the north-east showed units of gravel and brown, coarse-grained, shelly and coaly sand interbedded with reddish brown, fine-grained silt. These beds, with a total thickness of about 15 m, are sharply folded in a series of periclines (Plate 13). The nearby old gravel pits at Kelsey

Plate 12   Keyingham Gravel Pit [2378 2546].
Close-up view of part of a working face in flat-lying Kelsey Hill Beds showing the typical gravel-sand facies
(the worked mineral), here affected by a layer of manganiferous pan precipitation. The secondary
mineralisation highlights the upper parts of a cross-bedded unit showing current flow from north-east to
south-west. 20 June 1988.

Hill [c.238 266] and northwards to Burstwick Grange [244 278], described by Prestwich (1861) and later workers, are now mostly backfilled or flooded. Reid (1885) remarked that a thickness of more than 60 feet (18.3 m) of gravels were proved at the former locality by combined quarry and borehole sections.

Farther south-west, towards the Humber, the Kelsey Hill Beds appear to fan out into a hummocky mélange of deposits interbedded with till, although they are largely covered by Flandrian alluvium through which the silt, sand, gravel and till protrude to form isolated hills. The distribution below the alluvium is difficult to ascertain because there are few boreholes in the area. A borehole at Paull Fort [1699 2534] drilled directly into Kelsey Hill Beds proved 17.72 m of sands and gravels interbedded with laminated clays and sandy silts to a depth of about 7 m below OD, underlain by a 'sandy clay with gravel', which is probably Skipsea Till.

It is now generally agreed that the marine fauna can only have originated in the broad Humberside embayment of the Ipswichian interglacial sea, but its remarkable abundance and preservation remains an enigma. The shells may have remained unscathed during the Devensian glaciation by preservation in iceborne frozen rafts but no evidence for such erratics has been recognised in the local Devensian tills. Alternatively they may have been subject only to transportation in water, but that seems unlikely because some are very well preserved. In addition, emplacement at as much as 10 m above OD means that former Ipswichian deposits have been lifted, either by ice, by water under hydrostatic pressure or by postdepositional tectonics such as icepushing.

However the 'Marine Gravels' were initially formed and then brought to their present locations, their geographical distribution suggests that they were deposited at or near the ice margin, perhaps during a retreat pause. The de-

Plate 13   Keyingham Gravel Pit [2418 2562].

Interbedded clay, silt and fine-grained sand of the Kelsey Hill Beds showing structural deformation. A tight
fold, with an axial plane dipping at a low angle to the north-east, is cut by a high-angle fault with
downthrow to the west. 20 June 1988.

posits along the Keyingham Drain and Burstwick Drain
valleys are disposed in linear tracts normal to the supposed icefront, implying englacial deposition as eskers.
The contortions of the bedding as seen at Keyingham
could be indicative of gravity-related collapse and slumping as the ice melted in situ. The fluvioglacial gravels
south of the Humber Estuary and the Kelsey Hill Beds immediately to the north of it, around Paull, have a lobe-like
arrangement (Figure 25) and probably represent ice-mar-
ginal deposits. The presence of laminated silts and clays in
the Kelsey Hill Beds in this locality could thus be ex-
plained as deposits of proglacial lakes at or close to the ice
margin.

DEVENSIAN TO FLANDRIAN

The lithological units described in this section are believed to date back to the close of the Dimlington Stadial,

though their deposition continued through into the
Flandrian.

Older Blown Sand

The south-western margins of the district include a
small proportion of the extensive spread of Lincolnshire Cover Sands (Straw, 1963). The main agent of dis-
persal of these widespread sands, which are especially
thickly built up against the west-facing cuesta scarps of
North Lincolnshire, is considered to have been westerly
winds crossing barren central England during the cold,
dry climate of the Loch Lomond Stadial, which closed
the Devensian ice age between 10 000 and 11 000 years
ago.

   In this district, these blown sands appear as a thin cover
over the Upper Jurassic outcrop at the scarp foot north of
Walesby, at the extreme south-west corner of the Grimsby
(90) sheet, and also as an 'overspill' across the top of the

scarp at Caistor, down into the upper parts of a valley leading eastwards through Cabourne towards Swallow. The deposits have been and still are subject to partial redistribution whenever weather conditions are appropriate, and especially when vegetation cover is poor. The result is a development of 'dunes' along hedges and an admixture of sand in the topsoil wherever landforms to their leeward favour local slackening of windspeed. As the sand is lifted from its 'source' areas around Caistor, they are probably restocked, in their turn, by further supplies blown in from the west. Some of the outcrops of sand contain a proportion of angular flint fragments in the topsoil; these may be remnants of artificial marling with flint-bearing chalk to reduce the acidity of the sandy soil.

Head

Head is a periglacial solifluction deposit, the product of long-term permafrost action decomposing and partly mass-moving a zone of surface rock. In many parts of southern Britain, head formed throughout the Devensian glacial period. The greater part of this district, however, was scoured by the Dimlingtonian ice sheet and/or its meltwaters, and most of the head was probably deposited subsequently, in late Devensian to early Flandrian times.

Head is most readily recognised in this district where it rests on or adjacent to solid rock, i.e. within the Wolds. Its occurrence on drift deposits is rarely distinguishable because parent material and product may differ only in degree of compaction and weathering, features characteristic of a normal soil profile. Occasionally, however, there is field evidence that its presence may be widespread, albeit as an unmapped thin skin less than a metre thick. Examples include the sand and gravel body cut by the sea cliff at Old Hive [380 231], Holderness, where a thin layer of contrasting diamicton forms the top of the section, and a valley side [136 011] in the Wolds near Cabourne where chalky clay has crept downhill over blown sand.

This second example highlights the fact that Head, where mapped in this district, almost certainly includes a proportion and perhaps a dominance of post-Devensian sediment, since the earliest blown sand probably dates from the final Devensian stadial (see below). It is in fact impracticable to separate true head (periglacial) from products of later (postglacial) solifluction processes that continue at present. Thus some mapped head includes banks of material up to 2 m high that have accumulated on chalk hillsides along hedges which mark long-standing estate and/or parish boundaries.

The content of head deposits varies according to the source rock. In the Wolds it commonly consists of clay rich in angular chalk and flint fragments, and shows a crude bedding structure imparted by mass flow. It most commonly occurs as a scree-like apron separating steep chalk valley sides from a central strip of Alluvium or Dry valley Deposits.

Dry Valley Deposits

This term refers to detritus accumulated along the floors of upper tributary valleys in the Wolds, which lack surface water except during heavy storms. The cross-section of such valleys is commonly a shallow vee, rounded at the base by a build-up of these deposits, which comprise clay rich in fragments of flint and chalk (head), mixed with sandy, partially sorted flash-flood deposits. They are thus a mixed product of solifluction and fluviatile sedimentation. The thickness is variable but is normally up to 2 or 3 m; however, reservoir excavations [155 010] near Rothwell proved a soil thickness of only 0.6 m on chalk, where the topography suggested that mappable Dry Valley Deposits should have been present.

Downstream in any given valley, these deposits normally pass into true alluvium; commonly this occurs above the present spring line. The reason is a low present-day water table that is as likely to have been caused by artificial water extraction as by seasonal weather or longer term climatic changes. The presence of true alluvium in a valley bottom is normally signalled by the development of a distinct flat-topped flood plain, even where surface water no longer runs within it.

Lacustrine Alluvium

Enclosed hollows on the till outcrop are commonly floored by stoneless clays, silts and fine sands which in some places are interbedded with or overlie peat. These deposits are assumed to have accumulated in late- and post-glacial lakes or 'meres' by a variety of means including solifluction under periglacial conditions, hillwash, alluvial fan and delta formation and, in the case of laminated silt and clay, sedimentation from suspension. No 'meres' remain within the district, although some survived until at least the thirteenth century (Sheppard, 1957). The hollows are particularly abundant where the till surface is most hummocky, i.e. near the boundary between the Withernsea and Skipsea till outcrops in Holderness and in a 5 km-wide belt from Tetney and Humberston to Laceby. The arc-like shape of both tracts suggests they mark the position of glacial retreat stillstands. Many of the smaller hollows could be kettle holes. Some small depressions with surrounding till ramparts next to the Roos Drain valley in Holderness are interpreted as collapsed pingoes, probably fed by water from the chalk aquifer via 'blow-wells'. The larger depressions merely reflect the unevenness of Devensian glacial deposition and the juvenile nature of the landscape.

Previous 'mere' hollows in the urban areas may have been filled in, so that they are detectable only in boreholes. For example, at Grimsby Technical College [2651 0794], 3.05 m of clay, possibly including some made ground as well as lacustrine deposits, were recorded overlying a 0.46 m-thick peat in a barely perceptible depression. Modern farming methods are rapidly removing evidence of their previous occurrence in rural areas as well.

Between Aylesby and Stallingborough there are larger spreads of lacustrine silts, clays and peats in a series of linked hollows. They have been incised by the present drainage system leaving the top of the lacustrine deposits as a terrace slightly above the modern floodplains.

The two best-documented sequences of 'mere' deposits in the district are at The Bog [2736 2888], Roos and The

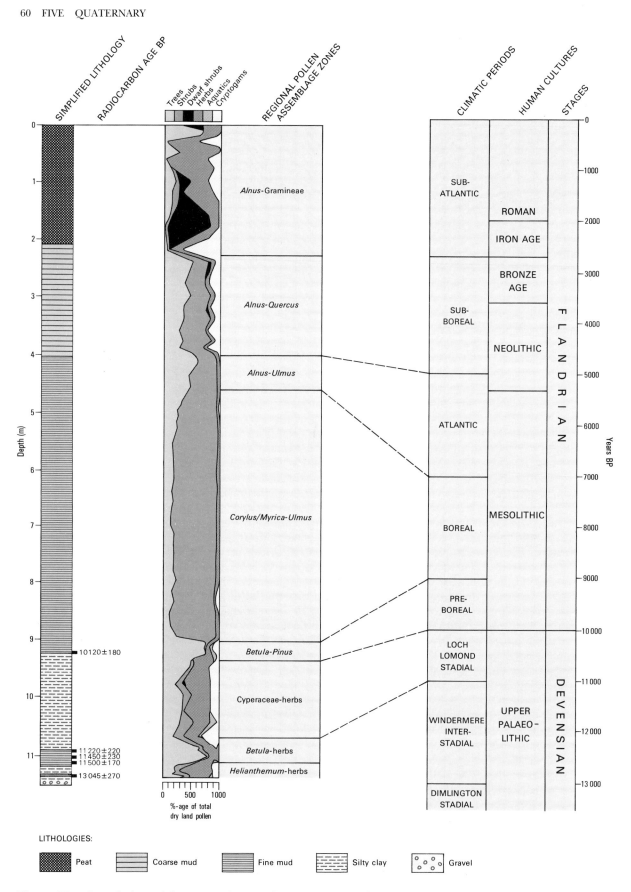

Figure 26 Correlation of the succession at The Bog, Roos with generalised postglacial climatic and archaeological chronology. (Pollen analysis and radiocarbon dating after Beckett 1981, Blackham et al., 1984).

Runnell [3669 2480], Holmpton, both in Holderness. The palynological study and radiocarbon dating of material from the former site (Beckett, 1981; Blackham et al., 1984) provide the most complete record of the postglacial vegetational and climatic history of the district (Figure 26) as well as showing the transition from open water mere to swamp and then to a final reflooding at the site itself. At The Runnell, a 'mere' depression 350 m long and 200 m wide is truncated by eroding coastal cliffs and shows lacustrine deposits up to 2.8 m thick (Plate 14). The following section was measured in 1986 (all beds tend to thin towards the mere edges, hence the thicknesses are maxima):

	Thickness m
Silt, yellowish-brown; prismatic joints; gradational base	1.0
Silt, buff grading down to grey; laminated	0.7
Peat, silt and shell marl; interbedded and fissile	0.25
Silt, grey, laminated, with organic and ferruginous staining	0.6
Peat, laminated, silty (reworked)	0.2
Silt, grey, shelly (local)	0 to 0.05
Clay, bluish grey, plastic, with some shells	0.2

In places the basal clay is floored by traces of gravel, and the underlying Withernsea Till is locally bleached bluish grey to a depth of 5 cm (Plate 14).

Peat and Submerged Forest

Postglacial peat is widespread in the district but uncommon at surface. It occurs interbedded with lacustrine al-

Plate 14   The Runnell, Holmpton [3669 2480].

A low sea cliff cut through the centre of a postglacial mere deposit of Lacustrine Alluvium into underlying Withernsea Till. The older parts of the mere deposit, below the hammer head, are conspicuously rich in organic material, notably in a peaty layer near the base and in the prominent pale layer just below the hammer. The latter consists of fissile peat interlayered with shell marl. Note the colour change from brown to grey in the till subjacent to the alluvium, presumably caused by chemical reduction, and also the deformation of the subvertical prismatic jointing in the lower part of the alluvial sequence. 20 June 1988.

luvium in enclosed hollows on the top of the till (see Figure 26 and Plate 14) and in generally more persistent beds within or immediately below the mostly marine and estuarine sequences deposited following the Flandrian transgression. Some of the thickest peats belong to both categories, i.e. where they occupy hollows in the till surface and underlie estuarine alluvium. Two examples are the 6.4 m-thick peat from about 2 m below OD downwards at Holme Hill, Grimsby [TA 2791 0877], and the 3.35 m-thick peat more than 6 m below OD at New Delights, Tetney [3313 0099].

The postglacial peat beds below the coastal plain either predate the Flandrian marine transgression or indicate subsequent regressions. They are most common on the south side of the Humber Estuary from north Grimsby to North Killingholme, and on the north side around Salt End and Paull, although a few boreholes have proved peat immediately overlying the till below the more inland parts of the Lincolnshire 'Outmarsh' south of Cleethorpes. Elsewhere, notably around Skitter Ness, in the Sunk Island area, and near the coast south of Cleethorpes, peat either did not accumulate or, more probably, developed but was subsequently removed by tidal channel scour or coastal erosion.

The average thickness of the basal postglacial peat beds is 0.5 to 1.0 m; they are only rarely 2 m or more, as for example below the docks of north Grimsby. These basal peats range in height relative to sea level from about OD to 10 m below OD and are most commonly recorded at about 5 m below OD. Radiocarbon dates of postglacial peats within that height range around the Humber estuary were listed by Gaunt and Tooley (1974); they varied from 6970 ± 100 to 2552 ± 120 years BP. The peats yielded Alder/Elm/Lime/Oak pollen assemblages indicating Flandrian Zones II and III (see Figure 26).

The local peats which are interbedded with, rather than underlying, marine and estuarine sediments are thin and of very variable height relative to OD, and appear to be of limited geographical extent. Consequently, they are unsuitable as marker beds for constructing a Flandrian lithostratigraphical or chronostratigraphical classification for the district. Gaunt and Tooley (1974) cited an age of 6681 ± 130 BP for a piece of alder wood from a peat bed at 9 m below OD within a brackish-water sequence at Immingham Docks [c.197 146] and 6170 ± 180 BP for a sample from the base of a peat resting on clay with marine shells at 2.40 m below OD on the foreshore of the North Sea side of Spurn [4235 1385]. The latter date was supported by pollen analysis of the peat, placing it in Flandrian Zone II.

Some other biogenic beds recorded from the foreshore of the Holderness North Sea coast were all probably exhumed from the basal part of 'mere' sequences which have been breached by coastal erosion. Two of them, one at Sand-le-Mere [3204 3110] and the other resting on till off the north end of Spurn [4230 1442], were observed during the resurvey. The remainder, inferred from references to 'Submerged Forest' or 'Noah's Wood' on the Ordnance Survey 1:10 000 maps, are assumed to have been comparable with the 'Submerged Forest' at Sand-le-Mere where the stumps of several trees, apparently more or less in situ, are set in peaty clay immediately overlying till.

Landslip

Landslip is a significant phenomenon in this district in two specific environments: the more important of these is the North Sea cliff zone of Holderness, and the other is the south-west facing Wolds scarp face, of which only a short stretch occurs in the extreme south-west corner of the district. Here, there is a tendency for the outcropping sandstone and limestone formations (Spilsby Sandstone, Tealby Limestone, Carstone and Chalk) to camber over and then slip across the weaker intervening argillaceous formations. The latter are themselves subject to landslip as a result of lubrication by water from the sandstone aquifers. There might appear to be potential for slippage on the eastern margin of the Wolds, southwards from Barnoldby le Beck, where till is banked up against the old chalk sea cliff, but there is little evidence that such slippage has occurred; however, some movement can be seen in an analogous situation on the north-facing flank of the Irby Dales glacial channel [192 053; 196 062].

Landslips in the drift at the Holderness seashore are integral to problems of coastal erosion and are discussed in that context (p.73).

FLANDRIAN

Most of the Flandrian deposits in the district are associated with the postglacial rise in sea level which resulted from the melting of the Pleistocene ice sheets. From near the end of the Devensian, 10 300 years ago, until 7000 years BP, the relative level of the southern North Sea rose from 65 m to less than 10 m below OD (Jelgersma, 1979). During the next 3500 years it rose more slowly with some temporary reversals, since when it has fluctuated within about 2 m of OD, although within this district the overall movement continues upwards. The sea entered the district about 7500 years ago and, between then and the present day, marine and estuarine clays, silts, sands and shingle up to 15 m thick have been deposited in the coastal areas on the underlying glacial tills, sands and gravels.

Following the retreat of the late Devensian ice about 13 000 years ago (Beckett, 1981), the Humber and its tributaries, draining to a much lower base level than now, incised the undulating till landscape left by the ice to produce a branching system of narrow, steep-sided valleys grading down to as low as 20 m below OD in this district. The main Humber valley of that period appears to be followed by the deep channel of the present-day estuary, though the original longitudinal gradient has been modified by tidal scour (Figure 27). The postglacial initial transgression may have first simply flooded the incised valleys to produce a ria (Figure 28.1). Subsequently, as the sea advanced, processes of marine erosion and deposition began to modify the inundated surfaces.

Borehole and geophysical evidence suggests that the Flandrian deposits (Figure 27) rest on a gently undulat-

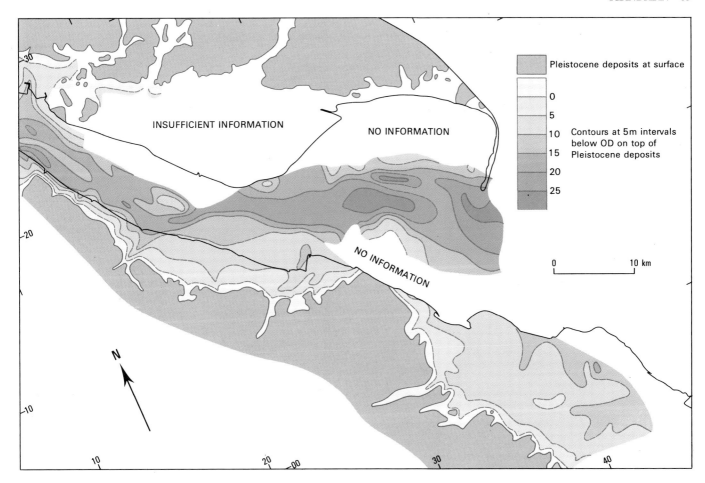

Figure 27 Contours on the concealed surface of Pleistocene deposits below and beside the lower Humber estuary.

ing postglacial surface which varies from 5 m below OD to between 10 and 15 m below OD; this surface contrasts markedly with the steeper slope on its landward side to the west. This distinction is most marked in the Lincolnshire Marsh area, where the sub-Flandrian platform in the 'Outmarsh' meets the sloping surface of the till in the 'Middle Marsh', which extends to the Wolds. The contrast is less distinct elsewhere, but is discernible along the edge of the 'Outmarsh' north-west of Grimsby and north of the Humber around Hedon, and especially so, near Winestead, although data are sparse here. The abrupt landward edge of the sub-Flandrian platform suggests that it originated as a wave-cut shore feature. A comparable surface below the Flandrian sediments of Fenland has been attributed by Gallois (1988) to late Pleistocene erosion by a lake or shallow sea. As none of the radiocarbon-dated peats of the Humber district can unequivocally be said to rest on the platform, it cannot at this time be given a precise age. It may be a product of accelerated erosion under periglacial conditions along the shore of a late Devensian lake dammed by either ice or moraine. The suggestion of a valley leading towards Saltfleet on the till surface below the 'Outmarsh' points to a pre-transgression origin for the platform. Alternatively, it may have been

cut by wave action during an extended pause in the advance of the Flandrian sea. In the latter case, its general height in relation to sea-level rise data for the region suggests an age of about 6000 to 5000 years BP (Gaunt and Tooley, 1974), although peats as old as 7690 ± 400 BP have been recorded resting on the comparable surface at the base of the Fenland Flandrian succession (Horton, 1989).

It can be inferred that the sea probably reached its maximum lateral extent in the district about 3500 BP when its height first approached that prevailing now. Subsequent deposition has extended the land surface within the Humber estuary area and in the Lincolnshire Outmarsh. The deposits are varied, but boreholes are locally too sparse and potential marker horizons, notably peats, are so impersistent that neither a chronological sequence nor a lithostratigraphical classification can be established. Figure 28 is a speculative interpretation of the evolution of the Humber estuary since 7500 BP.

Alluvium

The deposits shown as alluvium on the maps of the district vary from stream-channel gravels to overbank, very peaty clays deposited in fluviatile environments ranging

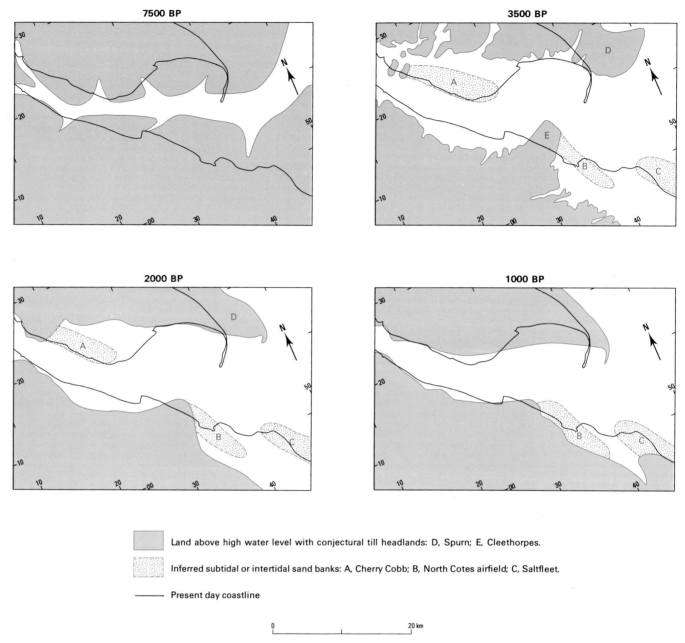

Figure 28 Conjectural evolution of the lower Humber estuary during the Flandrian.

from intermittently flowing Wolds streams to coastal-plain creeks near high tide level. No boundary is drawn on the map between freshwater alluvium and estuarine alluvium. The two merge imperceptibly near the junctions of the river valley and coastal floodplains, the nature of deposition thereabouts having varied with the many changes of sea level and shifts of the tidal channels. In the Wolds valleys the distinction between Dry Valley Deposits and alluvium is based on their inferred origin; a flat surface is taken to indicate a floodplain and hence an alluvial deposit, even if there is no permanent surface water present now. The surface alluvium in hollows on the till plateaux of the Lincolnshire 'Middle Marsh' and Holderness, mostly silt and clay, is assumed

to be fluviatile if associated with streams now draining to the sea, although it probably overlies lacustrine clay or peat, deposited when the hollow had no permanent outlet. Many valleys are floored by modern alluvial clay and silt overlying sand and gravel, which may also be of Flandrian age in part but which could not be distinguished from Devensian fluvioglacial deposits. Postglacial fluviatile deposits predating the Flandrian transgression may underlie the marine and estuarine sediments of the Humber estuary and Lincolnshire 'Outmarsh', although they are unlikely to be widespread if marine planation preceded sedimentation as suggested on p. 62.

The principal areas of mapped alluvium are the valleys of the Burstwick, Keyingham and Winestead drains north of the Humber and of Skitter Beck, Laceby Beck/River Freshney and Waithe Beck on the south side. There is little borehole data on alluvium thicknesses. In the Holderness valleys there is about 2 m of mostly stiff clay, below which alluvial clay is probably largely intercalated with estuarine clay and silt. The varied alluvial clay, silt, sand and gravel of the Skitter Beck and River Freshney valleys are closely associated with fluvioglacial deposits, which hinders an estimation of their thickness; it is probably in the order of 2 to 3 m. A characteristic sequence in the alluvium of the Waithe Beck valley across the 'Middle Marsh' is brown silt and clay overlying gravel with a total thickness ranging from about 2.5 m near the Wolds to 5 m near Tetney. It is possible that at least some of the gravel is of Devensian age.

MARINE AND ESTUARINE ALLUVIUM

It is convenient to describe these deposits under two headings, reflecting the absence and presence of influence of the Humber estuary respectively. The relatively coarse- and fine-grained variants distinguished on the maps are both discussed here.

Marine and Estuarine Alluvium of the Lincolnshire Outmarsh south of Cleethorpes

The Marine and Estuarine Alluvium of the 'Outmarsh' reflects a depositional environment more open to marine influence than the estuarine Humber shore deposits. Over most of the area they are about 10 to 15 m

thick and they thin significantly only within one or two kilometres of the inland edge of the marsh. Seemingly random variation of lithology is common, but a feature that does emerge from the well records is the existence of two linear bodies of relatively coarse-grained sediment aligned *en échelon* and approximately parallel to the present coast (Figures 28.2, 28.3 and 28.4). They are here referred to as 'sand bodies' although 'silt' is sometimes the dominant lithology mentioned in the logs. Both bodies appear to be at least partly underlain by finer-grained deposits, especially on the landward side (Figure 29).

The North Cotes Airfield sand body runs south-south-eastward from an outcrop of till on the sea bed off Cleethorpes, which may be the planated remains of the postulated former promontory there. The sand does not reach surface onshore although it is covered by less than a metre of clay or silt in the North Cotes area and possibly only by man-made saltern mounds east of Marshchapel. The Saltfleet sand body is partly overlain by finer-grained deposits as well, but it also provides a base for the old North Somercotes/Saltfleet storm beach and the modern beaches south of Donna Nook. The two sand bodies are separated by a belt with clays and silts, 10 m or more thick, around the distributaries of the River Lud. Inland from the sand bodies is a 4 to 5 km-wide area underlain by clays, commonly described as 'black' in well records and thus probably of high organic content. East of Tetney and south-west of Marshchapel, the clay is un-

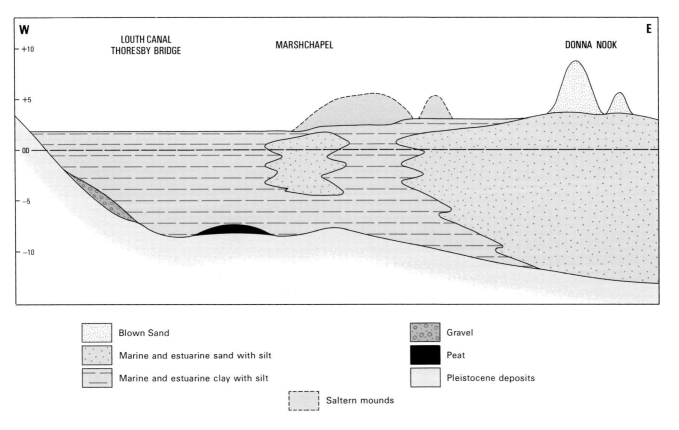

Figure 29 Diagrammatic west to east section through the Flandrian deposits of the Lincolnshire Outmarsh

derlain by peat. These finer-grained inland deposits are little known but are probably comparable with the 'Scrobicularia' and 'Triglochin' clays described by Swinnerton (1931) farther south along the Lincolnshire coast.

The sand bodies appear to represent a persistent coastal barrier system bordered on the landward side by intertidal mud flats or a lagoon. It is possible that the sand bodies postdate and have partly replaced a wider intertidal flat or lagoonal strip, but their *en échelon* relationship and the finer-grained deposits between them below the Lud estuary suggest that both the sand bodies and the position of that estuary are fairly long-lived. There has been some broadening of the sand bodies by progressive onlapping of the clays to the west.

Most of the surface deposits on the alluvial flats are characteristic of saltmarsh. They comprise interbedded silty clay and clayey silt with some sand laminae and much organic material, including decayed saltmarsh vegetation and algal mats, and whole and comminuted shell debris. The dendritic pattern of former tidal creeks is clearly visible in air photographs but less so on the ground. They are usually marked by shallow, sinuous, dry channels commonly less than 0.4 m deep and rarely as much as one metre. No significant differences were noted between the sediments inside and outside them.

As around the Humber shore, mapping of marine sand and shingle has distinguished between 'Storm Beaches', characterised by a positive topographical expression and described hereafter, and 'Marine Alluvium; sand, gravel or shingle'. In addition to the superficial deposits on the seaward side of old sea walls, as for example in the 'Outmarsh' west of Porter's Sluice [415 996] and around the oldest part of Sunk Island, the latter category also includes blown sand mixed with the alluvial clay and silt on the landward side of sand dunes, as at Humberston Fitties [331 055].

Marine and Estuarine Alluvium of the Humber estuary area (inland from Spurn and Cleethorpes)

Flandrian deposition in the Humber shore areas has been in a largely estuarine environment, probably protected from the open sea by the postulated former till promontories east of Spurn and north-east of Cleethorpes (see Figure 28.2). The Flandrian deposits of onshore areas are up to 13 m thick and their variability reflects continuing changes in sea level and tidal channel courses, as well as reclamation work by man. Fine-grained sediments predominate, except on the north side of the Humber below Cherry Cobb Sands and the southern part of Sunk Island (Figure 30).

In the latter area, the greater part of the postglacial succession consists of brown, fine-grained sands. They are vaguely laminated in part, mostly calcareous and contain fragmentary shells. These sands are thought to represent a linear sand shoal linked at its upstream end to the 'islands' of glacial till and gravels near Paull (see Figures 28.2 and 28.3). However, due to a local paucity of boreholes and the superposition of the Flandrian sands on lithologically similar Pleistocene sands with marine shells, the exact location of both the upstream link of the shoal sands and their north-eastern and lower limits are questionable. The sands are covered by 1 to 5 m of laminated silty clays and sands, with organic layers especially near the top, probably deposited in saltmarsh environments in the last 400 years. These 'warp' deposits are well exposed along the south-east side of Sunk Island, east of Hawkin's Point, in low cliffs undercut by a northward movement of the Sunk Roads channel (Plate 15). The local term 'warp' is used here in the general sense, describing all fine-grained estuarine sediments, rather than in the restricted sense implying artificially induced deposition.

Elsewhere around the Humber shores, the Flandrian sediments reflect lower energy levels, although there are some sand and gravel intercalations, probably deposited either as bars marginal to tidal channels or as storm beaches resulting from short-lived surges. A discontinuous basal sand bed, up to 1.2 m thick in the north Grimsby to Immingham area, may be reworked aeolian 'coversands' or periglacial Head.

Storm Beach Deposits

Storm Beach Deposits of sand and shingle fringe much of the present-day North Sea coast of this district. They commonly either overlie and obscure a man-made sea wall or are themselves covered by blown sand, as at Spurn Head and Donna Nook. Older storm beaches have been recognised up to 6 km inland and, in places, they too form a base for sand dunes. It is convenient to describe the mapped 'Storm Beach Deposits' and 'Older Storm Beach Deposits' together because they differ significantly only in their position relative to the present-day coastline. Some of the beaches, such as the one at Spurn and those east of a line from Humberston to Conisholme, are less than 400 years old and their historically documented development, in association with the general evolution of the coast, has been described by de Boer (1964, 1981) and Robinson (1970, 1984) (Figure 31). The discontinuous line of old beaches between Conisholme and Humberston probably originated along the medieval sea wall. It continues northwards along the eastern and northern edges of the elevated till area of central Cleethorpes, forming a terrace feature around, and probably partly on the till.

Other storm beaches, such as the east to west tract near Keyingham and Patrington Haven (Figure 31) and the southern end of the Saltfleet/North Somercotes beach, may have originated 2000 to 3000 years ago, although they were probably considerably modified by subsequent storm action, notably between the late twelfth and early fourteenth centuries. The storm surges of that period, referred to by Robinson (1970) as the 'stormy centuries', had a great effect on the general configuration of North Sea coasts (Berendsen and Zagwijn, 1984). The shell assemblages in the old storm beaches, in which *Hydrobia ulvae* (Pennant), *Cerastodema edule* (Linné) and *Macoma balthica* (Linné) are the most common species, are characteristic of a shallow-water, possibly intertidal environment.

One probable product of the 'stormy centuries' is the north-western (distal) end of the Saltfleet/North Somercotes beach, which is now separated from the sea by a

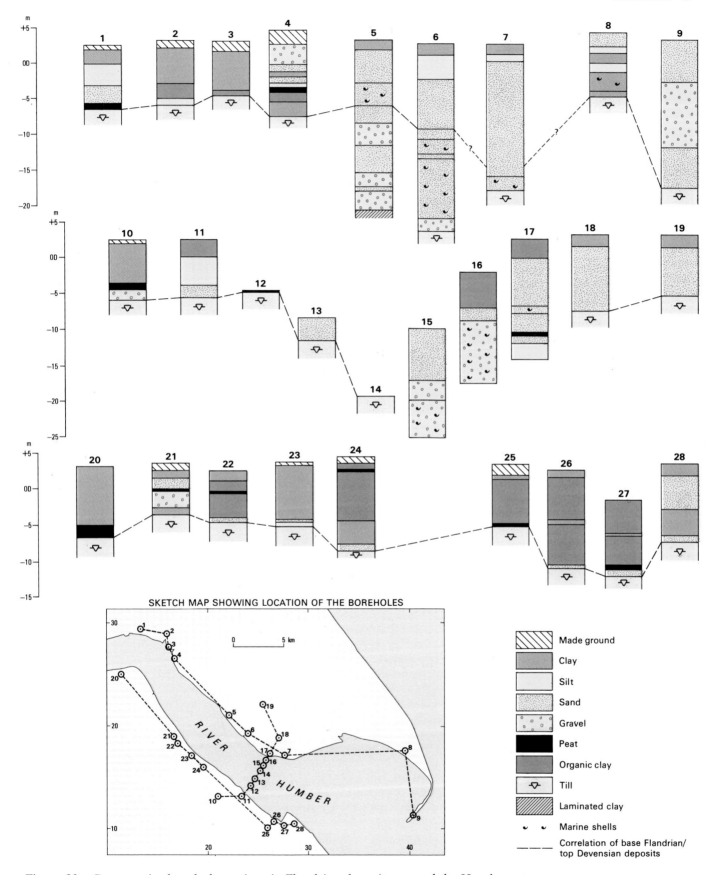

Figure 30   Comparative borehole sections in Flandrian deposits around the Humber estuary.

Plate 15   Humber shore, Sunk Island [2973 17040].

General view, looking west, showing erosion of Estuarine Alluvium and some of the methods used to combat that erosion. From the left, prominent features include a belt of *Spartina* grass, used to stabilise tidal mudflats; a belt of artificially laid limestone rubble ('berm') populated by *Fucus*; bluffs of eroded alluvium populated mainly by *Artemisia*; traces of shell shingle at high-water mark; and the modern sea wall, built mainly of till faced by 'rip-rap' of fresh Jurassic limestone, grassed over in part. 17 August 1988.

strip of agricultural land up to 2 km wide. The former beach is in the form of a complex spit with at least 17 separate westerly or north-westerly pointing fingers (Figure 30), some of them recurved; it appears to have grown in a north-westerly direction across the Lud estuary by the successive addition of new fingers, tangentially attached to its northern side. Its mode and alignment of growth imply longshore current strengths and direction markedly different from those prevailing now. The sand and shingle are up to 9 m thick at the Lakeside Lido [432 960] and 5 to 7 m below the centre of North Somercotes village. Sand predominates at surface along the north-east flank of the beach, but lag gravels comprising pebbles in a clay matrix are common on the southern edge. The youngest and shallowest extensions of the beach have been breached and removed by a distributary of the River Lud to the north-west of North Somercotes.

The cyclic evolution of Spurn Head has been described by de Boer (1964), as outlined in Chapter Six. Storm Beach sand and shingle are up to 20 m thick along the broad southern half of the peninsula, but thin to less than 10 m at the narrow northern neck, where they are largely covered by Blown Sand and Made Ground. A borehole [4007 1095] at the north end of the spatula-shaped tip of the spit proved 20.42 m of beach deposits as follows:

	Thickness m	*Depth* m
'Sand'	6.10	6.10
'Rough gravel'	8.84	14.94
'Sand and gravel'	5.48	20.42
'Till'		

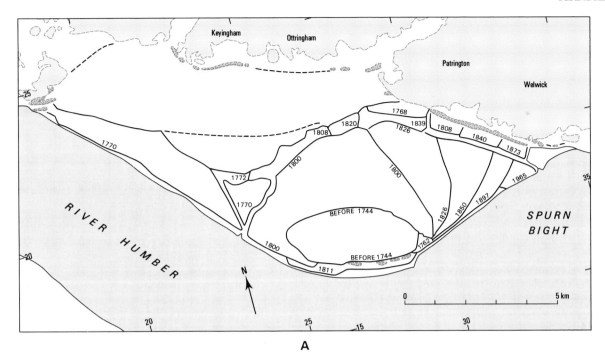

A

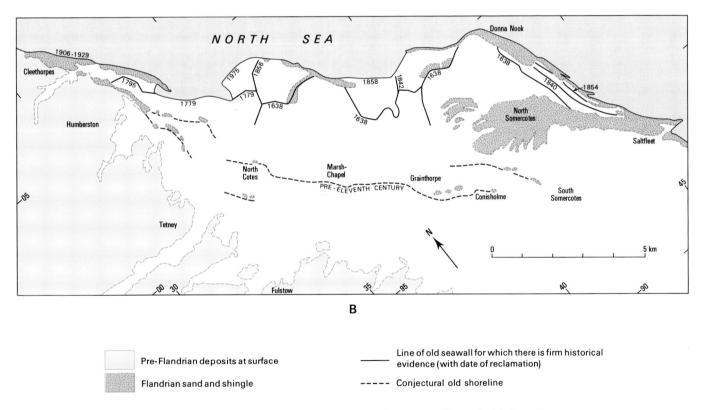

B

Pre-Flandrian deposits at surface

Flandrian sand and shingle

Line of old seawall for which there is firm historical evidence (with date of reclamation)

----- Conjectural old shoreline

Figure 31 History of land reclamation as defined by storm beaches, sea walls and old shorelines.
A. The area around Sunk Island.
B. Lincolnshire Outmarsh.

Coastal Blown Sand

Most of the coast south of Grimsby and around Easington, Kilnsea and Spurn has some wind-blown sand at surface but, in general, it is thick enough to be mapped only where it forms dunes on or next to storm beaches. There are also sand dunes on the old storm beach between Saltfleet and North Somercotes. In some of the more built-up areas, such as Cleethorpes, Humberston Fitties, North Somercotes and Saltfleet, sand dunes have been flattened, moulded in shape or completely removed by man. Elsewhere, they form some of the most undulating topography in the district outside the Wolds. The largest dunes, which are on Spurn, at Donna Nook and near Saltfleet, are over 9 m high.

The dunes originate along a line parallel to the coast on the landward side of unvegetated sand beach. The dune sand is stabilised by the growth of marram grass followed by shrubs, of which the most common is sea buckthorn. As both the southern part of Spurn and the coast south of Cleethorpes are prograding eastwards, they are fringed by a series of dune lines. The youngest line, nearest the sea, is mostly continuous. Older lines are progressively incised by blow-outs and are eventually converted, first to a serrated strip of crescentic dunes with broad slacks between seaward-facing promontories, and then to an irregular jumble of sand hills. The results of this process can be seen in the southern part of Spurn, on the coast between Donna Nook and Saltfleet Haven, and on the old beach north of Saltfleet village.

The speed of dune development is indicated by the presence in one area [443 972], south of Donna Nook, of three established parallel dune lines within a belt 200 m wide, together with a discontinuous line of incipient dunes about 50 m farther east, on the beach. All of these have presumably grown since the construction of the sea wall about 140 years ago, although it is possible that here, as elsewhere in the district, the growth of sand dunes has been enhanced by fixing fascines (bundles of brushwood) in the beach. At some places, such as at Donna Nook, it is probable that dune-growth was initiated by the construction of a sea wall which is now completely hidden. On Spurn, blown sand is commonly inextricably mixed with tipped 'boulder clay' and rubble that have been applied for coastal protection.

Present-day estuarine and marine sedimentation

This section discusses the sedimentary processes that are active today, together with their products, which have been mapped as Tidal Flat and Modern Beach Deposits, Beach and Shoreface Deposits, and Seabed and Tidal River Bed Deposits. These sediments are the active equivalents of onshore marine and estuarine deposits described between pp. 65 and 69.

SEDIMENTATION IN THE HUMBER ESTUARY

The River Humber is an estuary formed by the amalgamation of several rivers. It is approximately 63 km long from Trent Falls at its source to Spurn Point at its mouth. Over half of its length, therefore, falls within the area discribed in this memoir. The estuary is well mixed, with relatively little vertical variation in salinity (Denman, 1979), and macrotidal, with a tidal range of approximately 6 m at spring tides and 3 m at neaps. Tidal currents in the estuary are strong, with surface velocities up to 2.3 m/second (4.4 knots) on springs and 1.4 m/second (2.8 knots) on neap tides off Immingham. This compares with 1 m/second (2 knots) and 0.5 m/second (1 knot) respectively in the immediately adjacent offshore area. Strong currents are also found just south of Spurn Head, where they correspond with a scoured trough with water depths up to 23 m. Elsewhere in the estuary channel, depths are around 10 to 12 m.

Although the River Humber drains a catchment of about one fifth of the area of England (c.26 000 km^2), it only discharges about 0.1×10^6 tons of sediment into the North Sea each year (Veenstra, 1971). The majority of the sediment within the present estuary is therefore believed to have been transported in through the estuary mouth from the North Sea. O'Connor (1987) estimated that approximately 2.22×10^6 m^3 of sediment originates from the North Sea each year compared with 0.3×10^6 m^3 from upstream. It is likely that most of the sediment is derived from the erosion of the Pleistocene glacigenic sediments along the Holderness coast, where cliff recession may be up to 2 m each year (Valentin, 1971). McCave (1973) estimated that such coastal erosion may yield 0.4×10^6 tons of mud annually, although estimates are subject to a high degree of uncertainty. Offshore erosion of the sea bed is believed to be a relatively unimportant source of mud (McCave, 1987). Provenance studies based on heavy mineral grains in estuary sediments also point to sources along the Holderness coast (Al-Bakri, 1986).

TIDAL FLAT DEPOSITS

Tidal Flat Deposits fringe the entire estuary. Only where land-fill reclamation and harbour works are extensive, as in the vicinity of Kingston upon Hull, are modern tidal flats absent. Within Spurn Bight, the tidal flats are over 4 km wide, but along most of the estuary they are only a few hundreds of metres across.

Tidal flats are generally areas of sediment accretion due to the difference in erosional and depositional shear at times of high tide. Thus, sediment deposited from turbid waters at high tide is not re-entrained as the tide begins to ebb. Sediment may be resuspended during the following flood tide and moved farther inland. In this way, sorting of the sediment occurs, with the result that the finest muds are transported landward. The highest parts of the tidal flat are therefore dominated by mud. The muds are often very soft and brown in colour at the surface, but at depths of a few centimetres they are black and anoxic. The surface muds are generally extensively bioturbated by burrowing infauna and by the activity of wading birds.

The uppermost part of the tidal flat may become vegetated by halophytic plants (Plate 15), which serve to stabilise the mud and trap further sediment during high tides. Algae growing on the sediment surface also serve to bind the sediment and give some resistance to erosion. Decomposition of algae may be a contributing factor to the observed sediment anoxia at shallow depths. In many parts of the estuary, just seaward of the sea wall, more mature salt marsh, often with a surface of rough pasture, may be present, with a small cliff from 0.5 to 1 m high, occasionally up to 1.7 m high, at its seaward side. The cliff (Plate 15) often exposes finely laminated silts and clays with occasional pebble clasts, indicating erosion of former tidal flat sediments. Such erosion may be due to periodic changes in the locations of the main estuary channels. In some places, patches of older, firmer mud representing earlier mudflat deposits may be exposed as inliers within more recent mudflat.

In some parts of the estuary the tidal flats consist dominantly of sand. The most notable area of sandflats within this area is between Cleethorpes and Donna Nook, where they are up to 2.5 km wide and consist of well-sorted, very fine-grained sand. Other sandflats are mostly confined to the area of Spurn Bight, where two linear tracts of sand parallel to the coast are found. The inner one occurs near the high-water mark and is approximately 500 m wide; it consists of well-sorted, very fine-grained sand, which tends to fine towards the shoreline.

The outer area is broader and forms a low bank c.1.5 m above the level of the mudflat; it consists of well-sorted, fine-grained sand. These two sandy areas are separated from each other by a mudflat. The outer area is thought to have formed as a result of a clockwise eddy current across Spurn Bight at high water (Pethick, 1988) or as a sand bar originally protecting a lagoon-like area within Spurn Bight (Humphries, 1973).

An elongate body of barnacle-encrusted gravel within the Tidal Flat Deposits of Spurn Bight lies inside and parallel to the promontory of Spurn Head. This gravel body, known as 'Old Den' (see cover photograph), appears to be a relict feature which formed as a shoal after a breach in Spurn Head in historical times (De Boer, 1964).

The Tidal Flat Deposits are probably between 4 and 6 m thick in the estuary upstream of Immingham, but may be up to 9 m thick in Spurn Bight and over 12 m thick in the Grimsby area (see Figure 30). The surface of the sediments shelves gently down to the low-water mark, but then more steeply down to the river bed.

RIVER BED DEPOSITS

River Bed Deposits in the Humber Estuary are dominated by sands. The source of these sediments is also believed to be largely marine.

The sands are mostly medium or fine grained, and tend to fine upstream (British Geological Survey, 1990). They are often overlaid by a thin, possibly transient layer of mud (McQuillin et al., 1969). Patches of gravelly sediment are mostly associated with, and probably derived from exposures of till on the river bed. River Bed Deposits also include a number of sand banks which may separate flood and ebb channels.

Muddy sands and sandy muds are also present on the river bed, mostly close to the seaward edges of mudflats. These muddy sediments may correlate with areas of less vigorous tidal currents (McQuillin et al., 1969). In places they infill older river channels cut into the underlying Pleistocene till. The thickness of River Bed Deposits is very variable; the sandbanks, e.g. Foul Holme Spit, are up to 15 m thick, but in many places Pleistocene till may be exposed on the river bed, with little or no sediment cover.

SHOREFACE DEPOSITS

Shoreface Deposits along the Holderness coast to Spurn Head consist mostly of sand and gravelly sand. Gravelly sediments dominate towards the top of the beach, at the foot of the cliffs. Most of them may be derived directly from the erosion of the Pleistocene tills within these cliffs. Wave-induced sediment transport by longshore drift is to the south and has been responsible for the accumulation of the sand and shingle spit of Spurn Head. Some sediment may be transported offshore, for example in the area of the Binks (De Boer, 1964).

SEA-BED DEPOSITS

The North Sea just offshore is largely shallow, with a relatively flat sea bed. Water depths are typically between 10 and 15 m.

The Sea-bed Deposits are separated from the Shoreface Deposits along the Holderness coast by a narrow, c.200 to 500 m-wide strip of largely sediment-free, exposed till floor. They are dominantly gravels and sandy gravels, except in the area off the mouth of the Humber where the sediments are mostly sands. The gravels contain a mixture of lithologies dominated by Carboniferous sandstone and limestone, together with igneous and other rock types which generally indicate derivation from Palaeozoic formations of northern England and southern Scotland (Veenstra, 1971). These gravels may have originated as lag deposits derived from moraines or outwash fans, or additionally from erosion of till by wave action either from within the Holderness cliffs or from submarine exposures such as those already mentioned.

Made Ground

Materials deposited directly by human agency, either on the natural landsurface or as fill in man-made excavations, have been mapped as 'Made Ground'. As in all the more populated parts of Great Britain this includes large areas of public authority and commercial waste disposal, notably around Grimsby and east Hull, and landscaping 'fill' for industrial, housing or recreational projects. Most of the major industrial developments near the Humber estuary, for example at Salt End, Killingholme, Immingham, Pyewipe and West Marsh, have involved some large-scale dumping on low-lying marine alluvial flats, using brought-in material such as aggregate as well as clinker, fly-ash and other largely inert industrial waste. Much of the Made Ground of newer landscaped urban areas merely consists of the local Drift deposits transferred from one part of a site to another by earth-moving equipment. Similarly, Made Ground has been mapped at some rural localities, such as at Conisholme, where hummocky terrain marking old abandoned settlements is probably caused by very local transfer of material. The embankments of Covenham Reservoir are made of clay, mostly till, dug to a depth of more than 3 m from the floor of the site.

The largest backfilled excavations are some of the old brick pits on the south-west side of the Humber between Immingham and North Killingholme, which have been partly used as dumps for industrial waste. There are many smaller backfilled chalk, clay and gravel pits, including several old brickpits within the built-up area of Grimsby and Cleethorpes.

Much Made Ground in the district is associated with reclamation from, or defences against, the sea. This includes, for example, the till clays excavated from the Easington gas pipeline terminal site, which were used to reinforce the sand dunes at Kilnsea and the north end of Spurn, and also the till overburden from the gravel pit at Keyingham, which has been used to build the new sea wall at Sunk Island. The largest areas of Made Ground on former intertidal flats are the peninsula around Grimsby Royal Dock and fish docks, reclaimed in the mid-nineteenth century, and a strip along the north side of the Humber around the King George Dock, Hull, and eastwards to and including some of the Salt End industrial site, which is a twentieth-century reclamation.

The most distinctive Made Ground is formed by the waste mounds of the medieval salt industry, which operated until the seventeenth century on the Lincolnshire 'Outmarsh' (Robinson, 1970; Pattison and Williamson, 1986). The salt was obtained by evaporation of brines produced from washing highly saline silts scraped from the tidal flats after high spring tides; the mounds are the discarded silt. The older ones merge to form a low plateau about 4 m higher than the surrounding alluvial flat, on the east side of the main road through North Cotes, Marshchapel and Grainthorpe, which follows the line of the pre-seventeenth-century sea wall. The younger mounds in that area, which are nearer the present-day coast, are more isolated, steep-sided hillocks with characteristic rosette-like shapes when seen from above. There are more of these 'saltern' mounds scattered around the edges of the old North Somercotes storm beach and northwards from North Cotes to Humberston. There are also historical records of salterns on the Humber shore north of Grimsby (Rudkin and Owen, 1960), but these had closed down long before those of the Marshchapel area and appear to have left no surface trace. Some small, steep-sided mounds rising above the alluvial flat near Skeffling on the north side of the Humber may also be saltern mounds.

SIX
Coastal changes

Studies of local sea-level change (e.g. Gaunt and Tooley, 1974) confirm that, as part of the southern North Sea region, this district is subject to rising relative sea level as a consequence of eustatic change and crustal subsidence. This effect, however, seems to be of only minor importance to local short-term coastal changes, which include both the rapid erosion of the Holderness North Sea cliffs and the seaward advance of the north-east Lincolnshire coast.

Between Cleethorpes and the south-east corner of the district, the relative sinking of the land surface is more than counterbalanced by accretion. This is probably due to both the continuing supply of new marine sediment from the eroding Holderness till, with local retention by the protective effect of the south Holderness peninsula, and the convergence of northward- and southward-flowing residual currents south of the Humber estuary. The consequent prograding of the coast is effected by beach deposition, the spread of saltmarsh vegetation and the accumulation of blown sand. In the past, these processes have been consolidated by man-made sea walls and reclamation for agriculture, but in recent years much of the intertidal and sand dune areas have been preserved for military use or nature conservation. However, despite the seaward advance of the coast in the last 400 years (Figure 31), the area behind the sea walls, which is commonly below the level of the highest spring tides (and that includes virtually all the alluvial flat of the Lincolnshire 'Outmarsh'), is subject to the threat of marine flooding, a threat which increases with the continuing rise in mean sea level. Barnes and King (1953) have chronicled the historic floods of the 'Outmarsh', culminating in the February 1953 storm flood which inundated large areas, both along the south-west side of the Humber north-west of Grimsby, and farther south, west and south of Donna Nook.

Throughout recorded history extensive areas of land have been lost along the Holderness North Sea coast, with an average retreat rate of the order of 1 to 2 m per year. At any given point and time, the rate of retreat is controlled by local factors such as the presence of beach deposits and the height of the cliff, but the fundamental cause of retreat is removal of material from the foot of the cliff. This leads to cliff failure and to the deposition of more material on the beach for the sea to remove.

The cliff landslips (Plate 5) were described in detail by Pickwell (1878) who quotes cliff failures 200 to 600 yards (183 to 549 m) long by 20 to 50 yards (18 to 46 m) deep of cliffs 60 feet (18 m) high. He gives specific examples to the north of the district at Hilston, Grimston, Thorp and Aldborough, the last being a slip 900 yards (823 m) long and 50 to 60 yards (46 to 55 m) wide. The engravings which illustrate these sites show that the landslips

are rotational. They are sometimes restricted to the tills above the Basement Till, but deeper rotational failures locally affect the Basement Till, where the plane of failure extends down to, and below the cliff base. Successive failures are enhanced by secondary mudflows and slides of slipped material that have been saturated by sea spray, rain and drainage water.

The role of water draining from the land adversely affecting cliff stability by gullying and softening the till was noted by Steers (1953) and Valentin (1971). Water seeping through sandy layers in the till may promote instability by seepage erosion, causing undercutting of the cliff face.

Hutchinson (1986) confirmed that instability of the cliffs resulted in deep-seated rotational landslips. He noted that the rate of debris removal is greater than the rate of supply by mudslides and other shallow mass movements and is, on average, greater than the supply from deep-seated movements. Hutchinson examined the processes involved in marine erosion, such as the formation of small caves, notches at the base of the cliff, scour around erratic blocks, frost wedging, and softening of the till due to pore-pressure reduction as a result of unloading by marine erosion. He also claimed to identify a 12-year cycle governing the rate of southward movement of beach material as oblique wave forms, which remove support from the base of the cliff in the troughs (locally called ords) and expose the till cliff to the direct erosive action of the sea; any one site is exposed to maximum wave attack at 12-year intervals, but is protected by beach wave crests in the interim. The mode of sediment transport and its implications for cliff erosion are described in detail by Pringle (1981, 1985).

Valentin (1971) drew attention to the role of Dimlington High Ground, the highest point on the Holderness coast, as the southern fulcrum in its geographical 's'-shape. The highest cliffs yield most debris at their base and are thus more likely to be protected from further attack. Dimlington cliffs thus protrude as a headland because of their height. However, because they protrude, they are more exposed to storm waves. As long as the height of the cliffs remains constant as the coast retreats, the balance between these two factors is retained; consequently, the coastline maintains its shape. If, however, the height of the cliff decreases, the balance is upset and the rate of retreat accelerates. This appears to be happening at Dimlington where the highest point was over 42 m above OD 140 years ago, but is now about 37 m (Figure 23) and is likely to decrease to below 30 m in the next 50 to 100 years. Measurements of coastal recession kept by Holderness District Council show that, while the coast between Kilnsea and Tunstall as a whole is retreating at an average rate of about 1.3 m a year, the recent rate around Dimlington exceeds that considerably.

The potential for similar acceleration of retreat also seems to exist at three points on the coast between Dimlington and Spurn where relatively high cliffs now forming secondary fulcrums will decrease in height as the coast recedes. The southernmost of these is How Hill [420 153], which is of critical importance as the till base to which the sand and shingle spit of the present-day Spurn peninsula is attached. The crucial role of this till headland at the north end of Spurn in the latter's cyclical evolution has been discussed by de Boer (1964, 1981). Historical evidence shows that the present peninsula is only the latest of a series of curved spits to have projected from the north across the mouth of the Humber. Each, in succession, has progressively grown in length, been breached and subsequently re-formed farther west over a recorded period of about 250 years. The present headland has survived more than 100 years longer than its predecessors because of human intervention. However, the present scale of the intervention, despite the dumping of large quantities of 'boulder clay' excavated from the Easington hydrocarbon terminal site, appears to be increasingly inadequate in maintaining Spurn as a peninsula.

Pethick (1988) pointed out that, as Spurn is merely the raised eastern edge of the Spurn Bight intertidal flats, a breach of the spit would not alter the overall shape of the Humber estuary. However, the longer term problem of erosion on the Holderness coast farther north is one which, if unresolved, will increase in severity as the coastline recedes, because at present it coincides with the highest land in the area.

A summary is given below of the engineering properties of the tills that are subject to rapid erosion on the Holderness coast.

GEOTECHNICAL PROPERTIES OF HOLDERNESS TILLS

Engineering properties of Holderness tills have been studied at the Building Research Establishment, Cowden (Marsland and Powell, 1985; Atkinson et al., 1985), in site investigations at Easington, and by Bell and Forster (1989). Workers agree, in general, on the ranges of values of the parameters determined, but only Bell and Forster were able to distinguish all three of the named tills on these criteria.

All of the tills have fine-grained fractions (sand size and less) greater than 60 per cent and are therefore matrix-dominated tills. Bell and Forster (1991) indicated that the grading curves for the three tills (Basement, Skipsea and Withernsea), although similar, may be used to distinguish between them, thus confirming Madgett and Catt's (1978) grading analyses.

The clay minerals which comprise the clay-grade fraction (<2 μm) are predominantly illite and kaolinite; the former is dominant, except in weathered material where kaolinite dominates. Natural moisture contents of the fresh tills lie in the range 12 to 20 per cent, with a mean of about 16 per cent; where they are weathered, this increases to 18 to 26 per cent, with a mean of 23 per cent. Atterberg limits are: plastic limit 14 to 21 per cent, liquid limit 20 to 39 per cent for Skipsea and Withernsea Till and slightly higher for Basement Till (PL 16 to 23 per cent, LL 28 to 42 per cent). Values for weathered material are higher still (PL 20 to 26 per cent, LL 38 to 53 per cent). Natural moisture content of fresh tills is at or below the plastic limit value and indicates a state of over-consolidation. The Skipsea and Withernsea Tills are generally of low plasticity, while the Basement Till is of low to intermediate plasticity. When weathered, till increases in plasticity to intermediate to high values.

Unconfined compressive strength data (Bell and Forster, 1991) indicate the Withernsea Till to be stiff to very stiff and the Skipsea and Basement tills to be very stiff: strength values increase down through the sequence and reflect the greater degree of over-consolidation. Remoulded strength values are close to the undisturbed values, which indicate a low sensitivity. The strength behaviour of the tills is described in detail by Marsland and Powell (1985).

Weathered till, formerly identified as Hessle Till, differs in geotechnical properties from unweathered material in line with the findings of Eyles and Sladen (1981), who worked on the lodgement till in Northumberland. The weathered material is oxidised and decalcified, and has higher moisture content and plastic and liquid limit values, with lower strength values than unweathered material of the same till.

SEVEN
Economic geology

BRICK CLAY

There are many disused pits in the district which worked clay for making bricks, tiles and drainage pipes. They used Devensian glacial till and glacial lake deposits and Flandrian Marine and Estuarine Alluvium.

Most of the till workings were around Grimsby and are now largely filled and built over. It is probable that, in common with till clay pits elsewhere in the region, only the near-surface decalcified beds ('Hessle Till') were used. Many of the Grimsby/Cleethorpes pits, including those at Holme Hill [277 089], Mill Road [302 085], Chapmans Road [300 095] and Conyards Road [302 092], closed about the time of the First World War. The glaciolacustrine clays within the till near Waltham [251 034] were worked more recently; former deposits of glaciolacustrine clay at Great Limber have been effectively worked out.

The biggest concentration of Flandrian clay workings was along the south-west side of the Humber estuary between Immingham and East Halton. There were also clay pits in the 'warp' at Winestead in Holderness, in operation until about 1950, and at several places in the Lincolnshire 'Outmarsh', such as Fulstow, Grainthorpe Fen and near South Somercotes, which probably all closed before the Second World War. The worked clays tended to be of estuarine rather than marine facies; consequently, they had a low sand and silt content, and probably included much organic matter. They were probably plastic clays liable to shrinkage on drying, but their fine grain size would have made them especially suitable for tile manufacture and their organic content may have reduced fuel costs during firing.

CHALK

The Lincolnshire Wolds are peppered with disused small 'marling' pits and medium-sized quarries from which chalk has been dug by farmers for agricultural lime and hard core. Some hard beds in the Ferriby Chalk around Louth were quarried in the past on a small scale for building stone. There are also several larger chalk quarries in this district, all now closed, of which the most recently operated were at Riby [174 063] and North Ormsby [288 936]. Riby was worked from the 1940s to the 1970s, mostly for fill aggregate, with maximum output in the 1960s of up to 30 000 tons per month. It was reopened in the 1980s to supply fill for the construction of the A180 road. North Ormsby Quarry, which produced about 50 000 tons of chalk a year, largely for agricultural lime and industrial fillers, closed around 1970. Both operations mostly worked the lower part of the Burnham Chalk.

The chalk of the Welton and Burnham Formations, which form the greater part of the readily accessible Wolds chalk, is generally stronger than the chalk of southern England and is suitable for hard core, although its potentially high moisture content makes it susceptible to frost damage; it is thus commercially unacceptable for near-surface use.

COAL

The Tetney Lock Borehole established the presence of an important coal-bearing Westphalian sequence in the district, comparable to those of the working coalfields east of the Pennines (Howitt and Brunstrom, 1966). However, the Coal Measures are deeply buried, ranging from a minimum of around 1.3 km in the south-west of the district to more than 2.2 km in the north-east (Figures 6 and 7b). The Top Hard or Barnsley Coal is at a depth of about 1.7 km in the south-west, increasing to more than 2.5 km in the east (Figure 7a). Such depths are well beyond current economic limits (1.2 km) for the mining of coal in Britain. Any exploitation would present major problems because of the engineering properties of the beds at depth, and the need to solve the difficulties posed by the high temperatures (50 to 80°C) at these depths. Exploitation may eventually be possible by means of gasification.

EVAPORITES

Very large volumes of anhydrite and halite occur within the Permian rocks of the district, below depths in excess of 1200 m (Figure 13). Younger Triassic anhydrites are less deeply buried at depths of little more than 700 m. The limited current demand for these raw materials and their shallower availability elsewhere, suggest that there is little likelihood of exploitation in the foreseeable future.

GEOTHERMAL ENERGY

Studies of the low-enthalpy geothermal potential of the Carboniferous (Holliday, 1986) and post-Carboniferous (Gale et al., 1983; Smith 1986) rocks of eastern England have been summarised by Gale and Holliday (1985). The main conclusion of this work was that the Permo-Triassic sandstones of the Grimsby and Cleethorpes area have the greatest potential within the region. This was tested by the Cleethorpes Borehole, and a preliminary assessment of the resource was made by Downing et al. (1985). They concluded that the Sherwood Sandstone had a transmissivity of at least 60 darcy-metres (Dm), yielding brine with a salinity of 35 to 80/grams per litre (g/l) at a temperature of 53°C. The exploitation of this resource is currently regarded as uneconomic, although locally in the Paris Basin, low-enthalpy resources only a few degrees warmer (less than 60°C) are currently used. Energy costs need to rise appreciably before the Sherwood Sandstone brines could become a feasible economic proposition. The Basal Permian Sands at Cleethorpes proved to have a much lower transmissivity, less than 2 Dm, although temperatures of 64°C were recorded.

The relatively high geothermal gradients in the Upper Carboniferous and younger rocks of the district, around 30°C/per kilometre (Downing et al., 1985), suggest that temperatures of 100°C could be obtained at depths of a little more than 3 km in largely impermeable Lower Carboniferous rocks. The exploitation of this heat source for domestic purposes might prove possible by use of the 'hot dry rock' method. However, the high geothermal gradients are not believed to continue to deeper levels because of the effects of the high thermal conductivities of the Dinantian limestones and the underlying 'basement' rocks. Estimates of temperatures at depths of 7 km (taken as the practical limit of drilling) under the district are in the range 160 to 180°C (Gale and Rollin, 1986; British Geological Survey, 1987), less than the 200°C necessary for electricity generation using the 'hot dry rock' approach.

HYDROCARBONS

The district lies in the area between the oilfields of the East Midlands, in which the reservoirs are sandstones of Namurian and Westphalian age, and the gasfields of the Southern North Sea Basin, in which the reservoirs are of the Basal Permian Sands. Despite this, only limited exploration activity has been carried out within the district beyond the stage of seismic reflection surveys. The Winestead Borehole is the only one in the district to have been drilled directly for hydrocarbons, the Tetney Lock Borehole having been sunk as a deep stratigraphical test. A number of exploration boreholes have been drilled close by in adjacent districts but, like Winestead, have been declared dry.

Vitrinite reflectance data from the Cleethorpes Borehole (Kirby, 1985) show that the Permian and Mesozoic parts of the section are immature for hydrocarbon generation. Similarly, unpublished results from the Nettleton Bottom, Nettleton and Winestead boreholes show vitrinite reflectance values rarely greater than 0.5 per cent from rocks of that age. However, similar data from the Carboniferous rocks show them to be more mature.

Oil and gas generation within the Carboniferous rocks of eastern England has been reviewed by Cornford (1986), Kirby et al. (1987) and Fraser et al. (1990). Most of the Upper Carboniferous rocks contain terrestrial plant material, particularly the Coal Measures, and are thus believed to have gas-generating potential. However, the vitrinite reflectance values from Cleethorpes (Kirby,

1985) and adjacent boreholes suggest that the Westphalian and Namurian rocks of the district are mature only for oil generation (ranging up to 0.9 per cent). This suggests that only limited quantities of locally sourced gas have been generated, and that major accumulations of such are unlikely. However, up-dip migration of gas from more deeply buried and more mature Upper Carboniferous rocks offshore cannot be ruled out. The major oil-source rocks of the East Midlands oilfields are believed to be early Namurian shales. It has not yet been established that such rocks occur within the district but, if present, they are likely to be mature for oil generation (vitrinite reflectance values 0.9 to 1.0 per cent). Sandstones in the overlying Namurian and Westphalian sequences, in suitable structural positions, are the likely main reservoir rocks.

HYDROGEOLOGY AND WATER SUPPLY

The district includes parts of hydrometric areas 26 and 29, and is divided by the Humber estuary into the Holderness region to the north and Lincolnshire to the south. In both areas the Chalk is the most important aquifer; other water-bearing formations are of relatively little importance. Chalk groundwater has always been an important source of supply, but large-scale development has only taken place since the 1940s.

In 1987, the total licensed groundwater abstraction south of the Humber was 71.64 million cubic metres per annum (m³/a) and the licensed surface water abstraction was 14.32 million m³/a. North of the Humber estuary, surface water abstraction is relatively more important; the total licensed take from surface and groundwater (entirely Chalk) sources are 12.76 million m³/a and 1.26 million m³/a respectively.

The mean annual rainfall varies from as low as 600 mm over the Holderness area to more than 750 mm along the high ground of the Lincolnshire Wolds, which rise to an altitude of over 150 m above mean sea level (Figure 1). Potential evapotranspiration averages 425 millimetres per year (mm/yr), but the effective infiltration is highly variable, being primarily dependent upon the permeability of the cover material. On the Wolds, nearly all effective rainfall infiltrates the Chalk, at an average rate of 250 mm/yr, and this is reflected in the nature of the river regimes which are all almost entirely groundwater fed. The average annual infiltration through the superficial deposits of Holderness is only 52 mm, with high surface run-off through artificial channels.

The hydrogeology of the district was first described in Geological Survey publications by Reid (1885), Woodward (1904) and Fox-Strangways (1906). Since then, numerous reports concerning specific aspects of the groundwater resources have been written, notably by Price (1957), Foster (1968) and Foster et al. (1974). Birmingham University has undertaken surveys of the hydrogeology both north and south of the Humber (Anon, 1978, 1985) and has developed mathematical models of the aquifer systems. The district is also covered by the hydrogeological maps for North and East Lincolnshire and for East Yorkshire (Institute of Geological Sciences, 1967, 1980).

A description of the hydrogeological importance of the formations observed at or near outcrop follows.

The 'Ancholme Clay Group' is for the most part an aquiclude. The **Elsham Sandstone**, a thin, confined, water-bearing unit within the group, is not used for water supply at present but the quality is good, although of the sodium bicarbonate type, and it is a potentially useful aquifer for small supplies.

The **Spilsby Sandstone** crops out as a narrow strip along the base of the Wolds scarp face and thus direct recharge is limited. The unit is bound above and below by impermeable strata and there is only limited hydraulic continuity with the Lower Cretaceous and Chalk aquifers. The Spilsby Sandstone is used for water supply only where Chalk water is not readily available.

There are no public supply sources in the Spilsby Sandstone in this district and nearly all records are for boreholes drilled through 35 to 60 m of unsaturated Chalk just east of the Wolds scarp face, notably around Rothwell [152 996].

Flow is intergranular and well screens are necessary to prevent borehole collapse, while development of the completed borehole is by surging and pumping. Despite the numerous private supply boreholes and a small number of springs, there is little yield information available, and most of this is for boreholes which tap the Carstone as well. The available data suggest that yields improve to the south as the aquifer thickens: a borehole just north of Cabourne [140 018] yields only 1100 cubic metres per day (m^3/d) for a 7 m drawdown, while south of Sheet 90, the sandstone supports major public supply sources.

The quality of the groundwater is good, with a total hardness of between 200 and 250 mg/l; the concentrations of chloride, sulphate and nitrate are significantly lower than in the Chalk in the same area.

The **Carstone** is the only useful and distinct aquifer within the well documented parts of the Lower Cretaceous, but there is some evidence that much of the underlying **Tealby Formation** may be arenaceous in the central and south-eastern parts of the district. The **Tealby Limestone** is a thin water-bearing formation but is not used for supply. The Upper and Lower Tealby Clays and the Claxby Ironstone are aquicludes and they separate the Lower Cretaceous aquifers from the Spilsby Sandstone.

The Carstone is in hydraulic continuity with the overlying Red Chalk (part of the Chalk aquifer) and has a small outcrop area along the Wolds scarp face, but it also crops out to the east in the deeper valleys. The small quantity of direct replenishment is augmented by downward leakage of Chalk groundwater, and, as much of the Chalk in the south-western area is unsaturated, infiltrating water ultimately replenishes the Lower Cretaceous aquifer. Flow is toward the north-east, but much of the groundwater re-emerges as baseflow to the Waithe Beck and other rivers, or moves upward into the Chalk.

Development of this aquifer is confined to the south-western part of the Wolds, where the Chalk is unsaturated or has a minimal saturated thickness. The Carstone is

exploited in a large number of private boreholes. Along the scarp face, borehole yields are relatively low, typically ranging from 430 to 760 m^3/d for about 10 m drawdown. In the valleys, higher transmissivity zones have developed as a consequence of high through-flow, and although the saturated thickness is rarely greater than 4 m, yields range between 840 and 2400 m^3/d. There is also a public supply source at Binbrook, in the Waithe Beck valley. Both intergranular and fissure flow occur and sand screens are used.

In the areas where the Carstone is used for supply, the groundwater quality is generally good and reflects the long travel time through the thick unsaturated zone of the Chalk; it is a calcium-bicarbonate water with low sodium chloride and nitrate (a representative analysis is shown in Table 1). In the south-eastern area, the groundwater throughput in the Carstone is slow and considerable softening by ion-exchange has taken place to give sodium bicarbonate waters. This water is not used for supply.

The **Chalk** group is treated as a single hydrogeological unit. The permeability of the Chalk matrix is very low and groundwater flow occurs mainly through fissures, such as bedding planes and joints, which have been preferentially widened by solution. Fissure development has occurred mainly in the near-surface and groundwater movement is concentrated in this zone. The effective aquifer is thus thin relative to the stratigraphical thickness of the Chalk, varying probably from 50 m (under the higher ground) to 100 m (under the lower ground). In the unconfined areas, the water table fluctuates through as much as 30 m and transmissivities may double between low and high groundwater levels; in the confined Chalk these fluctuations are smaller.

In the past, the Chalk aquifer, both north and south of the Humber, was overdeveloped, causing saline intrusion in some coastal areas. However, reduction in the licensed abstraction has now reduced outflows to approximately the same quantity as recharge. Despite this, 75 per cent of the discharge is by pumping and the extensive artesian conditions that existed in coastal areas prior to 1940 are rare today. Natural discharge occurs through a small number of springs, although significant flow is limited to exceptionally high winter groundwater levels, and via 'blow wells' (Chalk-water springs occurring where high groundwater pressure has forced a flow path upward through the confining boulder clay and gravel). In the past, blow wells were widespread, but now they only flow in a few areas, notably around Tetney where they supply good quality water, as at Littlecoates Pumping Station [253 085].

There is a very wide range of transmissivity and borehole yield values but, unlike other Chalk areas in England, the variation in this district does not appear to be directly related to the present or fossil valley system. The bulk of abstraction is from the confined Chalk in the coastal areas between Grimsby and North Killingholme [142 170] and around Kingston upon Hull; in these areas, transmissivities average 4000 m^2/d and may attain more than 10 000 m^2/d. Other areas of high transmissivity are often associated with the presence of gravels directly overlying the Chalk. In contrast, the transmissivity of the Chalk in the south-west of the Lincolnshire Wolds and beneath the entire Holderness peninsula may be less than 50 m²/d.

Analysis of 75 borehole records for the district reveals that for a 300 mm diameter borehole with an effective saturated thickness of 50 m, the mean yield is 460 m³/d per metre-drawdown (m-dd), and there is a 20 per cent probability of obtaining more than 1260 m³/d per m-dd. The low transmissivity areas are poorly represented in these records and have much lower yields; the unconfined Chalk south of the Caistor Monocline has a very thin saturated thickness, the water-table level being lowered by the deep river system, and the mean yield from each of six boreholes was just over 50 m³/d per m-dd. Very large (> 0.5 m) diameter public supply boreholes yield over 4000 m³/d and where horizontal adits have been constructed may yield up to 20 000 m³/d. There are no licensed abstractions in the Holderness area of this district and a trial 300 mm diameter borehole yielded 125 m³/d for a drawdown of 57 m.

It is generally unnecessary to line boreholes in the Chalk, excepting the upper 10 m to prevent possible infiltration of contaminated surface waters. Newly constructed boreholes are normally developed with hydrochloric acid to remove the slurry caused by drilling, and this process may double the yields.

Hydrochemical and water-level data confirm that the effective aquifer is thin and help define groundwater flow directions and velocities. High nitrate and tritiated water occur only at shallow depths (up to 30 m below the water table in the unconfined Chalk and 7 m where confined) and tritium was found in groundwater at Grimsby as early as 1967, indicating rapid flow from the Wolds recharge zone. South of the Humber, rapid flow occurs in a north-easterly direction towards the major abstraction sites, but south of the Waithe Beck there is minimal flow in both the confined and unconfined Chalk. North of the Humber, groundwater converges on Kingston upon Hull due to concentration of abstraction sites, but little flow occurs in the Chalk beneath the till of Holderness.

Chalk groundwater may be divided into a number of hydrochemical types and representative analyses are shown in Table 1. Throughout the unconfined Chalk of the Wolds, reasonable quality, recent recharge waters with alkalinity of between 190 and 230 mg/l exist. North of Cuxwold [173 011] calcium sulphate waters dominate, with levels of chloride, sulphate and nitrate ions having increased over the last twenty years, apparently as a result of modern farming practices; chloride concentrations are generally over 30 mg/l, sulphate frequently greater than 100 mg/l and nitrate (as N) exceeds 10 mg/l. In the southern area, the very thick unsaturated zone results in better quality, calcium bicarbonate waters with lower concentrations of these ions.

The chemistry of the confined groundwaters also varies from north to south. North of the Waithe Beck, rapid flow towards the coastal abstraction sites results in modern, low chloride, low nitrate, calcium bicarbonate

Table 1   Representative chemical analyses of groundwater from confined Chalk (cck), outcrop Chalk, (ck), and Carstone (cs) from the Patrington and Grimsby district.

Location	Salt End	Hollym	Grimsby	Cleethorpes	Bradley	Beelsby	Limber	Binbrook
National Grid reference	162 276	352 250	256 108	280 089	240 062	200 032	149 063	208 934
Analyst	YWA	YWA	AWA	AWA	AWA	AWA	AWA	AWA
Date	Jul 1980	Apr 1979	Nov 1988	Nov 1988	Nov 1988	Nov 1988	Nov 1988	Oct 1986
Aquifer	cck	cck	cck	cck	ck	ck	ck	cs
pH	7.30	8.23	7.35	7.28	7.29	7.20	7.36	8.00
Electrical conductivity at 25°C	5700	6090	1240	590	530	615	350	520
Total hardness (as CaCO₃)	818	762	320	243	246	296	152	268
Alkalinity (as CaCO₃)	426	256	200	210	193	195	140	157
Calcium (as Ca)	109	103	113	89.4	82.8	124	47.3	98
Magnesium (as Mg)	131	123	14.3	7.33	6.16	5.09	10.4	6.0
Sodium (as Na)	1070	990	95.4	17.8	8.4	8.8	13.3	10.0
Potassium (as K)	95	51.6	3.62	2.82	1.85	0.99	3.13	0.8
Sulphate (as SO₄)	373	567	39.2	14.2	25.9	44.1	21.1	4.0
Chloride (as Cl)	2066	1500	213	31.7	20.8	24.5	12.5	22
Nitrate (as N)	20.1	0.01	3.33	3.4	6.63	11.6	<0.5	0.01
Fluoride (as F)	–	–	0.11	0.19	0.13	<0.1	0.20	0.12
Total iron (as Fe)	–	13.5	3.07	0.06	0.03	0.18	0.08	–
Manganese (as Mn)	–	9	<10	<10	<10	<10	<10	<10

YWA: Yorkshire Water Authority. AWA: Anglian Water Authority. Units are milligrammes per litre except for manganese (which is in microgrammes per litre), pH (which is in pH units) and electrical conductivity (which is in microsiemens per cubic centimetre).

waters, but monitoring has shown that the chloride and nitrate levels have risen. South of the Waithe Beck, flow is restricted and the longer residence times have produced sodium waters through ion-exchange.

Saline waters exist in two zones south of the Humber and throughout the northern area; they have been studied using major and minor ion chemistry, carbon and tritium isotopes, geophysical logging and depth sampling.

The most extensive saline zone comprises the entire Holderness peninsula south and east of Hedon [190 285]. This is a stable body of saline groundwater dating from the Ipswichian interglacial (Anon, 1978), which shows that there is minimal flow in this part of the Chalk. The Chalk of Kingston upon Hull and the area from Skitter Ness [130 254] to North Killingholme [142 170] contains a mixture of old and modern saline waters with chloride concentrations exceeding 1000 mg/l[-1] in places. Old saline water is present at depth and induced intrusion of modern sea-water took place prior to 1950. Monitoring of the chemistry has shown that the saline bodies have been stablised as a result of controlled pumping.

The Grimsby saline zone, extending from Immingham [185 145] south-east to Cleethorpes [308 085], developed largely as a result of abstraction-induced intrusion from the Humber Estuary. The relationship between fresh and saline water is complex, but monitoring of chloride concentrations over the past 40 years shows that there was a dramatic increase in salinity as a direct consequence of increased pumping between 1950 and 1970. Since that time reductions in abstraction have improved the water quality considerably. The saline intrusion was facilitated by areas of exposed chalk on the sea bed; throughout the rest of the district, thick impermeable boulder clay and alluvial cover, together with low transmissivity Chalk, have hindered the inflow of sea-water.

Impermeable tills clays are the thickest and most widespread **Superficial Deposits**, and are important in that they confine the Chalk and limit recharge over large areas. Glacigenic sands and gravels form locally important water-bearing deposits and, being often overlain by till, are more extensive than their outcrop area suggests (see Figures 23–25). Although widely used for private supply in the past, risk of pollution from surface sources limits their usage today. Nevertheless, where these highly permeable deposits are both saturated and in hydraulic continuity with the Chalk, they act as an important storage reservoir and significantly increase the transmissivity of the aquifer system. This is particularly important along the unconfined–confined boundary where deposits lying against the buried (pre-Devensian) cliff are frequently over 10 m thick. A pump test in a gravel borehole at Laceby [222 066] showed a transmissivity of 1100 m²/d, and a test in unconfined gravel near Keelby [158 111] calculated the storage coefficient as 0.02 (Anon, 1978).

IRONSTONE

Ferruginous ooliths are a characteristic component of strata between the Spilsby Sandstone and the Carstone.

They are most abundant in the Roach Formation and the Claxby Ironstone. Trial levels in The Roach at Otby [c.139 935] were mentioned by Ussher et al. (1888, p.100), but the iron ore was said to be 'not worth extraction'. The Claxby Ironstone, however, has been mined in underground workings which extend into this district from the Nettleton Bottom Mine of the adjoining Brigg district (Gaunt et al., 1991); production had ceased by 1969. Trials, including a 1200 m-long heading [from 1346 9290], were made after the First World War in the Claxby Ironstone of the Walesby/Otby area, but undulations in the bedding made working impractical. The commercial ore of the Claxby Ironstone is in a 2 m-thick band in the lower part of the formation and consists of berthierinic ooliths in a sideritic and berthierinitic matrix. Its siliceous nature was balanced by mixing it with Frodingham Ironstone from the Scunthorpe area, thus moderating the latter's high calcareous content (Slater and Highley, 1977).

Rapid depletion of Frodingham Ironstone reserves at and near outcrop during the time of peak production around 1960 led to investigation of its potential at depth around Brocklesby, on the western edge of this district. Five boreholes proved thicknesses of the Frodingham Ironstone between 6.2 and 10 m, at depths between 410 and 474 m, with a chemical composition which was variable, but comparable with the ironstone at outcrop. However, the influx of high-grade imported ore during the 1960s prevented any exploitation of the resource.

PHOSPHATES

Bands of phosphatic nodules are common in several of the sub-Chalk formations of the Lincolnshire Wolds area, including the Spilsby Sandstone, the Claxby Ironstone, the Roach and the Carstone. An investigation during World War Two suggested that a bed at the base of the Spilsby Sandstone was the most promising as a source of phosphates (Oakley, 1941). Another possibility was considered to be the extraction of phosphates during the processing of Claxby Ironstone, which had been found to contain ferruginous limestone nodules with 11.2 per cent phosphate content. A review of phosphate resources in the late 1970s (Notholt et al., 1979) implied a lack of commercial value for any of the phosphate occurrences in this district. Circumstances have not significantly altered since then.

SAND AND GRAVEL

Although there are considerable reserves of Quaternary sand and gravel in the district, there is only one currently active pit. It is at Mill Hill, Keyingham [243 253], where Kelsey Hill Beds up to 4.5 m thick are extracted to produce washed sand and gravel for general building use. Pebble lithologies in the gravel are as varied as in the associated tills and include quartzite, flint, chalk, Carboniferous and Jurassic limestones and sandstones, dolerite and other igneous and metamorphic rocks. The coal fragments and marine shells which commonly form a scientifically signficant part of the Kelsey Hill Beds are relatively scarce and present no major obstacle to usability of the product. The till overburden from the pit has also been used locally in general construction work such as the building of sea walls and the Hedon bypass. The most accessible Kelsey Hill Beds, along the lower valley of Keyingham Drain, have been largely worked out. Higher up the valley, they appear to be thinner and include much interbedded silt, but the large outcrops between Paull and Thorngumbald may represent further valuable resources.

The largest reserves of sand and gravel south of the Humber are the fluvioglacial terrace deposits from Habrough to Laceby which continue below till and alluvial overburden towards Grimsby. They have been worked at Keelby [1514 1004] where 2.5 m of fairly well-sorted sand with interbedded chalk and flint pebble gravel overlie till; thicknesses may exceed 15 m elsewhere. The high chalk, marine shell and coal contents may limit the use of these deposits as aggregates for concrete. Smaller bodies of Fluvioglacial and Glacial Sand and Gravel are scattered throughout the till-covered areas, especially near Roos [292 296], around Waltham and along the east side of the Lincolnshire Wolds. Former workings include sites near Laceby [201 068], Waltham [263 039] and Utterby [3062 9290]. The glacial deposits are generally less well sorted and contain more clay than the fluvioglacial deposits.

Modern and older Flandrian beach deposits have also been worked for sand and gravel in several places. Two of the largest and most recent operations were at North Somercotes [432 960 to 426 965] and near Patrington Haven [3246 1985 to 3288 1956]. The gravels are generally poorly sorted and contain abundant marine shells. Most of these workings have been stopped by sterilisation of remaining resources by residential and commercial development, as at Cleethorpes and North Somercotes,

or because they aggravated coastal erosion, for example at Spurn. Thicknesses of up to 15 m of sand are recorded at places within the Flandrian marine alluvium of Sunk Island and the Lincolnshire Marsh coast, but the deposits may be too fine grained on the whole to be of significant economic use.

Dredged gravel from offshore deposits, which is landed at several wharves in Hull, comes from licensed areas east of this district. It is probably mostly from thin (1 to 2 m) lag gravels originating from winnowed till, but thicker gravels near New Sand Hole, about 10 km east of Kilnsea, may have been produced by tidal scour and deposition (Nunny and Chillingworth, 1986).

TIDAL POWER

Tentative proposals, the most recent in 1986–1987 by the Association of Yorkshire and Humberside Chambers of Commerce, have been made to harness the tidal energy of the Humber estuary by building a barrage across it at some point between Grimsby and Hull. At the time of writing there appears to be no immediate prospect of any plan being implemented.

UNDERGROUND STORAGE

The Welton Chalk formation beneath South Killingholme has been found to have an ideal combination of physical factors (proximity to an oil refinery, sufficient depth to maintain pressure, effective impermeability because of moisture content, and workability) to act as a host for storage caverns (The Quarterly Journal of Engineering Geology, 1985) to hold liquified hydrocarbon gases such as propane and butane. The fuels are held in a liquid state at minimal expense, without recourse to artificial maintenance processes such as freezing or pumping.

APPENDIX 1

Key boreholes

* indicates boreholes from which BGS holds core and/or samples
† indicates boreholes for which BGS holds geophysical logs

* **Thoresway Borehole** (TF19NE/14) [1640 9632] 79 m
Ferriby Chalk, Carstone, Roach, Tealby Formation, Claxby Ironstone, Spilsby Sandstone.

* **Kilnsea Fort Borehole** (TA41NW/3B) [4171 1617] 305 m
Skipsea Till, Basement Till, glacial and/or interglacial sand and gravel, Flamborough Chalk.

† **Winestead Borehole** (TA22SE/7) [2741 2433] 2004.06 m
Skipsea Till, glacial and/or interglacial sand and gravel, Kirmington Channel deposits (laminated clay), Flamborough to Ferriby Chalk formations, 'Ancholme Clay Group', 'Redbourne Group', Lias, Penarth Group, Mercia Mudstone Group, Sherwood Sandstone Group, Zechstein, Basal Permian Sands, Coal Measures.

†* **Cleethorpes Borehole** (TA30NW/51) [3023 0709] 2100.1 m
Drift deposits including Skipsea Till, Flamborough to Ferriby Chalk formations, Carstone, Roach, Tealby Formation, Claxby Ironstone, Spilsby Sandstone, 'Ancholme Clay Group', 'Redbourne Group', Lias, Penarth Group, Mercia Mudstone Group, Sherwood Sandstone Group, Zechstein, Basal Permian Sands, Coal Measures.

†* **Tetney Lock Borehole** (TA30SW/83) [3325 0090] 2851.4 m
Marine and Estuarine Alluvium, Skipsea Till, Burnham to Ferriby Chalk formations, Carstone, Roach, Tealby Formation, Claxby Ironstone, Spilsby Sandstone Group, 'Ancholme Clay Group', 'Redbourne Group', Lias, Penarth Group, Mercia Mudstone Group, Sherwood Sandstone Group, Zechstein, Basal Permian Sands, Coal Measures, Millstone Grit.

†* **South Killingholme (Geostore) SK1 Borehole** (TA11NE/113) [1783 1764] 211.97 m
Marine and Estuarine Alluvium, Glacial Sand and Gravel, Skipsea Till, Burnham to Ferriby Chalk formations, Carstone.

†* **Killingholme (NIREX) Boreholes:**
DG1 [1498 1908] 206.15 m
Skipsea Till, Burnham, Welton and Ferribly Chalk fomaions, Carstone, 'Ancholme Clay Group'.

BH37 [1732 1905] 127.16 m
Marine and Estuarine Alluvium, Skipsea Till, Flamborough and Burnham Chalk formations.

* **IGS North Humberside Boreholes:**
No. 1 (TA21NW/14) [2348 1899] 64.62 m
Marine and Estuarine Alluvium, Skipsea Till, ?Kirmington Channel deposits (laminated clay), ?Anglian till, Flamborough and ?Burnham Chalk formations.

† No. 3. (TA21NE/10) [2756 1677] 167.64 m
Marine and Estuarine Alluvium, Skipsea Till, ?interglacial sand and gravel, Flamborough and Burnham Chalk formations.

No. 4 (TA31NE/7) [3931 1719] 56.39 m
Blown Sand, Storm Beach Deposits, Marine and Estuarine Alluvium, Skipsea Till, Basement Till, glacial and ?interglacial silt and sand, Flamborough Chalk.

Brocklesby area (Richard Thomas and Baldwin) Boreholes:
* No 9 (Habrough) (TA11SW/10b) [1458 1350] 473.05 m
Drift; Burnham, Welton and Ferriby Chalk formations, Carone, 'Ancholme Clay Group', 'Redbourne Group', Lias.

* No 10 (Brocklesby) (TA11SW/10c) [1418 1103] 478.38 m
Drift; Burnham, Welton and Ferriby Chalk formations, Carstone, 'Ancholme Clay Group', 'Redbourne Group', Lias.

†* No 11 (Roxton Wood) (TA11SE/119) [1651 1180] 515.42 m
Drift; Burnham, Welton and Ferriby Chalk formations, Carstone, Tealby Formation, Claxby Ironstone, Spilsby Sandstone, 'Ancholme Clay Group', 'Redbourne Group', Lias.

* No 14 (Carr Leys Wood) (TA11SW/86) [1429 1245] 467.26 m
Drift; Burnham, Welton and Ferriby Chalk formations, Carstone, 'Ancholme Clay Group', 'Redbourne Group', Lias.

Salt End: Many site investigation boreholes showing diverse Pleistocene sequences, e.g.:

Air Products Ltd Borehole No 4 (TA12NE/70) [1633 2858] 48.25 m
Marine and Estuarine Alluvium, Skipsea Till, glacial and/or interglacial sand and gravel, channel deposits (laminated clay), ?Anglian till, Flamborough Chalk.

BP Chemicals Ammonia Plant Borehole No 80 (TA12NE/100) [1606 2751] 30.41 m
Marine and Estuarine Alluvium, Peat, Skipsea Till including glacial sand and gravel bed, glacial and/or interglacial sand and gravel including a peat bed, Flamborough Chalk.

Key sections

a   Cliffs along the North Sea coast of Holderness from Sand-le-Mere [3202 3099] to Easington [4082 1873] and at Kilnsea Fort [4175 1624 to 4814 1600]: Drift, mostly Devensian till. Due to coastal erosion the exposures are constantly changing. Especially noteworthy during the resurvey were sections at The Runnell [368 248]: Devensian/Flandrian 'mere' deposits; Old Hive [3803 2306]: Skipsea and Withernsea tills with associated sand and gravel; Dimlington High Ground and neighbourhood [385 225 to 403 197]: Basement, Skipsea and Withernsea tills,Devensian Glacial Sand and Gravel and the ?proglacial Dimlington Silts.

b   Keyingham Gravel Pit [242 255]: Skipsea and Withernsea tills, Kelsey Hill Gravels.

c   Shoreline [2890 1667 to 3144 1777] near East Bank Farm, Sunk Island: low cliffs in Flandrian estuarine sediments.

d   Geostore gas storage caverns, South Killingholme [TA 174 172]: no longer accessible, but they provided important information on the Welton Chalk Formation during the resurvey (see *Quarterly Journal of Engineering Geology*, 1985).

e   Sand pits [151 100] at The Grange, Keelby: Glacial Sand and Gravel.

f   Irby Dale Quarry [1923 0518]: Welton and Burnham Chalk formations.

g   Quarry at Swallow Vale [174 043]: Welton Chalk.

h   West Ravendale Main Pit [227 000]: basal Burnham Chalk.

i   'Ludborough Quarry' [282 944]: Welton and Burnham Chalk formations.

j   North Ormsby Quarry [288 935]: Welton and Burnham Chalk formations.

APPENDIX 2

BGS photographs

Copies of these photographs are deposited in the library of the British Geological Survey, Keyworth, Nottingham NG12 5GG, the library at the BGS, Murchison House, West Mains Road, Edinburgh, EH9 3LA, and in the BGS Information Office at the Geological Museum, Exhibition Road, London, SW7 2DE. Prints and slides of most subjects can be supplied at a standard tariff.

Series A

5430   The Spurn Peninsula at Kilnsea Warren
14850   Ludborough Quarry, North Ormsby, general view. [2817 9441]
14851   Ludborough Quarry, North Ormsby, part of the quarry face. [2817 9441]
14852   Ludborough Quarry, North Ormsby, as above, different lighting. [2817 9441]
14853   Ludborough Quarry, North Ormsby, part of the quarry face. [2817 9441]
14855   Ludborough Quarry, part of the Burnham Chalk Formation. [2820 9441]
14856   Ludborough Quarry, showing good development of the North Ormsby Marl [2822 9441]
14857   Ludborough Quarry, upper quarry face, looking north-west. [2822 9441]
14858   Ludborough Quarry, upper quarry face, looking north-west. [2822 9441]
14859   Ludborough Quarry, upper quarry face, looking north-north-east. [2822 9441]
14860   Ludborough Quarry, North Ormsby Marl, with platy chalk above and below. [2822 9441]
14861   North Ormsby Quarry, showing part of the Burnham Chalk Formation. [2864 9356]
14862   North Ormsby Quarry, showing part of the quarry face. [2864 9356]
14863   North Ormsby Quarry, closer view of face shown in the two foregoing photographs [2864 9356]
14864   North Ormsby Quarry, showing Burnham Chalk Formation. [286 935]
14865   North Ormsby Quarry, showing Burnham Chalk Formation, closer view. [286 935]
14866   North Ormsby Quarry, lower face of the quarry. [2872 9350]
14867   West Ravendale Quarry, Burnham Chalk–Welton Chalk boundary. [227 000]
14868   West Ravendale Quarry, closer view of the foregoing field of view. [227 000]
14869   Hatcliffe–Ravendale Road: Round Hill and Home Walk Plantations. [216 003]
14870   Hatcliffe–Ravendale Road: Round Hill and Home Walk Plantations. [216 003]

14871   Irby Dale, Irby upon Humber. [1950 0500]
14872   250 m NNW of Dimlington High Land. [3897 2189]
14873   Foreshore, north of Easington. [4037 1970]
14874   Low-tide foreshore, north of Easington. [4046 1959]
14875   Low-tide foreshore, north of Easington. [4046 1959]
14876   Cliff foot, Dimlington High Land. [3910 2169]
14877   Cliff foot, Dimlington High Land, looking approximately NW. [3910 2169]
14878   Foreshore, north of Holmpton, near Withernsea. [370 244]
14879   Close-up of a site just off the field of the above photograph. [370 244]
14880   Old Hive, Holmpton, near Withernsea. [3806 2306]
14881   Close-up of part of the above field of view. [3806 2306]
14882   West side of Keyingham Sand and Gravel Pit. [2378 2546]
14883   West side of Keyingham Sand and Gravel Pit. [2378 2546]
14884   East side of Keyingham Sand and Gravel Pit. [2418 2562]
14885   View of strata in right angle section to the photograph above. [2418 2562]
14886   The Runnell, Holmpton, near Withernsea. [3669 2480]
14887   Humber Estuary coast on south side of Sunk Island. [2973 1704]
14888   Humber Estuary coast on south side of Sunk Island, view looking west. [2973 1704]
14889   Low sea cliffs on south side of Sunk Island. [2967 1703]
14890   Low sea cliffs on south side of Sunk Island. [2976 1707]

Series L

1598   Chalk sequence Middle to Upper Chalk, Ulceby. [107 134]
2994   Sand and gravel pit, Keelby. [1517 1006]
2995   Sand and gravel pit, Keelby. [1517 1006]
2996   Sand and gravel pit, Keelby. [1515 1005]
2997   Sand and gravel pit, Keelby. [151 100]
2998   Sand and gravel pit, Keelby. [151 100]
2999   Sand and gravel pit, Keelby. [151 100]
3000   Sand and gravel pit, Keelby. [151 100]
3001   Sand and gravel pit, Keelby. [151 098]
3002   Chalk pit Irby Dale. [1930 0515]
3003   Chalk pit Irby Dale. [1925 0520]
3004   Chalk pit Irby Dale. [190 053]
3005   Glacial meltwater channel, Irby Dale. [190 053]
3006   Irby Dale, small chalk pits. [193 954]
3007   Irby Dale, Chalk and Glacial Sand and Gravel. [1935 0545]
3008   Glacial features, Irby Dale. [193 054]
3009   Raised-beach feature, Humberston. [3275 0565]

REFERENCES

Most of the references listed below are held in the Library of the British Geological Survey at Keyworth, Nottingham. Copies of the references can be purchased subject to the current copyright legislation.

ALABASTER, C, and STRAW, A. 1976. The Pleistocene context of faunal remains and artefacts discovered at Welton-le-Wold, Lincolnshire. *Proceedings of the Yorkshire Geological Society*, Vol. 41, 75–94.

AL-BAKRI, D H. 1980. The sediments of the Humber estuary mouth and the adjacent coastline. Unpublished PhD thesis, University of Sheffield.

ALLISON, K J (editor). 1984. *A history of the county of York, East Riding. Volume V, Holderness: southern part.* (Oxford: Oxford University Press.)

AMBROSE K, and IVIMEY-COOK, H I C. 1982. The Barby (IGS) Borehole, near Daventry, Northamptonshire. *Report of the Institute of Geological Sciences*, No. 82/1, 36–40.

ANON. 1978. *South Humberbank Salinity Research Project: Final Report to the Anglian Water Authority.* Study carried out by the Department of Geological Sciences and the Department of Civil Engineering, University of Birmingham.

ANON. 1985. *Yorkshire Chalk groundwater model study: final report to the Yorkshire Water Authority, Leeds.* Study carried out by the Department of Geological Sciences and the Department of Civil Engineering, University of Birmingham.

ASHTON, M. 1980. The stratigraphy of the Lincolnshire Limestone Formation (Bajocian) in Lincolnshire and Rutland (Leicestershire). *Proceedings of the Geologists' Association*, Vol. 91, 203–233.

ATKINSON, J H, LEWIN, P I, and NG, C L. 1985. Undrained strength and consolidation of a clay till. *Proceedings of the International Conference on Construction in glacial tills, Edinburgh, 1985*, 49–54.

BARKER, R D, LLOYD, J W, and PEACH, D W. 1984. The use of resistivity and gamma logging in lithostratigraphical studies of the Chalk in Lincolnshire and South Humberside. *The Quarterly Journal of Engineering Geology*, Vol. 17, 71–80.

BARNES, F A, and KING, A M. 1953. The Lincolnshire coastline and the 1953 storm flood. *Geography*, Vol. 38, 141–160.

BECKETT, S C. 1981. Pollen diagrams from Holderness, North Humberside. *Journal of Biogeography*, Vol. 8, 177–198.

BELL, F G, and FORSTER, A. 1991. The clay deposits of Holderness. 111–118 in Quaternary Engineering Geology. *Proceedings of the 25th Annual Conference of the Engineering Group of the Geological Society (London), Edinburgh, 1989.*

BERENDSEN, H J A, and ZAGWIJN, W H. 1984. Some conclusions reached at the symposium on geological changes in the western Netherlands during the period 1100–1300 AD. 225–229 in Geological changes in the western Netherlands during the period 1000–1300 AD. BERENDSEN, H J A, and ZAGWIJN, W H (editors). *Geologie en Mijnbouw*, Vol. 63.

BERRIDGE, N G. 1985. Geological notes and local details for 1:10 000 Sheets TA10SW (part) and 10SE: Cabourne and Swallow. *British Geological Survey Technical Report*, WA/88/8.

— 1986. Geological notes and local details for 1:10 000 Sheets TA10NW (part), TA10NE and TA20NW: Great Limber, Riby and Laceby. *British Geological Survey Technical Report*, WA/88/7.

— 1987a. *Geological notes and local details for 1:10 560 Sheet TA20SW: Beelsby and Barnoldby le Beck.* (Keyworth: British Geological Survey.)

—1987b. Geological notes and local details for 1:10 000 Sheets TF29NW, TF29NE and TF29SE(N): Wold Newton and Ludborough. *British Geological Survey Technical Report*, WA/88/19.

— 1988. Geological notes and local details for 1:10 000 Sheets TA32 and TA33: Tunstall, Withernsea, Patrington and Dimlington. *British Geological Survey Technical Report*, WA/88/16.

BISAT, W S. 1939. The relationship of the 'Basement Clays' of Dimlington, Bridlington and Filey bays. *The Naturalist* (Hull), 133–135 and 161–168.

— 1940. Older and newer drift in East Yorkshire. *Proceedings of the Yorkshire Geological Society*, Vol. 24, 137–151.

— and DELL, J A. 1941. On the occurrence of a bed containing moss in the boulder clays of Dimlington. *Proceedings of the Yorkshire Geological Society*, Vol. 24, 219–222.

BLACKHAM, A, FLENLEY, J R, and HALL, A. 1984. The Flandrian vegetational history of the meres of Holderness. Chapter 7 of Late Quaternary environments and Man in Holderness. GILBERTSON, D D and others. *British Archaeological Reports, British Series*, No. 134.

BOTT, M H P. 1988. The Market Weighton anomaly — granite or graben? *Proceedings of the Yorkshire Geological Society*, Vol. 47, 47–53.

— ROBINSON, J, and KOHNSTAMM, M A. 1978. Granite beneath Market Weighton, east Yorkshire. *Journal of the Geological Society of London*, Vol.135, 535–543.

— SWINBURN, P M, and LONG, R E. 1984. Deep structure and origin of the Northumberland and Stainmore troughs. *Proceedings of the Yorkshire Geological Society*, Vol. 44, 479–495.

BOWEN, D Q, RICHMOND, G M, FULLERTON, D S, SIBRAVA, V, FULTON, R J, and VELICHKO, A A. 1986a. Correlation of Quaternary glaciation in the Northern Hemisphere. Chart in Quaternary glaciations in the Northern Hemisphere. SIBRAVA, V, BOWEN, D Q, and RICHMOND, G M (editors). *Quaternary Science Reviews*, Vol. 5.

— ROSE, J, McCABE, A M, and SUTHERLAND, D G. 1986b. Correlation of Quaternary glaciations in England, Ireland, Scotland and Wales. 229–339 in Quaternary glaciations in the Northern Hemisphere. SIBRAVA, V, BOWEN, D Q, and RICHMOND, G M (editors). *Quaternary Science Reviews*, Vol. 5.

BOWER, C R, and FARMERY, J R. 1910. The zones of the Lower Chalk of Lincolnshire. *Proceedings of the Geologists' Association*, Vol. 21, 333–359.

BOYLAN, P J. 1966. The Pleistocene deposits of Kirmington, Lincolnshire. *Mercian Geologist*, Vol. 1, 339–350.

BRADSHAW, M J, and BATE, R H. 1982. Lincolnshire borehole proves greater extent of the Scarborough Formation (Jurassic Bajocian). *Journal of Micropalaeontology*, Vol. 1, 141–147.

— and PENNEY, S R. 1982. A cored Jurassic sequence from north Lincolnshire: stratigraphy, facies analysis and regional context. *Geological Magazine*, Vol. 119, 113–134.

BRANDON, A, SUMBLER, M G, and IVIMEY-COOK, H I C. 1990. A revised lithostratigraphy for the Lower and Middle Lias (Lower Jurassic) east of Nottingham, England. *Proceedings of the Yorkshire Geological Society,* Vol. 48, 121–141.

BRITISH GEOLOGICAL SURVEY. 1987. *Hot dry rock potential of the United Kingdom. Investigation of the geothermal potential of the UK.* (Keyworth, Nottingham: British Geological Survey.)

— 1990. Spurn. Sheet 53°N–00° including part of Humber–Trent. Sheet 53°N–02°W. Sea bed sediments. 1:250 000. (Southampton: Ordnance Survey for British Geological Survey.)

BROMLEY, R G, SCHULZ, M-G, and PEAKE, N B. 1975. Paramoudras: giant flints, long burrows and the early diagenesis of chalks. *Det Kongelige Danske Videnskabernes Selskab Biologiske Skrifter*, Vol. 20, Pt 10, 31 pp.

BURNETT, A. 1904. The Upper Chalk of north Lincolnshire. *Geological Magazine*, Decade 5, Vol. 1.

CASEY, R. 1973. The ammonite succession at the Jurassic–Cretaceous boundary in eastern England. 193–266 *in* The Boreal Lower Cretaceous. CASEY, R and RAWSON, P F (editors). *Geological Journal Special Issue*, No. 5.

CATT, J A, and DIGBY, P G N. 1988. Boreholes in the Wolstonian Basement Till at Easington, Holderness. *Proceedings of the Yorkshire Geological Society*, Vol. 47, 21–27.

— and MADGETT, P A. 1981. The work of W S Bisat FRS on the Yorkshire Coast. 119–136 in *The Quaternary in Britain*. NEALE, J and FLENLEY, J (editors). (Oxford: Pergamon Press.)

— and PENNY, L F. 1966. The Pleistocene deposits of Holderness, East Yorkshire. *Proceedings of the Yorkshire Geological Society*, Vol. 35, 375–420.

CENTRAL ELECTRICITY GENERATING BOARD and UK NIREX LIMITED. 1987. *NIREX preapplication studies: Killingholme Site Investigation (1986) Contract KHN/C/200: Factual Report.* Volume 2: Borehole Records and Volume 10: Geophysical Borehole Logging.

CHADWICK, R A. 1985a. End Jurassic–early Cretaceous sedimentation and subsidence (late Portlandian to Barremian), and the late-Cimmerian unconformity. Chapter 12 in *Atlas of onshore sedimentary basins in England and Wales*. WHITTAKER, A W (editor). (Glasgow: Blackie.)

— 1985b. Overview. Chapter 16 in *Atlas of onshore sedimentary basins in England and Wales*. WHITTAKER, A W (editor). (Glasgow: Blackie.)

— PHARAOH, T C, and SMITH, N J P. 1989. Lower crustal heterogeneity beneath Britain from deep seismic reflection data. *Journal of the Geological Society of London*, Vol. 146, 617–630.

CLAYTON, C J. 1986. The chemical environment of flint formation in Upper Cretaceous chalks. 43–54 in *The scientific study of flint and chalk: proceedings of the Fourth International Flint Symposium, 1983*. SIEVEKING, G de G, and HART, M B (editors). (Cambridge: Cambridge University Press.)

COPE, J C W, GETTY, T A, HOWARTH, M K, MORTON, N, and TORRENS, H S. 1980a. A correlation of the Jurassic rocks in the British Isles. Part One: Introduction and Lower Jurassic. *Special Report of the Geological Society of London*, No. 14.

— DUFF, K L, PARSONS, C F, TORRENS, H S, WIMBLEDON, W A, and WRIGHT, J K. 1980b. A correlation of the Jurassic rocks in the British Isles. Part Two: Middle and Upper Jurassic. *Special Report of the Geological Society of London*, No. 15.

CORNFORD, C. 1986. Source rocks and hydrocarbons of the North Sea. 197–236 in *Introduction to the petroleum geology of the North Sea*. GLENNIE, K W (editor). (Oxford: Blackwell Scientific Publications.)

CORNWELL, J D, and WALKER, A S D. 1989. Geophysical investigations. 25–51 in *Metallogenic models and exploration criteria for buried carbonate-hosted ore deposits — a multidisciplinary study in eastern England*. PLANT, J A and JONES, D G (editors). (Keyworth, Nottingham: British Geological Survey and London: The Institution of Mining and Metallurgy.)

COX, B M, and GALLOIS, R W. 1981. The stratigraphy of the Kimmeridge Clay of the Dorset type area and its correlation with some other Kimmeridgian sequences. *Report of the Institute of Geological Sciences*, No. 80/4, 1–44.

DE BOER, G. 1964. Spurn Head: its history and evolution. *Transactions of the Institute of British Geographers*, Vol. 34, 71–89.

— 1981. Spurn Point: erosion and protection after 1849. 206–215 in *The Quaternary in Britain*. NEALE, J W, and FLENLEY, J (editors). (Oxford: Pergamon Press.)

DENMAN, N E. 1979. Physical characters of the Humber. *Natural Environment Research Council Publication*, Series C, No. 20, 5–8.

DERBYSHIRE, E, FOSTER, C, LOVE, M A, and EDGE, M J. 1984. Pleistocene lithostratigraphy of north-east England: a sedimentological approach to the Holderness sequence. 371–384 in *Correlation of Quaternary chronologies*. MAHANEY, W C (editor). (Norwich: Geo Books.)

DONATO, J A, and MEGSON, J B. 1990. A buried granite batholith beneath the East Midland Shelf of the Southern North Sea Basin. *Journal of the Geological Society of London*, Vol. 147, 133–140.

DOWNING, R A, and HOWITT, F. 1969. Saline ground-waters in the Carboniferous rocks of the English East Midlands in relation to the geology. *Quarterly Journal of Engineering Geology*, Vol. 1, 241–269.

— ALLEN, D J, BIRD, M J, GALE, I N, KAY, R L F, and SMITH, I F. 1985. *Cleethorpes No. 1 Geothermal Well — a preliminary assessment of the resource. Investigation of the geothermal potential of the UK.* (London: HMSO for British Geological Survey.)

EVANS, C J, KIMBELL, G S, and ROLLIN, K E. 1988. *Hot dry rock potential in urban areas. Investigation of the geothermal potential of the UK.* (Keyworth, Nottingham: British Geological Survey.)

EYLES, N, and SLADEN, J A. 1981. Stratigraphy and geotechnical properties of weathered lodgement till in Northumberland, England. *Quarterly Journal of Engineering Geology*, Vol. 14, 129–141.

FISHER, M J. 1986. Triassic. 113–132 in *Introduction to the petroleum geology of the North Sea*. GLENNIE, K W (editor). (Oxford: Blackwell Scientific Publications.)

FLETCHER, T P. 1988. Geological notes and local details for 1:10 560 Sheet TF 19 SE and the northern part of 1:10 000 Sheet TF 29 SW: Tealby, Kirmond le Mire and Binbrook. *British Geological Survey Technical Report* WA/88/18.

FOSTER, S S D. 1968. Report on the groundwater hydrology and Resources of Hydrometric Area 26 (Hull Rivers): Part I —The Jurassic rocks between Market Weighton and the Humber. *Institute of Geological Sciences Open-File Report* WD/68/4.

— PARRY, E L, and CHILTON, P J. 1974. Groundwater resources development and saline water intrusion in the Chalk aquifer of

North Humberside. *Institute of Geological Sciences Open-File Report,* WD/74/4.

FOX-STRANGWAYS, C. 1906. The water supply (from underground sources) of the East Riding of Yorkshire. *Memoir of the Geological Survey of England and Wales.*

FRASER, A J, NASH, D F, STEELE, R P, and EBDON, C C. 1990. A regional assessment of the intra-Carboniferous play of northern England. 417–439 *in* Classic petroleum provinces. BROOK, J (editor). *Special Publication of the Geological Society of London,* No. 50.

GALE, I N, SMITH, I F, and DOWNING, R A. 1983. *The post-Carboniferous rocks of the East Yorkshire and Lincolnshire Basin. Investigation of the geothermal potential of the UK.* (London: HMSO for Institute of Geological Sciences.)

— and HOLLIDAY, D W. 1985. The geothermal resources of eastern England. 55–63 in *European Geothermal Update. Proceedings of the 3rd International Seminar on the results of EC Geothermal Energy Research.* STRUB, A S, and UNGEMACH, P (editors). (Dordrecht: D Reidel.)

— and ROLLIN, K E. 1986. Assessment of the geothermal resources. 132–147 in *Geothermal energy — the potential in the United Kingdom.* DOWNING, R A, and GRAY, D A (editors). (London: HMSO.)

GALLOIS, R W. 1979. Geological investigations for the Wash Water Storage Scheme. *Report of the Institute of Geological Sciences,* No. 78/19.

— 1988. Geology of the country around Ely. *Memoir of the British Geological Survey,* Sheet 173 (England and Wales).

— and COX, B M. 1976. The stratigraphy of the Lower Kimmeridge Clay of eastern England. *Proceedings of the Yorkshire Geological Society,* Vol. 41, 13–26.

— — 1977. The stratigraphy of the Middle and Upper Oxfordian sediments of Fenland. *Proceedings of the Geologists' Association,* Vol. 88, 207–228.

GAUNT, G D, FLETCHER, T P, and WOOD, C J. 1992. Geology of the country around Kingston upon Hull and Brigg. *Memoir of the British Geological Survey,* Sheets 80 and 89 (England and Wales).

— IVIMEY-COOK, H C, PENN, I E, and COX, B M. 1980. Mesozoic rocks proved by IGS boreholes in the Humber and Acklam areas. *Report of the Institute of Geological Sciences,* No. 79/13, 1–34.

— and SMITH, E G. 1978. 38 in *Annual report for 1977.* (London: Institute of Geological Sciences.)

— and TOOLEY, M J. 1974. Flandrian sea-level changes in the Humber estuary. *Bulletin of the Geological Survey of Great Britain,* No. 48, 25–40.

GLENNIE, K W. 1986. Early Permian-Rotliegend. 63–85 in *Introduction to the petroleum geology of the North Sea.* GLENNIE, K W (editor). (Oxford: Blackwell Scientific Publications.)

GRAY, D A. 1958. Electrical resistivity marker bands in the Lower and Middle Chalk of the London Basin. *Bulletin of the Geological Survey of Great Britain,* No. 15, 85–95.

HANCOCK, J M. 1975. The petrology of the Chalk. *Proceedings of the Geologists' Association,* Vol. 86, 499–535.

HARLAND, R, and DOWNIE, C. 1969. The dinoflagellates of the interglacial deposits at Kirmington, Lincolnshire. *Proceedings of the Yorkshire Geological Society,* Vol. 37, 231–237.

HARWOOD, G M, and SMITH D B (editors). 1986. The English Zechstein and related topics. *Special Publication of the Geological Society of London,* No. 22.

HILL, W. 1888. On the lower beds of the Upper Cretaceous Series in Lincolnshire and Yorkshire. *Quarterly Journal of the Geological Society of London,* No. 44, 320–367.

HOLLIDAY, D W. 1986. Devonian and Carboniferous basins. 84–110 in *Geothermal energy — the potential in the United Kingdom.* DOWNING R A and GRAY, D A (editors). (London: HMSO.)

HOLLOWAY, S. 1985. Triassic: Sherwood Sandstone Group (excluding the Kinerton Sandstone and the Lenton Sandstone Formation). Chapter 5 in *Atlas of onshore sedimentary basins in England and Wales.* WHITTAKER, A W (editor). (Glasgow: Blackie.)

HORTON, A. 1989. Geology of the Peterborough district. *Memoir of the British Geological Survey,* Sheet 158 (England and Wales).

— and POOLE, E G. 1977. The lithostratigraphy of three geophysical marker horizons in the Lower Lias of Oxfordshire. *Bulletin of the Geological Survey of Great Britain,* Vol. 62, 13–24.

— SHEPHARD-THORN, E R, and THURRELL, R G. 1974. The geology of the new town of Milton Keynes. *Report of the Institute of Geological Sciences,* No. 74/16.

HOWARTH, M K. 1980. The Toarcian age of the upper part of the Marlstone Rock Bed of England. *Palaeontology,* Vol. 23, 637–656.

— and RAWSON, P F. 1965. The Liassic succession in a clay pit at Kirton Lindsey, north Lincolnshire. *Geological Magazine,* Vol. 102, 261–266

HOWITT, F, and BRUNSTROM, R G W. 1966. The continuation of the East Midlands Coal Measures into Lincolnshire. *Proceedings of the Yorkshire Geological Society,* Vol. 35, 549–564.

HUMPHRIES, D W. 1973. The sedimentology of the Humber Estuary. [6 pages] in *The Humber Estuary: Proceedings of a joint symposium [of] the University of Hull/Humber Advisory group. December 12–13, 1973.* JONES, N V (editor). (Hull: University of Hull.)

HUTCHINSON, J N. 1986. Cliffs and shores in cohesive materials: geotechnical and engineering aspects. 1–44 in *Proceedings of a Symposium on Cohesive Shores, Burlington, Ontario.* SKAFEL, M G (editor). (Burlington: Associate Committee for Research on Shoreline Erosions and Sedimentation and National Research Council, Canada.)

INSTITUTE OF GEOLOGICAL SCIENCES. 1967. Hydrogeological map of North and East Lincolnshire. 1:126 720. (London: Cook, Hammond and Kell Ltd for Institute of Geological Sciences.)

— 1980. Hydrogeological map of East Yorkshire. 1:100 000. (Southampton: Ordnance Survey for Institute of Geological Sciences.)

JEANS C V. 1973. The Market Weighton structure: tectonics, sedimentation and diagenesis during the Cretaceous. *Proceedings of the Yorkshire Geological Society,* Vol. 39, 409–444.

— 1980. Early submarine lithification in the Red Chalk and Lower Chalk of eastern England: a bacterial control model and its implications. *Proceedings of the Yorkshire Geological Society,* Vol. 43, 81–157.

JELGERSMA, S. 1979. Sea-level changes in the North Sea basin. 233–248 in The Quaternary history of the North Sea. OELE, E SCHUTTENHELM,, R T E, and WIGGERS, A J (editors). *Acta Universitatis Upsaliensis Symposia Universitatis Upsaliensis Annum Quingentesimum Celebrantis,* No. 2.

JUDD, J W. 1867. On the strata which form the base of the Lincolnshire Wolds. *Quarterly Journal of the Geological Society of London,* Vol. 23, 227–251.

JUKES-BROWNE, A J. 1885. The boulder-clays of Lincolnshire. *Quarterly Journal of the Geological Society of London*, No. 41, 114–132.

— and HILL, W. 1900–1904. The Cretaceous rocks of Britain. *Memoir of the Geological Survey of Great Britain* [in 3 volumes].

KELLY, S R A, and RAWSON, P F. 1979. Some late Jurassic–mid-Cretaceous sections on the East Midlands Shelf, England, as demonstrated on a field meeting, 18–20 May, 1979. *Proceedings of the Geologists' Association*, Vol. 94, 65–73.

KENT, P E. 1953. The Rhaetic Beds of the north-east Midlands. *Proceedings of the Yorkshire Geological Society*, Vol. 29, 117–119.

— 1955. The Market Weighton Structure. *Proceedings of the Yorkshire Geological Society*, Vol. 30, 197–227.

— 1966. The structure of the concealed Carboniferous rocks of north-eastern England. *Proceedings of the Yorkshire Geological Society*, Vol. 35, 323–352.

— 1967. A contour map of the sub-Carboniferous surface in the north-east Midlands. *Proceedings of the Yorkshire Geological Society*, Vol 36, 127–133.

— 1974. Structural history. 13–28 in *The geology and mineral resources of Yorkshire*. RAYNER, D H, and HEMINGWAY, J E (editors). (Leeds: Yorkshire Geological Society.)

— 1980a. Subsidence and uplift in east Yorkshire and Lincolnshire: a double inversion. *Proceedings of the Yorkshire Geological Society*, Vol. 42, 505–524.

— 1980b. *British regional geology: eastern England from the Tees to the Wash* (2nd edition). (London: HMSO for the Institute of Geological Sciences.)

KIRBY, G A. 1985. *Cleethorpes No. 1 Geothermal Well: geological well completion report. Investigation of the geothermal potential of the UK.* (Keyworth: British Geological Survey.)

— SMITH, K, SMITH, N J P, and SWALLOW, P. 1987. Oil and gas generation in eastern England. 171–180 in *Petroleum geology of north-west Europe*, Vol. 1. BROOKS, J, and GLENNIE, K W (editors). (London: Graham and Trotman.)

— and SWALLOW, P W. 1987. Tectonism and sedimentation in the Flamborough Head region of north-east England. *Proceedings of the Yorkshire Geological Society*, Vol. 46, 301–309.

LAMPLUGH, G W. 1881. On the Bridlington and Dimlington glacial shell-beds. *Geological Magazine*, Decade 2, Vol. 8, 535–546.

— 1896. On the Speeton Series in Yorkshire and Lincolnshire. *Quarterly Journal of the Geological Society of London*, Vol. 52, 179–220.

— 1919. On a boring at Kilnsea, Holderness. *Summary of Progress of the Geological Survey of Great Britain for 1918*, 63–64.

LEEDER, M R. 1982. Upper Palaeozoic Basins of the British Isles — Caledonide inheritance versus Hercynian plate margin processes. *Journal of the Geological Society of London*, Vol. 139, 479–491.

LOTT, G K, and WARRINGTON, G. 1988. A review of the latest Triassic succession in the UK sector of the Southern North Sea Basin. *Proceedings of the Yorkshire Geological Society*, Vol. 47, 139–147.

McCAVE, I N. 1973. Mud in the North Sea. 75–100 in *North Sea science*. GOLDBERG, E D (editor). (Cambridge, Mass.: MIT Press.)

— 1987. Fine sediment sources and sinks around the East Anglian coast (UK). *Journal of the Geological Society of London*, Vol. 144, 149–152.

McQUILLIN, R, ARNOLD, S E, TULLY, M C, and HULL, J H. 1969. Cruise report, Humber investigations, 1968. *Report of the Institute of Geological Sciences*, No. 69/3.

MADGETT, P A, and CATT, J A. 1978. Petrography, stratigraphy and weathering of Late Pleistocene tills in East Yorkshire, Lincolnshire and north Norfolk. *Proceedings of the Yorkshire Geological Society*, Vol. 42, 55–108.

MARIE, J P P. 1975. Rotliegendes stratigraphy and diagenesis. 205–211 in *Petroleum and the continental shelf of north-west Europe, Vol. 1, Geology*. WOODLAND, A W (editor). (London: Applied Science Publishers Ltd.)

MARSLAND, A, and POWELL, J J M. 1985. Field and laboratory investigations of the clay tills at the Building Research Establishment test site at Cowden, Holderness. *Proceedings of the International Conference on Construction in glacial tills, Edinburgh, 1985*, 147–168.

MORTIMORE, R N, and WOOD, C J. 1986. The distribution of flint in the English Chalk with particular reference to the 'Brandon Flint Series' and the high Turonian flint maximum. 7–20 in *The scientific study of flint and chalk: proceedings of the Fourth International Flint Symposium, 1983*. SIEVEKING, G DE G, and HART, M B (editors). (Cambridge: Cambridge University Press.)

MURRAY, K H. 1982. Correlation of electrical resistivity marker bands in the Cenomanian and Turonian Chalk from the London Basin to the Market Weighton area, Yorkshire. *Hydrogeological Department Report, Institute of Geological Sciences*, No. WD/82/5.

— 1986. Correlation of resistivity marker bands in the Cenomanian and Turonian Chalk from the London Basin to east Yorkshire. *Report of the British Geological Survey*, Vol. 17, No. 8.

NOTHOLT, A R G, HIGHLEY, D E, and SLANSKY, M. 1979. Phosphate. *Raw Materials Research and Development Dossiers of the Commission of the European Communities, Brussels*, No. 4.

NUNNY, R S, and CHILLINGWORTH, P C H. 1986. *Marine dredging for sand and gravel*. (London: HMSO for Department of the Environment Minerals Division.)

OAKLEY, K P. 1941. British phosphates Part 3: Lower Cretaceous phosphorites, Isle of Wight to Yorkshire, with supplementary notes on Lincolnshire. *Wartime Pamphlet of the Geological Survey of Great Britain*, No 8.

O'CONNOR, B A. 1987. Short and long term changes in estuary capacity. *Journal of the Geological Society of London*, Vol. 144, 187–195.

PACEY, N R. 1984. Bentonites in the Chalk of central eastern England and their relation to the opening of the north-east Atlantic. *Earth and Planetary Science Letters*, Vol. 67, 48–60.

PATTISON, J, and WILLIAMSON, I T. 1986. The saltern mounds of north-east Lincolnshire. *Proceedings of the Yorkshire Geological Society*, Vol. 46, 77–79.

PENN, I E, COX, B M, and GALLOIS, R W. 1986. Towards precision in stratigraphy: geophysical log correlation of upper Jurassic (including Callovian) strata of the Eastern England Shelf. *Journal of the Geological Society of London*, Vol. 143, 381–410.

PENNY, L F. 1974. Quaternary. 245–264 in *The geology and mineral resources of Yorkshire*. RAYNER, D H, and HEMINGWAY, J E (editors). (Leeds: Yorkshire Geological Society.)

— COOPE, G R, and CATT, J A. 1969. Age and insect fauna of the Dimlington Silts, East Yorkshire. *Nature, London*, Vol. 224, 65–67.

—and RAWSON, P F. 1969. Field meeting in east Yorkshire and north Lincolnshire. *Proceedings of the Geologists' Association*, Vol. 80, 193–218.

PETHICK, J S. 1988. The physical characteristics of the Humber. 31–45 in *A dynamic estuary. Man, nature and the Humber.* JONES, N V (editor). (Hull: Hull University Press.)

PHARAOH, T C, MERRIMAN, R J, WEBB, P C, and BECKINSALE, R D. 1987. The concealed Caledonides of eastern England: preliminary results of a multidisciplinary study. *Proceedings of the Yorkshire Geological Society*, Vol. 46, 355–369.

PHILLIPS, J. 1829. *Illustrations of the geology of Yorkshire. Part 1. The Yorkshire coast.* (York: printed privately.)

PICKWELL, R. 1878. The encroachment of the sea from Spurn Point to Flamborough Head and the works executed to prevent the loss of land. *Proceedings of the Institute of Civil Engineers*, Vol. 51, 191–212.

PRESTWICH, J. 1861. On the occurrence of *Cyrena fluminalis* together with marine shells of Recent species, in beds of sand and gravel over beds of boulder clay near Hull. *Quarterly Journal of the Geological Society of London*, Vol. 17, 446–456.

PRICE, J H. 1957. The hydrogeology of the Spilsby Sandstone. *Hydrogeological Department Report, Institute of Geological Sciences*, No. WD/57/6.

PRINGLE, A W. 1981. Beach development and coastal erosion in Holderness, North Humberside. 194–205 in *The Quaternary in Britain.* NEALE, J, and FLENLEY, J (editors). (Oxford: Pergamon Press.)

— 1985. Holderness coastal erosion and the significance of the ords. *Earth Surface Processes and Landforms*, Vol. 10, 107–124.

QUARTERLY JOURNAL OF ENGINEERING GEOLOGY. 1985. Photographic feature: Liquified petroleum gas caverns at South Killingholme. *The Quarterly Journal of Engineering Geology*, Vol. 18, ii–iv.

REID, C. 1885. The geology of Holderness and the adjoining parts of Yorkshire and Lincolnshire. *Memoir of the Geological Survey of England and Wales*, Sheets 85 and 86 [old series].

RHYS, G H (compiler). 1974. A proposed standard lithostratigraphic nomenclature for the southern North Sea and an outline structural nomenclature for the whole of the (UK) North Sea. *Report of the Institute of Geological Sciences*, No. 74/8, 1–14.

ROBINSON, A H W. 1964. The inshore waters, sediment supply and coastal changes of part of Lincolnshire. *East Midland Geographer*, Vol. 3, 307–321.

ROBINSON, D N. 1970. Coastal evolution in north-east Lincolnshire. *East Midland Geographer*, Vol. 5, 62–70.

— 1984. The Saltfleetby–Theddlethorpe coastline. *Transactions of the Lincolnshire Naturalists' Union*, Vol. 21, 1–12.

ROSE, J. 1985. The Dimlington Stadial/Dimlington Chronozone: a proposal for naming the main glacial episode of the Late Devensian in Britain. *Boreas*, Vol. 14, 225–230.

ROWE, A W. 1929. The zones of the White Chalk of Lincolnshire. *Naturalist*, No. 875, 411–439.

RUDKIN, E H, and OWEN, D M. 1960. The medieval salt industry in the Lindsey Marshland. *Reports and Papers of the Lincolnshire Architectural and Archaeological Society*, Vol. 8, 76–84.

SHEPPARD, J A. 1957. The medieval meres of Holderness. *Transactions of the Institute of British Geographers*, Vol. 23, 75–86.

SLATER, D, and HIGHLEY, D E. 1977. The iron ore deposits in the United Kingdom of Great Britain and Northern Ireland.

393–409 in *The iron ore deposits of Europe and adjacent areas*, Vol. 1. Zitzmann, A (editor). (Hannover: Bundesanstalt für Geowissenschaften und Rohstoffe.)

SMITH, D B. 1989. The late Permian palaeogeography of north-east England. *Proceedings of the Yorkshire Geological Society*, Vol. 47, 285–312.

— BRUNSTROM, R G W, MANNING, P I, SIMPSON, S, and SHOTTON, F W. 1974. Correlation of the Permian rocks of the British Isles. *Special Report of the Geological Society of London*, No. 5.

— HARWOOD, G M, PATTISON, J, and PETTIGREW, T H. 1986. A revised nomenclature for Upper Permian strata in eastern England. 9–17 *in* The English Zechstein and related topics. *Special Publication of the Geological Society of London*, No. 22.

SMITH, I F. 1986. Mesozoic basins. 42–83 in *Geothermal energy — the potential in the United Kingdom.* DOWNING, R A, and GRAY, D A (editors). (London: HMSO.)

SMITH, N J P (compiler). 1985. Pre-Permian geology of the United Kingdom (South), Map 1. 1:100 000. (Keyworth, Nottingham: British Geological Survey.)

SMITH, W. 1821. Geological map of Yorkshire. 4 sheets. (London: J Cary.)

STEERS, J A. 1953. Erosion and accretion: evidence of coastal changes. Chapter 3 *in* The Sea Coast. *New Naturalist*, No. 25.

STRAHAN, A. 1886. Notes on the relations of the Lincolnshire Carstone. *Quarterly Journal of the Geological Society of London*, Vol. 42, 486–493.

STRAW, A. 1961. The erosion surfaces of east Lincolnshire. *Proceedings of the Yorkshire Geological Society*, Vol. 33, 149–172.

— 1963. Some observations on the 'Cover Sands' of north Lincolnshire. *Transactions of the Lincolnshire Naturalists' Union*, Vol. 15, 260–269.

— 1969. Pleistocene events in Lincolnshire. *Transactions of the Lincolnshire Naturalists' Union*, Vol 17, 85–98.

— 1979. Eastern England. 1–139 in *The geomorphology of the British Isles: eastern and central England.* (London: Methuen.)

SWINNERTON, H H. 1931. The post-glacial deposits of the Lincolnshire coast. *Quarterly Journal of the Geological Society of London*, Vol. 87, 360–375.

— 1935. The rocks below the Red Chalk of Lincolnshire and their cephalopod faunas. *Quarterly Journal of the Geological Society of London*, Vol. 91, 1–46.

— 1941. Further observations on the Lower Cretaceous rocks of Lincolnshire. *Proceedings of the Geologists' Association*, Vol. 52, 198–207.

— and KENT, P E. 1976. The geology of Lincolnshire. (2nd edition). *Lincolnshire Natural History Brochure*, No. 7.

SYLVESTER-BRADLEY, P C, and FORD, T D. 1968. *The geology of the East Midlands.* (Leicester: Leicester University Press.)

TAYLOR, J C M. 1986. Late Permian–Zechstein. 87–111 in *Introduction to the petroleum geology of the North Sea.* GLENNIE, K W (editor). (Oxford: Blackwood Scientific Publications.)

TURNER, J S. 1949. The deeper structure of central and northern England. *Proceedings of the Yorkshire Geological Society*, Vol. 27, 280–297.

USSHER, W A E. 1890. The geology of parts of north Lincolnshire and south Yorkshire. *Memoir of the Geological Survey of England and Wales*, Sheet 86 [old series].

— JUKES-BROWNE, A J, and STRAHAN, A. 1888. The geology of the country around Lincoln. *Memoir of the Geological Survey of England and Wales*, Sheet 83 [old series].

VALENTÍN, H. 1971. Land loss at Holderness. 116–137 in *Applied coastal geomorphology*. STEERS, J A (editor). (London: MacMillan.)

VEENSTRA, H J. 1971. Sediments of the southern North Sea. *Report of the Institute of Geological Sciences*, No. 70/15, 9–23.

VERSEY, H C. 1934. Saxonian movements in East Yorkshire and Lincolnshire. *Proceedings of the Yorkshire Geological Society*, Vol. 22, 52–58.

WARRINGTON, G. 1974. Trias. 145–160 in *The geology and mineral resources of Yorkshire*. RAYNER, D H, and HEMINGWAY, J E (editors). (Leeds: Yorkshire Geological Society.)

— and eight others. 1980. A correlation of Triassic rocks in the British Isles. *Special Report of the Geological Society of London*, No. 13.

WATTS, W A. 1959. Pollen spectra from the interglacial deposits at Kirmington, Lincolnshire. *Proceedings of the Yorkshire Geological Society*, Vol. 32, 145–151.

WHITTAKER, A W (editor). 1985. *Atlas of onshore sedimentary basins in England and Wales*. (Glasgow: Blackie.)

— and CHADWICK, R A. 1984. The large-scale structure of the Earth's crust beneath southern Britain. *Geological Magazine*, Vol. 121, 621–624.

— — and PENN, I E. 1986. Deep crustal traverse across southern Britain from seismic reflection profiles. *Bulletin de la Société Géologique de France*, Series 8, Vol. 2, 55–68.

— HOLLIDAY, D W, and PENN, I E. 1985. Geophysical logs in British stratigraphy. *Special Report of the Geological Society of London*, No. 18.

WILLIAMSON, I T. 1983. *Geological reports for DoE: land use planning. South Humberside Project.* (Leeds: Institute of Geological Sciences.)

WINGFIELD, R T R. 1989. Glacial incisions indicating Middle and Upper Pleistocene limits off Britain. *Terra Nova*, Vol. 1, 538–548.

— 1990. The origin of major incisions within Pleistocene deposits of the North Sea. *Marine Geology*, Vol. 91, 31–52.

WOOD, C J, and SMITH, E G. 1978. Lithostratigraphical classification of the Chalk in North Yorkshire, Humberside and Lincolnshire. *Proceedings of the Yorkshire Geological Society*, Vol. 42, 263–287.

WOOD, S V, and ROME, J L. 1868. On the glacial and post-glacial structure of Lincolnshire and south-east Yorkshire. *Quarterly Journal of the Geological Society of London*, Vol. 24, 146–184.

WOODWARD, H B. 1904. The water supply of Lincolnshire from underground sources. *Memoir of the Geological Survey of England and Wales*.

FOSSIL INDEX

Acanthocythereis dunelmensis (Norman)   42
Arctica islandica (Linné)   43
Arctica sp.   40

Bolivina sp.   42

Cassidulina reniforme   42
Cassidulina teretis Tappan   42
Cerastodema edule (Linné)   66
Corbicula fluminalis   56
Crassipora kosanke (Potonié and
   Kemp) Bharadwaj   10

'Cyprina islandica'   43
'Cyprina sp.'   40
Cytheropteron latissimum (Norman)   42

'Dentalium'   43

Elofsonella concinna (Jones)   42
Elphidium clavatum Cushman   42
Eucytheridea macrolaminata
   (Elofson)   42
Euestheria sp.   11

Geisina arcuata   11

Haynesina orbiculare (Brady)   42
Hemicythere cillosa (Sars)   42
Hiatella arctica (Linné)   40
Hydrobia ulvae (Pennant)   66

Islandiella norcrossi (Cushman)   42

Lingula mytilloides J. Sowerby   10

Macoma balthica (Linné)   40, 66
Miliolinella subrotunda (Montagu)   42

Nonion labradoricum (Dawson)   42
Nonionella auricula Herron-Allen and
   Earland   42

Psiloceras   19
Psiloceras planorbis   19

Qinqueloculina stalkeri Loeblich and
   Toppan   42

'Tellina balthica'   40
Trifarina angulosa (Williamson)   42

GENERAL INDEX

Page numbers in italics refer to figures.
Page numbers in bold refer to tables.
Page numbers followed by 'P' refer to plates.

Aalenian Stage 22
Acanthoceras jukesbrownei Zone *31*
Acanthoceras rhotomagense Zone *31*
Aegiranum Marine Band 12
aeromagnetic anomaly map *9*
aeromagnetic data *5*
Air Products Ltd Borehole No. 4 81
Aislaby Group *14*, 15–16
Albian Stage 6, 25, *27*
albidum Zone *27*
Aldborough 73
Alder 62
algae 70
algal mats 66
alluvium 57, 59, 63–66
　estuarine 64, *68*P
　lacustrine *47*, 59, *61*P, 61–62
　marine 52
　marine and estuarine *39*, 65–66,
　　75, 81
Alnus-Graminae pollen assemblage
　Zone *60*
Alnus-Quercus pollen assemblage Zone
　60
Alnus-Ulnus pollen assemblage Zone
　60
Alum Shale Member *18*
amblygonium Zone *27*
Ampthill Clay *20*, 24–25
'Ancholme Clay Group' 24, 77, 81
Ancholme, Vale of 38
Anglian Stage 38, *39*, 40
　glaciation 38
　till 40, 81
anguiformis Zone *27*
angulata Zone *18*
anhydrite 15, 16, 17, 75
anoxia 70
Aptian Stage 6, 28
aquicludes 77
aquifer systems, mathematical models
　of 76
aquifers
　Chalk 76
　development of 77
　effective 77, 78
Artemisia *68*P
artesian conditions 77
Ash Holt 48
Ashby Hill 32, *33*
Atlantic climatic period *60*
Atterberg limits 74
Audleby 26
Aylesby 56, 59
Bajocian Stage *20*, 22

Barnby Member *18*, 19
Barnetby 30
Barnoldby le Beck 1, 43, 50, *51*, 62
　Waterdell House Quarry 32
Barnsley Coal *see* Top Hard/Barnsley
　Coal
Barnstone Member *18*, 19
Barremian Stage *27*
Barrow Flints *33*
Barton *41*
Barton Marls 32, *33*
Basal Permian Sands 13, *14*, 76, 81
Basement Boulder Clay 3
'Basement Clay' 43
Basement Till (of Holderness) 3, 38,
　39, 40, *42*P, 42–43, 44, *45*P,*47*, 73, 74,
　81
Bathonian Stage *20*, 22, 24
'beach deposit, calcreted' 43
beach deposits *39*, 73, 80
　Ipswichian 43
Beach and Shoreface Deposits 70
beaches 66, 68
Beacon Hill Marl *33*
Beckingham Member *18*
Beelsby 29, 30, *33*, **78**
Belmont Till 38
berm *68*P
berthierine 19, 22, 26
　oolith grainstone 19
Betula-herbs pollen assemblage
　Zone *60*
Betula-Pinus pollen assemblage
　Zone *60*
BGS photographs 82
bifrons Zone *18*
Bilinguites gracile Marine Band *11*
Bilinguites superbilingue Marine
　Band *11*
Billingham Anhydrite *14*, *15*, 16
Binbrook 26, 30, 38, 56, 78
Binks, The 71
bison 56
Black Band *31*, 32, *33*
Blea Wyke Sandstone Formation *18*
Blisworth Clay *20*, 23, 23–4
Blisworth Limestone *20*, 23, 24
blow-outs 70
blow-wells 59, 77
blown sand *39*, 58–59, 65, 66,
　68, 73
　Coastal 70
Blue Anchor Formation (Tea
　Green Marl) *14*, 17
bone beds, phosphatic 17
Boreal climatic period *60*
boreholes, key *81*
Bouguer anomaly map *9*
Boulby Halite *14*, *15*, 16
boulders 45
　lag *45*P, *49*P
BP Chemicals Ammonia Plant
　Borehole No. 80, 81
Bradley *51*, **78**
Brant Mudstone Formation *18*,
　19, *20*, 21
Brantingham Sandstone Formation
　24

brick clay 75
Bridlington 40, 43
'Bridlington Crag' 3, 43
Bröchelschiefer *14*, *15*, 16
Brocklesby 19, 26, 29, 40, 50, *51*, 79
Brocklesby area Boreholes
　No. 9 (Habrough) 19, 81
　No. 10 (Brocklesby) 81
　No. 11 (Roxton Wood) 19, 25,
　　81
　No. 14 (Carr Leys Wood) 19, 81
Brocklesby Park 50
Bronze age culture *60*
Brotherton Formation *14*, *15*,
　bucklandi zone *18*,
Building Research Establishment,
　Cowden 74
building stone 75
Burnham Chalk Formation *20*,
　32–37, *33*, *34*P, 36, *54*P, 75, 81, 82
Burnham Chalk–Flamborough
　Chalk junction 34, *36*
Burstwick 64
Burstwick Drain 56, 58
Burstwick Grange 57
butane 80

Cabourne 26, 28, 29, 59, 77
Cabourne Vale Farm 38, 40
Cabourne Woods 30
Cadeby Formation 13, *14*, *15*, 15
Cadeby Top Farm 32, *33*
Caistor 30, 38, 40, 59
Caistor Monocline 6, 32
Calethorpe Till 38
calcilutite 19
Callovian Stage 24
Calycoceras guerangeri Zone *31*
camber 62
Cambriense Marine Band 11, *12*
Campanian Stage 36, 37
'cannon shot' gravel 40
carbonate/evaporite cycles 13
Carboniferous 5, 10–11
　faulting 6
　Namurian 10
　Westphalian 10–11
Carboniferous Limestone 10, 11
Carlton Formation *14*, 17
Carnallitic Marl Formation *14*, *15*, 16
Carr Leys Wood Borehole 19, 81
Carstone Formation *27*, 28–29, 30,
　62, 77, 79, 81
'Carstone Grit' 28
Carstone Grit Member *27*
catchment, R Humber 70
caves 73
CEGB Borehole M7 34, 35, *36*
cementstones 21
Cenomanian *33*
　stratigraphy *31*
Central (North Sea) Fault zone 6
chalk 3, 29, 75
　with black flints 46
　blocks *46*P
　cataclastic fabric *49*P
　crushed 48
　quarries 75

Chalk aquifer 76
Chalk Bearings 50
Chalk Group 8, 20, 29–37, 62, 77
  Burnham Chalk 20, 32–37, 33, 34P, 36, 54P, 75, 81, 82
  Ferriby Chalk 20, 27, 30, 33, 75, 81,
  Flamborough Chalk 20, 33, 36, 37, 47, 81
  hilltop surface on 29, 38
  marker beds 29
  marl bands 32, 35, 37
  Northern Province 29
  Pink Bands 30, 31
  structure contours on 6, 8
  unsaturated 77
  Welton Chalk 20, 30, 32, 33, 34P, 54P, 75, 80, 81
Chalk surface, of Holderness 40
Chalky Boulder Clay 3
  see also Lowestoft Till
'Chalky Clay' 48
channel fills 56
channels, subglacial 48
Chapmans Road Pit, Cleethorpes 75
Cherry Cobb Sands 1, 64, 66
chloride content of water 77, 78
Cladoceramus undularo-plicatus Bed (band) 33, 36
clast-lithology ratios 48
Claxby Ironfield 26, 28, 29
Claxby Ironstone Formation 20, 20–28, 27, 77, 79, 81
clay 25, 29, 30, 40, 44, 53, 54, 56, 58P, 61, 64, 65, 66
  laminated 57, 66
  silty 45, 48, 66
  stoneless 59
  varved 54
clay minerals 74
Cleethorpes 1, 30, 32, 43, 51, 62, 64, 65–66, 66, 69, 70, 71, 72, 73, 75, 76, 78, 79, 80
  seismic reflection profile 4, 5, 57
Cleethorpes Borehole 10, 13, 14, 16, 17, 19, 20, 21, 23, 24, 25, 26, 28, 29, 75, 76, 81
Cleveland Basin 5, 22
Cleveland Ironstone Formation 18
Cliff Farm, Out Newton 42, 44, 47
cliff landslips see landslip
cliff line, pre-Devensian (Ipswichian) 50
cliff sections 48
  Easington to Tunstall 47
cliffs 71
  Holderness 40, 45
climatic history 61
climatic periods 60
clinker 71
Clixby 25
Cloughton Formation 22, 23
coal 23, 75, 79–80
  clastic 50
Coal Measures 10, 75, 81
Coalfield, South Yorkshire/Nottinghamshire/ Derbyshire 11
coaly fragments 22

Coastal Blown Sand 70
coastal erosion 73
  12-year cycle of 73
coastlines
  old 1
  see also Holderness, North Sea Coast, shorelines
cobbles 40, 45
coccoliths 29
Cockle Pits Borehole 19, 21
Coleby Mudstones Formation 18
collapse, gravity-related 58
Colwick Formation 14, 17
compression, Variscan 5
concretions, calcareous 21
conglomerate 27
  basal 29
Coniacian Stage 33, 36
Conisholme 66, 69, 71
Conyards Road Pit, Cleethorpes 75
Cornbrash 20, 23, 24
Corylus/Myrica-Ulnus pollen assemblage Zone 60
Cotham Member 14, 17
Covenham 30, 32
Covenham Reservoir 71
Cover Sands, Lincolnshire 58
Cretaceous 6, 26–37
  base of 25
  stratigraphy 20
  Lower Cretaceous 26-29
  Upper Cretaceous: The Chalk Group 29–37
Croxby 26, 29, 56
Croxby Pond 56
Croxton Marl 32, 33
crustal setting and tectonic history 5–9
cryoturbation 56
currents
  eddy 71
  longshore 68, 71
  tidal 70, 71
Cuxwold 78
Cuxwold Quarry 32, 33
cycles 23
cyclic repetition 19
Cymodoce Zone 25
Cyperaceae-herbs pollen assemblage Zone 60

Dales Bottom 28
davoei Zone 18
Deepdale Flint 32, 33
Deepdale Lower Marl 33
Deepdale Upper Marl 33
Defence, Ministry of 1
deformation, structural 58P
dentatus Zone 27
Devensian 3, 38, 43–58, 60
  Early 43
  late 59
Devensian to Flandrian 58–62
Dimlington 1, 50, 74
Dimlington High Ground 73, 81, 82
Dimlington Silts 3, 39, 40, 44–45, 45P, 47, 50
Dimlington Stadial 38, 43, 58, 60

Dimlingtonian ice sheet 44, 50
  see also Dimlington Stadial
Dinantian 10, 76
  structure 6
discharge, Humber R 70
discites Zone 23
dispar Zone 27
dolerite, Whin Sill type 38
dolomite 13, 15, 16
Don Group 13, 14, 15
Donna Nook 41, 65, 66, 69, 70, 71, 73
Dowsing Dolomitic Formation 17
Dowsing Fault zone 6
Drab Till 45, 50
drainage, proglacial 55
drainage channels, englacial 53
Dry Valley Deposits 39, 54P, 59, 64
Dudgeon Saliferous Formation 17
dunes 59, 66, 70

Easington 1, 40, 44, 50, 54, 70, 74, 82
  cliff section 47, 81
  Foreshore 45P
Easington Gas Terminal 43, 72
East Bank Farm, Sunk Island 81
East Halton 75
East Midlands Shelf 5
Eastern England Shelf 5
Easthorpe Tabular Flints 33
Edale Gulf 10
Edlington Formation 15, 15, 16
Edwalton Formation 14, 17
effective aquifer 77, 78
electrical conductivity 78
elephant 56
Elm 62
Elsham Sandstone Formation 24, 25, 77
Enthorpe Marls 32, 33
Enthorpe Oyster Bed 33
Eppleworth Flint 33
erosion
  by seepage 73
  coastal 73
  Dinantian 10
  Holderness coast 70
erratics, Liassic and Triassic 46
Esk (Rot) Halite 17
Eskdale Group 13, 14, 16
eskers 58
Estheria Band 11
evaoporites 16, 75
  minerals 13
evapotranspiration 76
exaratum Subzone 21
extension (crustal) 6

fabrics (rock)
  Basement Till 40
  cataclastic 49P
  planar 48
  platey, chalk 35P
  of tills 48
failure, rotational 73
falciferum Zone 18, 21
  exaratum Subzone 21
  falciferum Subzone 21
farming 1

fascines   70
faulting, Carboniferous   6
faults   *46*P, *58*P
fauna
  derived   56
  Ipswichian   56
  marine   57
Fenland   63
Ferribly Chalk Formation   20, 27, 30,
    33, 75, 81
Ferruginous Flint   *33*
'fill'   71
finger lakes   54–56, *55*
First Main Flint   32, *33*
fissiocostatum-rude Zone   27
fissure flow   77
Flamborough Chalk Formation   20,
    33, 36, 37, 47, 81
Flamborough Head   35
Flandrian   *39*, 57, 58, *60*, 62–72
  early   59
flexuring, peripheral   5
flints   29, 30, 48
  black   40, 46
  careous tabular   *33*, 35
  grey   35, *36*
  injection   32
  nodular   30, *34*P
  paramoundra   32
  tabular   *33, 34*P, *35*P, 35
  tabular bands   32
  white   35, *36*, 37
flow (water)
  fissure   77
  intergranular   77
flow, fabric in till   48
Fluvioglacial Sand and Gravel   *39*, 44,
    80
fly-ash   71
folds   *58*P
foliation, planar   *42*P
  see also fabric
Fordon Evaporites   *14, 15*, 16
Foston Member   *18*
Foul Holme Spit   71
Fox Cliff Member   *18*
Freshney, R   65
Frodingham Ironstone Member   *18,
    19, 20*, 79
Fucus   *68*P
Fulstow   30, *69*, 75

Gainborough Trough   5
Gainsborough Gulf   10
gasfields   76
gasification   75
Gastrioceras cancellatum Marine Band
    11, 12
Gastrioceras cumbriense Marine Band
    11, 12
geophysical log signatures   19, 30
geophysical records   29
geothermal energy   75–76
geothermal gradients   76
glacial lake deposits   75
Glacial Sand and Gravel   *39*, 43, *46*P,
    46, 50–53, 80, 81
Glacial Silt and Clay   53–54

glaciations   38
  see also ice sheets
Glen Parva Formation   *14*, 17
Glentham Formation   23
goëthite   26
gottschei Zone   27
grading, (particle size analysis) of
    tills   74
Grainthorpe   *69*, 72
Grainthorpe Fen   75
Granby Member   *18*, 19
The Grange, Keelby   50
  section in sandpits   81
granite,   6
Grantham Formation   20, 22
Grasby Marl   32, *33*
Grauer Salzron   *14*, 16
gravel   40, 44, *47*, 48, 50, 56, *57*P, 57,
    64, 65, 66, 68, 71, 79–80
  'cannon shot'   40
  dredged   80
Great Limber   30, 54, 75
Great Oolite Group   22, 23–24
Grey Shale Member   *18*
Grimsby   1, 28, 37, *41, 51*, 62, 63, 66,
    70, 71, 72, 73, 75, 77, **78**, 78, 80
  saline zone   79
Grimsby Royal Dock   72
Grimsby Technical College   59
Grimston   73
groundwater   76–79
gullying   73
Gunnerby   55, 56

Habrough   40, 80
Habrough No. 9 Borehole   19, 81
halite   17, 75
halophytic plants   70
Hardegsen Disconformity   16
Harlequin Formation   17
Hatcliffe   55, 56, 82
Hatcliffe Top Quarry   32, *33*
Hauterivian Stage   27
Hawkin's Point   66
Hayton Anhydrite   *14, 15*, 15
Head   *39*, 59
heavy minerals   70
heavy-mineral ratios   48
Hedon   63, 79, 80
Helianthemum-herbs pollen
    assemblage Zone   60
Hessle   *41*
Hessle Boulder Clay   3
'Hessle Clay'   48
Hessle Till   45, 48, 74, 75
Hettangian Stage   *18, 20*
Hibaldstow Limestones   20, 23
High Street   26
Hilston   73
Holaster subglobosus Zone   31
Holaster trecensis Zone   31
Holderness   1, 3, 48
  Chalk surface of   40
  cliffs   40
  coast   3
  North Sea Coast   62
  section   81
  shore sections   43

Tills, geotechnical properties of   74
hollows, enclosed   59, 62
Hollym   37, 50, **78**
Holme Hill, Grimsby   62
Holme Hill Pit, Cleethorpes   75
Holmpton   40, 53, 61, 82
  cliff section   *47*
  Foreshore   *49*P
Holocene   38, *39*
'hot dry rock' method   76
How Hill   74
Hoxnian   3, *39*, 40, 53
  artefacts   43
  interglacial   38
Hudlestoni Zone   25
Hull   1, 40, *41*, 70, 71, 77, 78, 79, 80
human cultures   60
Humber Basin   10
Humber estuary   1
  borehole sections, Flandrian
    deposits   67
  evolution of   64
  Marine and Estuarine Alluvium   66
  sedimentation in   70
Humberside (BGS) Borehole
    No. 3   *see* IGS
  North Humberside Borehole, No. 3
Humberston   59, 66, *69*, 72, 82
Humberston Fitties   66, 70
Humphriesianum Zone   23
Hunstanton Chalk Member   27, 29,
    30, *31*
hydrocarbons   76
  and new industries   1
hydrochemical types, Chalk
    groundwater   78
hydrochloric acid   78
hydrogeology   76–79

ibex Zone   18
ice pushing   57
ice sheets
  Devensian   43
  Dimlingtonian   *44*, 50, 59
  margin   58
  still-stand   50
ice-crevasses   53
icefront   58
igneous rocks, Caledonoid   38, 40
IGS North Humberside Boreholes
  No. 1   81
  No. 3   34, 35, *36*, 37, 81
  No. 4   81
IGS-83-1 profile   10 *see also*
    Cleethorpes seismic profile
illite   74
Immingham   1, 26, 40, *41, 51*, 66, 71,
    72, 75, 79
Immingham Docks   40, 62
industrial waste   71, 72
industries   1
Inferior Oolite Group   22–23
  Grantham Formation
  Lincolnshire Limestone   20, 22–23
  Northampton Sand   20, 22
infiltration (water)   76
inflatum Zone   27
Inoceramus digitatus band   *33*

interglacials, Hoxnian 38
inversum Zone 27
Ipswitchian 38, *39, 53, 79*
  faunas 56
Irby upon Humber 30, 55
Irby Dales, Irby upon Humber *54*P,
  82
  glacial channel 62
Irby Dales Quarry 32, *33*
  section *81*
Irby Dales Farm Quarry 32
iron-manganese oxide 48
ironstone 18, *27*, 28, 79

jamesoni Zone *18*
Jet Rock Member *18*
jointing, prismatic 61P
Jurassic 17–25
  stratigraphy *20*
  Lower (Lias Group) 17–22
  Middle 22–24
  Upper 24–25
Jurassic/Cretaceous boundary *20*
Jurassic/Triassic boundary *20*

kaolinite 74
Keelby 30, 53, 55, 79, 80
  sand and gravel pit 82
Kellaways Beds *20,* 24
Kellaways Clay 24
Kellaways Rock 24
Kellaways Sands 24
Kelsey Hill 56, 56–57
Kelsey Hill Beds 38, *39,* 43, 44, 50, *52,*
  53, 55P, 56–58, *57*P, *58*P, 79, 80
Kelsey Hill Gravels 3, 56, 81
Kelstern Airfield 38
kerberus Zone 27
kettle holes 59
Keyingham 1, 3, 58, 64, 66, *69,* 72
Keyingham Drain 55P, 56, 58, 80
Keyingham Gravel Pit 45, 55P, *57*P,
  *58*P, 82
Kilburn Sandstone *12*
Killingholme 1, 26, 30, 34, 50, 71
Killingholme gas storage *see* South
  Killingholme
Killingholme (NIREX) Boreholes
  BH36 81
  BH37 *33,* 34, 35, 36
  DG1 25, 28, 34, 35, *36,* 81
Kilnsea *41,* 70, 72, 73, 80
  cliff section *47*
Kilnsea Fort 37, 81
Kilnsea Fort Borehole 81
Kilnsea Warren, Spurn Peninsula 82
Kimmeridge Clay *20,* 24, 25, 29, 30
Kimmeridgian Stage *20,* 24
Kinderscoutian strata *10,* 11
Kingstone upon Hull *see* Hull
Kiplingcotes Flints *33*
Kiplingcotes Marl No. 1 36
  No. 3 35, 36
Kiplingcotes Marls 32, *33*
Kirk Ella Marls *33*
Kirkham Abbey Formation *14, 15,*
  15–16
Kirmington 19, *39, 41*

Channel
Kirmington Channel Deposits *39,* 50,
  51, 81
Kirmington Fjord *see* Kirmington
  Channel
Kirmington interglacial beds 3
Kirmond le Mire 26, 28, 56
Kirton Cement Shale 23
Kirton Cementstones *20,* 23

Laceby 28, 29, 30, *41,* 50, *51,* 53, 55,
  56, 59, 79, 80
  Oaklands Quarry 32
Laceby Beck/Freshney River 65
laeviuscula Zone 23
lag deposits 71 *see also* boulders,
  lag
lagoons 66, 71
lakes
  proglacial 58
  see also finger lakes; meres
Lakeside Lido 68
lamplughi Zone 27
land accretion 73
land reclamation *69,* 72
land-fill reclamation 70
landslip 1, *39,* 62, 73
Langport Member 17
larvikite 46
Late Albian Sub-stage 29
lautus Zone 27
Lebberston Member 23
Lenton Formation 16
levesquei Zone *18*
Lias Group 6, *8,* 17–22, *20,* 21
  Brant Mudstone Formation *18,* 19,
  20, 21
  Lower Lias *20*
  Marlstone Rock Formation *18,*
  19, *20, see also* Marlstone,
  Marlstone, Rock Member
  Scunthorpe Mudstones Formation
  18, 18–19, *19, 20*
  mudstones above Marlstone Rock
  Bed 21–22
liasicus Zone *18*
lignite 23
Lilstock Formation 17
Limber (= Great Limber) **78**
lime 62
limestone 17, 18, 19, 23, 26, *27,* 28, 29
limonite 26
Lincolnshire Cover Sands 58
Lincolnshire Limestone *20,* 22–23
Lincolnshire Marsh 32, 38
  Middle Marsh 1, 63, 64, 65
  Outmarsh 1, 62, 63, 64, 65–66, *69,* 72
  sand and gravel deposits *51*
Lincolnshire Wolds 1, 3
liquid limit 74
liquified-gas storage cavern, South
  Killingholme 32
Listeri Marine Band *11, 12*
Little Grimsby 26
Little Weighton Marls *33*
  No. 2 Marl 35
Littlebeck Anhydrite *13,* 15, 16
Littlebeck Formation *14*

Littlecoates Pumping Station 77
Loch Lomond Stadial climatic
  period *60*
logs 29
longshore drift 71
loricatus Zone 27
Louth 43
Louth Canal, Thoresby Bridge *65*
Low *Esteria* Band *12*
Lower Coal Measures 11, *12*
Lower Cretaceous *20,* 26–29
  Carstone Formation *27,* 28–29,30,
  62, 77, 79, 81
  Claxby Ironstone Formation *20,*
  26–28, *27,* 77, 79, 81
  Roach Formation *20,* 26, *27,* 28,
  28–29, 79
  Tealby Formation *20,* 26, *27,* 28, 77,
  81
  stratigraphy of *27*
Lower Inoceramus Bed *31*
Lower Lias *20*
Lower Orbirhynchia Bed *31*
Lower Palaeozoic basement 10
Lower Palaeozoic rocks *5*
Lower Permian Marl 15
Lower Pink Band *31*
Lower Roach Member 28
Lower Spilsby Sandstone Member
  20, 27
Lower Tealby Clay 26–27, 77
Lower Toarcian Substage 21
Lowestoft Till 38
Lud estuary 66, 68
Lud, R 65, 68
Ludborough 50, *51*
Ludborough Flints *33, 34*P
Ludborough Quarry 32, *33, 34*P, 35,
  82
  section *81*
Lud's Well 28, 29
lydite 28

Made Ground 68, 71–72
Magnesian Limestone 40
  see also Brotherton Formation;
  Cadeby Formation
mammillatum Zone 27
mammoth 56
manganiferous pan 57P
Manticeras dixoni Zone *31*
Manticeras mantelli Zone *31*
margaritatus Zone *18,* 21
marginatus Zone 27
'Marine Alluvium; sand, gravel or
  shingle' 66
Marine and Estuarine Alluvium 75, 81
'Marine Gravels' 56, 57
marine planation surfaces 38
Market Weighton Block 2, *5*
Market Weighton High 17
Market Weighton Structure 13, 18,
  22, 26, 28
Marl 29, 37
  bentonitic 30
  shell *61*P, 61
Marl Slate 13, *14,* 15
Marlstone Rock Formation *18, 19, 20*

Marlstone Rock Member   *18*
marram grass   70
Marsdenian Stage   *11*, 12
Marshchapel   65, *69*, 72
Marsupites testudinarius Zone   *36*
Marsupites testudinarius–Sphenoceramus
    lingua zone boundary   37
mélange   43, *46*P
Melton Ross   32
Melton Ross Marl   *33*
Mercia Mudstone Group   6, *8*, *14*,
    16–17, 81
mere deposits   59, 61, 81
meres   59
Mesolithic culture   *60*
metamorphic rocks, Caledonoid   38
Metoicoceras geslinianum Zone   *31*, 33
Micraster coranguinum Zone   *33*, 36
Micraster coranguinum–Uintacricus
    socialis zone boundary   37
Micraster cortestudinarium Zone   *33*, 36
Mid-Spilsby Nodule Bed   25
Middle Albian Sub-stage   29
Middle Chalk–upper Chalk
    boundary   *34*P
Middle Coal Measures   11, *12*
Middle Jurassic   22–24
    Great Oolite Group   22, 23–24
    Inferior Oolite Group   22–23
    Redbourne Group   *20*, 22, 81
Middle Toarcian sub stage   22
Middleton (East Halton) Marl   *33*, 35
Mill Hill, Keyingham   79
Mill Road Pit, Cleethorpes   75
'millet seed' grains   13
Millstone Grit   10, *12*, 81
Modern Beach Deposits   70
Mohorovičić discontinuity   5
moisture content, tills   74
moraine   55
mud   70, 71
mudflats   66, 71
    tidal   *68*P
mudflows   73
mudstone   16, 17, 18, 19, 21, 23, 24,
    26, *27*, 28, 29
    above Marlstone Rock Bed   21–22
    berthierine   19, 22
    bituminous   21
    fissile   21
Mytiloides labiatus Zone   *33*

Namurian strata   10, *11*, *12*
    structure   6
    Tetney Lock Borehole   *11*
natural gamma traces   29
Neolithic culture   *60*
Nettleton Borehole   10, 13, *14*, 15, 28,
    76
Nettleton Bottom Borehole   17, 18, 19,
    20, 21, 22, 23, 24, 25, 76
Nettleton Bottom Mine   79
Nettleton Limestone   23
Nettleton Pycnodonte Bed   *31*
Nettleton Sandstones   *20*
Nettleton Stone   *31*
Nevill's Drain *see* The Runnel,
    Holmpton

New Delights, Tetney   62
New Sand Hole   80
New Waltham   *51*
Newark Gypsum   17
Nitrate (in water)   77, 78
'Noah's Wood'   62
nodule bed   27
nodules, phosphatic   25
noricum Zone   27
Normanby Mill   25
North Carr Dales   50
North Cotes   *64*, 65, *69*, 72
North Cotes Airfield   65
North Killingholme   *41*, 62, 72, 77, 79
North Killingholme Borehole
    (DG1)   29
North Ormsby   30, 32, 38, 50, 75, 82
North Ormsby Marl   *33*, *34*P, *35*P
North Ormsby Quarry   *8*, 32, *33*
    section   81
North Sea coast   1
North Somercotes   1, 65, 66, 68, *69*,
    70, 72, 80
North Thoresby   50
Northampton Sand   *20*, 22
Nottingham Castle Formation   16

oak   62
Oaklands Quarry, Laceby   32, *33*
obtusum Zone   *18*, 19
oil shales   25
oilfields, Namurian   76
Old Den   71
Old Hive, Out Newton   50, *53*P, 59,
    81, 82
    drain outfall   *47*
Older Blown Sand   58–59
'Older Drift'   38
'Older Storm Beach Deposits'   66
ooliths, ferruginous   26
oppressus Zone   27
'Ord' channel   *45*P, *49*P
ords   73
Orford   56
orogenic belt, Caledonian   5
Otby   79
Otby Top   28
Ottringham   26, 37, 40, *69*
Out Newton   44
over-consolidation   74
Oxford Clay   *20*, 24
Oxfordian Stage   *20*, 24
oxynotum Zone   *18*, 19

packstone, calcarenite   19
Palaeozoic formations   71
palynological studies   61
Paradoxica or Sponge Bed   *31*
paramoudra flint   32
Patrington   *41*, 48, *69*
Patrington Haven   66, 80
Paull   58, 62, 66, 80
Paull Fort   57
Peak Mudstone Member   *18*
Peat   *39*, 59, *61*P, 61, 61–62, 64,*65*, 66
pebble lithologies   79
pebbles   40, 45
    Scandinavian   40

Pecten Ironstone Member   *18*, 19
Penarth Group   *14*, 17, *18*, *20*, 81
Permian rocks, lateral variation in
    thickness   13
Permian and Triassic   11, 13–17
Permian-Triassic boundary   13
phosphates   79
pingoes   59
pink bands (in chalk)   30, *31*
pits, backfilled   72
planorbis Zone   *18*
plastic limit   74
plate migration   2
platey fabric, chalk   *35*P
playas   16
Pleistocene   3, 38, *39*
    concealed surface of   *63*
Plenus Marls   32
Pliensbachian Stage   *18*, *20*, 21
pollen analysis   *60*
pollen assemblage zones
    Flandrian   62
    regional   *60*
Polyptychites spp. Zone   27
pore pressure   73
porphyrite, amygdaloidal   46
Porter's Sluice   66
Pre-Boreal climatic period   *60*
Precambrian basement   10
preplicomphalus Zone   27
Priestland Clay   23
primitivus Zone   27
proglacial deposits   54–56
propane   80
Purple Boulder Clay   3
Purple Till   48
putty chalk   *49*P
Pyewipe   71

quarries   82
    chalk   75
    key sections in   81
    Killingholme district   32
Quaternary   38–72
    Anglian   38, *39*, 40
    Devensian   38, 45–58, *60*
    Devensian to Flandrian   58–62
    Hoxnian   3, 38, *39*, 40, 43, 53
    Ipswichian   38, *39*, 43, 53, 56, 79
    'Wolstonian'   38, *39*, 40, 43

Radcliffe Formation   *14*, 17
radiocarbon dating   3, 44, *60*, 61, 62
rainfall   76
raricostatum Zone   *18*
Ravendale Flint   *33*, *34*P
Ravenscar Grou   22
Raventhorpe Beds   *20*, 22, 22–23
reclamation, land   66
Red Chalk   28, 29, 30, 77
    and Carstone   *20*
red clay   54
redbed facies, Permo-Triassic rocks   13
Redbourne Group   *20*, 22, 81
Redcar Mudstone Formation   *18*
reefs   15
regressions   62
reindeer   56

remoulding, fabric in till   48
reservoir rocks   76
resistivity logs   29
Retford Formation   *14*, 17
Rhaetian Stage   17, *18*
rhinoceros   56
Riby   29, 30, 50, 75
Riby Marl   *33*
Riby Quarry   32, *33*
rip-rap   *68*P
Riplingham Tabular Flints   *33*
River Bed Deposits   71
Roach Formation   *20*, 26, *27*, 28–29,
     79
Roach Stone Member   28
Roman culture   *60*
Roos, The Bog   59, *60, 80*
  chronology, climatic and
      archaeological   *60*
Roos Drain   59
rootlets   23
Rothwell   26, 28, 32, *33*, 59, 77
Roxby Formation   *14, 15*, 16
Roxton Wood No. 11 Borehole   19,
     25, 81
The Runnell, Holmpton   *47, 61*P, 61,
     81, 82
Ryazanian Stage   *27*

sabkas   16
saline intrusions   77, 79
saline water   79
salinity, Humber estuary   70
Salt End   1, 40, *41*, 62, 71, 72, **78**
Salt End Boreholes   81
salt marsh   71
saltern mounds   65, 72
Saltfleet   *41, 51, 63, 64*, 65, 69, 70
Saltfleet Haven   70
Saltfleet/North Somercotes
     beach   66
Saltfleetby Borehole   10, 11
saltmarsh   66, 73
sand   40, 44, 45, *47*, 48, 50, 56, *57*P,
     *58*P, 64, 65, 66, 68, 71
  blown see Blown Sand
  fine   59
  laminated   *46*P
sand bars   71
sand and gravel   79, 79–80
  Dimlington   *52*
  fluvioglacial   *39, 52*, 54–56
  glacial   *39, 43, 46*P, 46, 50–53, *52,
      53*P, 80, 81
  glacial/interglacial   81
  Lincolnshire Marsh   *51*
sand pits, The Grange, Keelby,
     section   81
Sand-le-Mere   62, 81
Sand-le-Mere Groyne   *47*
sandflats   71
'sands-and-clays'   28
sandstone   16, 17, 18, 19, 22, 23, 24,
     25, 26, *27*, 28, 29
  coaly   23
  glauconitic   21
  Permo-Triassic   75
  Upper Palaeozoic   38

Santon Oolite   23
Santonian Stage   33, 36, 37
saturated thickness   77
Scalby Formation   22
scarp, Lincolnshire Wolds   1
Scitulus Zone   25
scour   73
Scrobicularia clay   66
Scunthorpe Mudstones Formation   *18,*
     18–19, *19, 20*
Scythian Stage   17
sea buckthorn   70
sea cliff
  Dimlington High Land   *42*P
  Ipswichian   38, 43, 50
  see also cliffs
sea defences   72
sea level
  change in   73
  postglacial rise   62
sea walls   *69*, 70, 72, 73
  medieval   66
Sea-bed Deposits   70, 71
Searby   30
seatearths   23
Seaton Carew Formation   *14*, 17
sections, key   81
sediment accretion   70, 73
sediment sorting   70
sedimentation, present-day,
     estuarine and marine   70–71
seepage erosion   73
seismic reflection profiles   5, 10
  Cleethorpes   *4, 7*
semicostatum Zone   *18*, 19
Sewerby   43
Shafton Marine Band   *12*
shales, fissile   17
Sherburn Anhydrite   *15*, 16
Sherwood Sandstone Group   6, *8*, 13,
     14, 15, 16, 75–76, 81
shingle   66, 71
shoals   71
  sand   66
Shoreface Deposits   71
shorelines, old   *69 see also* coastlines
siderite   26
silt   40, *46*P, *47*, 48, 53, 56, 57, *58*P, 64,
     65, 66
silts and clays
  glaciolacustrine   *39*, 56
  laminated   58, 71
  Middle Lias   21
siltstone   13, 16, 17, 18, 19, 21, 22, 24,
     25
Sinemurian Stage   *18, 20*
Skeffling   72
Skipsea Till   3, *39*, 40, *42*P, 43, 44,
     45–46, *46*P, *47*, 48, 49P, 50, 53P, 56,
     57, 59, 74, 81
Skitter Beck   65
Skitter Ness   62, 79
Sleights Siltsone Formation   *14, 15*, 16
slides   73
Snitterby Limestone   23
solifluxion   59
sonic logs   29
source rocks (of till), Jurassic,

Triassic and Carboniferous   48
South Cave Borehole   21
South Cliff Road, Withernsea   *47*
South Killingholme   80
  liquified-gas storage caverns   32, *33*
  section, gas-storage caverns   81
South Killingholme (Geostore)
     SK1 Borehole   81
South Somercotes   *69*, 75
Southern North Sea Basin   5, 11, 13, 16
Spartina grass   *68*P
speetonensis Zone   *27*
Sphenoceramus lingua Zone
     (part)   *36*
Spilsby Sandstone Formation   25, *27*,
     29, 62, 77, 79, 81
spinatum Zone   *18*
spits   68
Spurn Bight   *69*, 70, 71, 74
Spurn/Head/Peninsula   1, 62, *64*, 66,
     68, 70, 71, 72, 74, 80
  evolution of   74
  Kilnsea Warren   82
Stainton le Vale   1, 28, 29, 56
Staintondale Group   *14*, 16
Staithes Sandstone Formation   *18*
Stallingborough   59
Sternotaxis planus Zone   33, *34*P, *36*
stillstands   55, 59
storage reservoir (water)   79
storm beach deposits   66, 68, 81
'Storm Beaches'   66
storm beaches   *69*
storm flooding   73
storm surges   66
strength
  compressive unconfined   74
  remoulded   74
structural deformation   *58*P
structure   5–9
Sub-Atlantic climatic period   *60*
sub-Flandrian platform   63
Subcrenatum Marine Band   10, *11, 12*
Submereged Forest   39, 62–62
subsidence
  Jurassic   6
  thermal   6
sulphate (in water)   77
Sunk Island   1, 34, 37, 62, 66, *68*P, *69*,
     72, 80, 82
Sunk Roads channel   66
surging   77
Swallow   29, 30, 32, 38, 59
Swallow Quarry   32, *33*
Swallow Vale Quarry   32, *33*
  section   81
Swinhope   29, 56

tardefurcata Zone   *27*
Tealby Formation   *20*, 26, *27*, 28, 77,
     81
Tealby Limestone Member   *27*, 28, 77
technical reports   *ix*
Teesside Group   *14*, 16
tenuicostatum Zone   *18*, 21
Terebratulina lata Zone   33, *34*P
terraces   59
  fluvioglacial sand and gravel   55

Tertiary Period   6
Tetney   50, *51*, 59, 65, *69*, 77
Tetney Lock Borehole   10, 13, *14*, 16,
    17, 19, *20*, 21, 23, 24, 25, 26, 28, 29,
    75, 76, 81
  Namurian strata   *11*
  Westphalian strata   *12*
thalwegs, undulating   48
Thoresway Borehole   28, 81
Thorncroft Sands   22, 23, 24
Thornanby   55, 56
Thorngumbald   80
Thornton Abbey   55
Thornton Curtis Marl   *33*
Thorpe   73
thouarsense Zone   *18*
tidal creeks   66
tidal currents   71
  Humber estuary   70
Tidal Flat Deposits   70–71
tidal power   80
tidal range, Humber estuary   70
Tidal River Bed Deposits   70
tills   3, 40, 44, *47*
  chalk-rich   *46*P
  Devensian   3, 29, *45*P, 75
  Dimlingtonian   48
  fabric of   48
  foliated   *46*P
  lodgement   48
  silt-to-clay ratio   48
  source rocks   48
Toarcian Stage   *18*, 20
Top Hard/Barnsley Coal   *8*, *12*, 75
topography   xii
Totterhoe Stone   *31*
transgressions, Flandrian   62
transmissivity, (of water)   77, 78, 79
Trent Falls   70
Trent Formation   *14*, 17
Triassic   11, 13–17, *20*
Triglochin clay   66
Triple Tabular Flints   *33*, *34*P, *35*P
tritium   78
Triton Anhydritic Formation   17
tunnel valleys   40
Tunstall   73
  cliff section   *47*
turneri Zone   *18*, 19
Turonian Stage   *33*, 36

Uitacrinus socialis Zone   *36*, 37
*Uintacrinus socialis–Marsupites
    testudinarius* zone boundary   37
Ulceby   19, 82
Ulceby Marl   *33*
Ulceby Oyster Bed   *33*
Ulceby Skitter   55
unconfined compressive strength   74
unconformities
  Albian   6
  basal-Permian   6, *8*
  regional   6

underground storage *see* South
    Killingholme
Upgang Formation   15, 16
Upper Bajocian substage   22
Upper Claxby Ironstone Member   *27*
Upper Coal Measures   *12*
Upper Cornbrash   22
Upper Cretaceous: the Chalk
    Group   19–37, *20*
Upper Estuarine Series (Beds)   *20*, 23,
    24
Upper Inoceramus Bed   *31*
Upper Jurassic   24–25, 27
  Ancholme Clay Group   24–25
Upper Lias   21
Upper Orbirhynchia Bed   *31*
Upper Palaeolithic culture   60
Upper Pink Band   *31*
Uppewr Roach Member   28
Upper Sinemurian Substage   21
Upper Spilsby Sandstone Member   *20*,
    27
Upper Telby Clay Member   *27*, 28, 77
Upper Toarcian substage   22
Utterby   26, 29, 80

Valangian Stage   *27*
Vale of Pickering–Flamborough
    Head Fault zone   6
The Valley Quarry, Wold Newton   32,
    33
valley bulging   28
valleys, subglacial   *54*P
Vanderbecki Marine Band   *12*
variabilis Zone   *18*, 27
Variscan Fold Belt   5
Variscan Orogeny   11
varves   54, 56
vitrinite reflectance   76
Volgian Stage   25
Volgian/Portlandian   27
Volviceramus involutus band   *33*

wackstones   26
Waithe Beck   1, 65, 78, 79
Walesby   79
Walesby Top Farm   38
Waltham   1, 50, 75, 80
Wanstead Borehole   *14*
warp deposits   66
waste disposal   71
water
  abstraction   76
  alkalinity   **78**, 78
  borehole yields   77, 78
  calcium bicarbonate   77, 78
  calcium sulphate   78
  chloride in   78
  hardness of   77
  hardness total   **78**
  nitrate in   77, 78
  saline   79

sodium   79
  total hardness of   **78**
  tritiated   78
  water supply   76–79
Waterdell House Quarry, Barnoldby le
    Beck   32, *33*
wave-cut platform, Ipswichian   40, 43,
    45, 50
Weichselian *see* Devensian
Welton Chalk Formation   *20*, 30, 32,
    33, *34*P, *54*P, 75, 80, 81
Welton–Burnham Chalk boundary   *34*P,
    *54*P
Welton-le-Wold   43
Welwick   *69*
West Marsh   71
West Ravendale Quarry   32, *33*, 82
  section   81
West Sole Group   22
West Walton Beds   *20*, 24
Westbury Formation   *14*, 17
Westphalian   10–11, 75, 76
  A   *11*, 11, *12*
  B   11, *12*
  C   11, *12*
  D   11, *12*
  Tetney Lock Borehole   *12*
Whitby Mudstone Formation   *18*
White Flint   *33*
Widmerpool Gulf   5, 10
Willerby Flints   *33*
Windermere Interstadial climatic
    period   60
Winestead   63, 64, 75
Winestead Borehole   10, 13, 17, 19, *20*,
    21, 23, 24, 24–25, 26, 28, 29, 30, 32,
    37, 40, *41*, 76, 81
Withernsea   1, 37, *41*
  cliff section   *47*
Withernsea Till   3, 40, *42*P, 43, 44, *46*P,
    47, 48, 50, 56, 59, *61*P, 61, 74, 81
Wold Newton   29, 30, 48
Wolds   29
Wolds-top planar surface   38 *see
    also* Chalk Group, hill top
    surface in
Wolstonian   *39*, 40, 43
Wolstonian glaciation   38
Wootton Marls   32, *33*

Yarburgh   30
Yeadonian   *12*
Yeadonian strata   *11*

Zechstein   81
Zechstein cycles
  English   13
  EZ1   13–15
  EZ2   15–16
  EZ3   16
  EZ4 and EZ5   16
Zechstein Sea   13

BRITISH GEOLOGICAL SURVEY

Keyworth, Nottingham NG12 5GG
(0602) 363100

Murchison House, West Mains Road, Edinburgh
EH9 3LA   031-667 1000

London Information Office, Natural History Museum
Earth Galleries, Exhibition Road, London SW7 2DE
071-589 4090

The full range of Survey publications is available through the
Sales Desks at Keyworth and at Murchison House, Edinburgh,
and in the BGS London Information Office in the Natural
History Museum Earth Galleries. The adjacent bookshop
stocks the more popular books for sale over the counter. Most
BGS books and reports are listed in HMSO's Sectional List 45,
and can be bought from HMSO and through HMSO agents
and retailers. Maps are listed in the BGS Map Catalogue, and
can be bought BGS approved stockists and agents as well as
direct from BGS.

*The British Geological Survey carries out the geological survey of Great
Britain and Northern Ireland (the latter as an agency service for the
government of Northern Ireland), and of the surrounding continental
shelf, as well as its basic research projects. It also undertakes
programmes of British technical aid in geology in developing countries
as arranged by the Overseas Development Administration.*

*The British Geological Survey is a component body of the Natural
Environment Research Council.*

HMSO publications are available from:

HMSO Publications Centre
(Mail, fax and telephone orders only)
PO Box 276, London SW8 5DT
Telephone orders 071-873 9090
General enquiries 071-873 0011
Queueing system in operation for both numbers
Fax orders 071-873 8200

HMSO Bookshops
49 High Holborn, London WC1V 6HB
(counter service only)
071-873 0011   Fax 071-873 8200
258 Broad Street, Birmingham B1 2HE
021-643 3740   Fax 021-643 6510
33 Wine Street, Bristol BS1 2BQ
0272-264306   Fax 0272-294515
9 Princess Street, Manchester M60 8AS
061-834 7201   Fax 061-833 0634
16 Arthur Street, Belfast BT1 4GD
0232-238451   Fax 0232-235401
71 Lothian Road, Edinburgh EH3 9AZ
031-228 4181   Fax 031-229 2734

HMSO's Accredited Agents
(see Yellow Pages)

And through good booksellers